Cross-Cultural Child Development for Social Workers

Cross-Cultural Child Development for Social Workers

An Introduction

Lena Robinson

First published 2007 by
PALGRAVE MACMILLAN
Houndmills, Basingstoke, Hampshire RG21 6XS and
175 Fifth Avenue, New York, N.Y. 10010
Companies and representatives throughout the world

PALGRAVE MACMILLAN is the global academic imprint of the
Palgrave Macmillan division of St. Martin's Press, LLC and of Palgrave
Macmillan Ltd. Macmillan® is a registered trademark in the United
States, United Kingdom and other countries. Palgrave is a registered
trademark in the European Union and other countries.

ISBN-13: 978–0–333–72610–5 paperback
ISBN 10: 0–333–72610–3   paperback

This book is printed on paper suitable for recycling and made
from fully managed and sustained forest sources.

A catalogue record for this book is available from the
British Library.

Library of Congress Cataloging-in-Publication Data
Robinson, Lena, 1957–
    Cross-cultural child development for social workers: an introduction/
Lena Robinson.
        p. cm.
    Includes bibliographical references and index.
    ISBN-10: 0-333-72610-3
    ISBN-13: 978-0-333-72610-5 (paper)
        1. Children of minorities—Great Britain. 2. Children of minorities—
United States. 3. Child development—Cross-cultural studies. 4 Social
work minorities—Great Britain. 5. Social work with minorities—United
States. 6. Family social work—Great Britain. 7. Family social work—
United States. I. Title.
HV751.A6R65 2007
362.708´0941—dc22   2006049769

10   9   8   7   6   5   4   3   2   1
16 15 14 13 12 11 10 09 08 07

Printed in China

Contents

Foreword

Cross-Cultural Child Development for Social Workers raises important and timely questions for those practising in a multicultural society with people whose origins are ethnically and culturally diverse. The failure of social workers to deal appropriately with the variety of ethnic identities within an anti-oppressive framework is a major preoccupation of this book. It focuses on child development as understood within psychology, but links its insights to working with black and Asian children and their families. Sadly, its many pages bring home, yet again, the message that despite the decades of work on anti-racist social work, racism continues to distort social work practice and deny children appropriate services.

Robinson seeks to explore the contributions to theory and practice that can emanate from the considerable body of research that black and cross-cultural scholars and practitioners have created for the field of psychology and the caring professions. Much of this literature will be unfamiliar to many white practitioners and academics and so the book serves the significant purpose of assisting these professionals in familiarizing themselves with existing research and scholarship in an easily accessible manner. Summary boxes help the reader check that they have understood the message in the preceding pages of the book and are helpful to students wishing to check that they have grasped the essentials.

Having established the failure of social workers to intervene appropriately in black families and thus contribute to the over-representation of their children in the care system, Robinson argues that understanding black and cross-cultural scholars' theories of child development would have had beneficial effects for the children concerned and prevented many of them from becoming 'looked after' in the care system. Additionally, their writings would have helped counter the problems of ignoring difference and diversity that is evident in popular Western theories of human development, particularly those concerning attachment as propounded by Bowlby. And, they would have offered insights into black and Asian children's internalization of the dominant culture unless their parents offer a strong racial socialization that engages with an alternative view of the world that better serves their needs.

Robinson's book methodically explores different key contributors to the debates about how to best support black and Asian children in developing a strong sense of themselves as racially aware beings, highlighting the importance of those authors who have developed models that contribute to our understanding of how black and Asian people living primarily in the USA and Britain reach the state of feeling comfortable with who they are and being capable of engaging with those who are different from them from a position of strength. These include the pioneers of theories of black development like Cross and subsequent critics of his work who went on to amen his work and develop theory further including Berry and Phinney.

To this end, Robinson explores Cross's model of nigrescence and the stages of development that a black person undergoes to reach the position of being proud of his or her identity at length and in considerable detail. She includes critiques of its basic tenets through Phinney's ethnic identity development model and Berry's acculturation model alongside Cross' revisions to his own model following reflection upon the issues raided by his critics. These critiques have indicated that Cross's model of identity cannot be understood as a simple linear progression towards an ideal state, but that different individuals and ethnicities respond differently to the processes of personal growth and development and have different needs in developing their black identity, particularly those elements linked to its buffering, bonding, bridging, codeswitching and individualizing functions. These concepts are explained in accessible language in the book.

Robinson draws on her own research on acculturation and racial identity. Black and Asian people's reaction to their cultural heritages become an important part of redefining the self, and a strong racially aware person will appreciate his or her heritage as well as not feeling threatened by others' views of their own culture. Combined with an extensive bibliography, this analysis enables Robinson to provide readers with a considerable body of literature that they can explore to improve their knowledge of the issues, including how black and Asian people address the problem of racism in society and what their possible responses, including therapeutic ones, might look like. Of particular relevance here is the question of racial socialization in Western societies and the roles that black and Asian parents play in helping their children deal with the impact of racism on their lives. Social workers can support such growth and development in black and Asian children's personalities if they understand the processes of racial socialization.

Robinson argues that the development of material here in the UK is hindered by the lack of research in this area and suggests that this gap should be made good, sooner rather than later. Those that have been seeking to address this issue are aware of the lack of funding and interest for these concerns.

For example, the Economic and Social Sciences Research Council (ESRC) has been talking about producing a special programme on 'race' and ethnicity for the past five years, but has yet to deliver on it. Lack of available funding is given as a reason and the matter has been kept under constant review. Meanwhile, other programmes that were not even on the drawing board five years ago have made it to implementation as funding for these has somehow been found. Some black scholars are wondering whether this means that the ESRC is fearful of engaging with one of the most disputed areas in the social sciences. Another difficulty is that many of the black scholars who started off in the UK are finding more prestigious positions in the American academy where the call to undertake research in a country that supports its scientific endeavours more than this one is hard to resist. This trend contributes to a 'brain drain' amongst black and Asian scholars and a loss of critical leadership and role models in their ranks here because their contributions to academia are not being made in the UK.

Each of the points that Robinson raises about the necessity of developing appropriate concepts and practices for social work professionals to become cross-culturally competent could itself be the subject of a complete tome. So, there remains much work to be done. Central to this endeavour is that of developing theories and practices of racial socialization and cognitive development that treat people as equals in an egalitarian society and value knowledge that is found amongst marginalized people themselves. Developing research partnerships with then is crucial in the project of creating that knowledge and the skills that would accompany it. In these, viewing the vase range of differences as strengths to work with in the task of finding commonalities and creating a better world for all are central. Also important is the task of ensuring that each grouping is seen as diverse. And so finding diversity and uniqueness within a unified grouping sits alongside the commonalities that exist amongst them.

Creating such a world requires that people being to think about other people as having agency, or the capacity to act as subjects able to organize their worlds in their own interests and relate to others as equal agents. Looking for allies across racial divides and the idea of rooting social work ecologically in an interdependent world where human rights, citizenship and social justice provide the broader context within which professional practice occurs, aims to achieve just that. And, it helps to empower service users, whoever they may be. Robinson's book is useful in getting British social workers started on or continuing with what is proving to be a long and difficult journey. The guidance it provides helps to clarify the direction that travellers seeking to become better practitioners should take.

Lena Dominelli
Professor of Applied Social Sciences
Durham University

1

Introduction

Introduction

As British society has become more heterogeneous, cross-cultural effectiveness has emerged as an essential skill for all social workers who work with children and young people. Over the past two decades, social scientists (mainly in the US) have become increasingly aware of the contributions that cross-cultural research findings can make to our understanding of human development. Little of the current social work literature in Britain has addressed the issue of cross-cultural child development. Articles and books written for social workers on child development are Eurocentric in nature and as a result require considerable adaptation before they can be responsive to some of the needs of black children. Kagitcibasi (1996) notes that developmental psychology textbooks 'tend not to include cultural differences, or they treat them as extraneous variables' (p. 4).

During the late 1980s, social work education in Britain 'became increasingly aware of the impact of oppression and discrimination on clients and communities' (Thompson, 1993, p. 1). For example, the Central Council for Education and Training of Social Workers (CCETSW) requirements for the DipSW award attached a high priority to an anti-discriminatory approach in college and placement teaching and assessment (see Central Council for Education and Training in Social Work Paper 30, 1991). The CCETSW document, which outlined the guidance notes for the teaching of childcare in the DipSW course, stressed that 'all social work students should have a sound knowledge of human growth and development, [and] the significance of race, culture and language in development must be understood' (Central Council for Education and Training in Social Work, 1991, p. 14). Although CCETSW does not state that these

1

theories are psychological or derived from psychology, it is obvious that these theories are psychological (Robinson, 1995).

The Children Act, 1989 (Department of Health, 1989) states that 'In making any such decision [regarding a child looked after or proposing to be looked after] a local authority shall give due consideration . . . to the child's religious persuasion, racial origin and cultural and linguistic background' (Section 22(5) (c)). Thus, the 'race', culture, language and religion of children and young people must be addressed in the provision of services. In order to meet the needs of and help the development of any child, black or white, it is essential that social workers operate with adequate knowledge, understanding and sensitivity (Robinson, 1998).

Traditional psychological theories have not had sufficient explanatory power to account for the behaviour of black children and young black people. Studies of child development and behaviour are deficiency based and offer an Eurocentric perspective. There is an absence of appropriate conceptual models or frameworks that address the diversity and strengths of the black population in Britain. Mainstream child psychology does not usually consider race and race awareness as an important variable on the child's mental, emotional and personality development (Wilson, 1978). Consequently, psychological theories of personality, intelligence, motivation, learning, language development, self-concept, etc. were standardized on whites and applied to black children. Woodhead (1999) points out that 'Intelligence testing, maternal deprivation, and cognitive development are but three of many topics in which developmental psychology has shaped beliefs and practices throughout Europe and North America' (Woodhead, 1999, p. 9).

This book will argue that a conceptual framework that incorporates a cross-cultural, ecological and black perspective for understanding the development of black children is critical to address omissions in existing theoretical formulations and research in the discipline of child development.

Cross-cultural psychologists (mainly in the USA) have presented alternative perspectives on black and minority child development (Gardiner, 1994; Greenfield and Cocking, 1994; Wilson, 1978). A number of psychologists in the US have recently begun to call for the inclusion of cross-cultural approaches to Western psychology (e.g., Segall et al., 1990). However, in Britain there is a lack of research from a cross-cultural perspective. The body of literature representing the deficit view of black children and families has most strongly influenced the professional and personal perceptions of social workers in Britain (see Robinson, 1995).

The failure to include black children in our conceptual thinking about service delivery has occurred in spite of strong empirical evidence supporting the need to integrate culturally sensitive perspectives in social work research and practice (Davis and Proctor 1989; Pinderhughes 1989). As a result, black children and families are seen by social workers whose standards of behaviour, often perceived as being the norm, have little or nothing to do with designing ways to ensure effective therapeutic outcomes for black children (Canino and Spurlock, 2000; Fontes, 1995; Pinderhughes, 1989).

A black psychological perspective challenges the Eurocentric theoretical formulations and research paradigms that have a potentially oppressive effect on black people. It attempts to build a theoretical model that organizes, explains, and leads to understanding the behaviour of black people. Research knowledge and information from a black psychological perspective on black family life, black children and young people are vital to the social work profession. Much of the work and research involved in developing a black perspective in psychology was initiated in the USA by black psychologists (Robinson, 1995). It may be some time before such perspectives are developed and articulated in Britain by psychologists and social workers, but, in the meantime, some understanding of current research and theory is needed to guide present understanding, action and research in Britain.

Some definitions

Throughout this book I use different labels to denote different ethnic and cultural groups. Sometimes I refer to black children, at other times, I use the term minority ethnic children or children from different cultural backgrounds. My choice of a specific label is based on the most appropriate term for the topic being discussed.

Black: The term 'black' has direct relevance to the discussion throughout this article, and has been used to describe people from South Asian, African and Caribbean backgrounds. While it is necessary to emphasize the heterogeneity of black people, of equal importance is the consideration of how black people in Britain differ from the white group. In Britain, 'Asian groups claim they are not "black" as part of their struggle to assert their own particularity in historical, cultural, ethical and linguistical terms' (Dominelli, 1997, pp. 7–8). This book does not, however, use the term 'black' to deny the uniqueness of different ethnic groups. It is used 'as an inclusive political term to counter the divisive aspects of racism' (Dominelli, 1997, p. 7). It is not my intention to exclude other groups but to point out that some of the issues concerning these groups also apply to other minority groups.

Race: Popular definitions of 'race' have conceptualized the term within a biological classification system. However, the validity of 'race' as a purely biological variable has been hotly debated and rejected, and 'race' has come to have a social and political meaning that, in part, is related to its original assumed biological roots (Yee et al., 1993). Smedley (1993, p. 22) notes that 'race'

> was the cultural invention of arbitrary meaning applied to what appeared to be natural divisions within the human species. The meaning has social value but no intrinsic relationship to the biological diversity itself. Race has a reality created in the human mind, not a reflection of objective truths . . . the physical differences were a major tool by which the dominant whites constructed and maintained social barriers and economic inequalities; that is, they consciously sought to create social stratification based on visible differences.

Ethnicity: A great deal of confusion surrounds the meaning of the term 'ethnic' or 'ethnicity'. Many uses and definitions of the terms can be found in the literature. My usage of the term 'ethnic group' parallels Yinger's (1976, p. 200) definition:

> A segment of a larger society whose members are thought, by themselves and/or others, to have a common origin and to share important segments of a common culture and who, in addition, participate in shared activities in which the common origin and culture are significant ingredients.

However, in the United States, ethnicity has been used as a euphemism for 'race' when referring to people of colour (that is, those persons whose ostensible ancestry is at least in part African,

Asian, Latin American, and/or combinations of these groups and/or white or European ancestry) and as a nonracial designation for whites (Betancourt and Lopez, 1993). Similar usages of the term 'ethnicity' can be found in Britain. Psychologists usually use the term ethnicity as a category to describe differences among people – reporting for example, ethnic differences in socialization.

Minority ethnic: My use of this term parallels Thoburn et al.'s (2000) use of the term in their study of family placement for children of minority ethnic origin. Children of minority ethnic origin 'were born to families who belonged to ethnic groups which are a minority in the UK [US] population' (p. 8).

Culture: The word ' "culture" denotes a way of life (family life, patterns of behaviour and belief, languages, etc.) but it is important to note that cultures are not static, especially in a community where there are people from several cultures living side by side' (Fernando, 1995, p. 5). Culture refers to 'child rearing habits, family systems, and ethical values or attitudes common to a group' (Fernando, 1991, p. 10).

According to Fernando (1991), culture is characterized by behaviour and attitudes; it is determined by upbringing and choice, and perceived as changeable (assimilation and acculturation). In contrast to the usual perception of relatively fixed 'cultures', Fernando argues that 'culture' needs to be considered as something that is subject to a fluidity of movement (Fernando, 1991). Indeed over the last decade and more the concept of culture has become a subject of critical debate in anthropology; and the idea of a stable, bounded and territorially specific culture has been transformed into a conception of culture as fluid, complex and transnational (Hannerz, 1996; Olwig and Hastrup, 1997).

Although cultural knowledge is important in helping social workers identify potential conflict areas, they must be careful not to apply cultural information in a stereotypic way. For example, white social workers need to identify possible gender differences within black groups. According to Ahmed (1996), 'black women negotiate between a number of cultures . . . the culture of "traditionalists" within black communities . . . [and] the culture of resistance to "traditionalism" . . . [However], above all, there is the culture of racism of the dominant society'. Likewise, practitioners also need to examine the impact of racism and discrimination on black child development. Locke (1992, p. 9) notes that 'Racism and prejudice are inextricably entwined in the oppression of culturally diverse groups in the US [and Britain]. Furthermore, 'culturally diverse individuals might be considered deviant with respect to socialization, religion, etc., and other areas' (Locke, 1992, p. 11).

Acculturation: Acculturation is a variable that must be considered in discussions of black child development (Robinson, 2001). The construct of acculturation has been used by psychologists in their efforts to describe within-group cultural differences. Acculturation may be defined 'in terms of the degree of integration of new cultural patterns into the original cultural patterns into the original cultural patterns' (Paniagua, 1994, p. 8). It therefore refers to the interaction between a dominant and a nondominant culture in which one is affected much more profoundly than the other. Psychologists have considered acculturation along a number of dimensions. One area of research has sought to understand the psychological impact of migration and acculturation (see Berry, 1980 for a detailed review). Another line of research has focused on 'levels of acculturation' as a way of delineating within-group cultural differences. This paradigm suggests that a person arriving in the United States or Britain, from Asia or Africa, gradually moves along the continuum from the nondominant pole toward the dominant pole, although numerous factors including age, gender and social class (Szapocznik et al., 1978; Ward, 2001) are thought to affect the rate at which this occurs. Paniagua (1994) notes that different acculturation scales have been developed to measure acculturation levels among different cultural groups, and presents examples of acculturation scales across four multicultural groups.

Ruiz (1981) has suggested a modification to the general 'levels of acculturation' – that is, that acculturation may be situational. Thus, a person might behave in a manner more closely associated with the dominant culture at work, but act in a way more congruent with the nondominant culture while at home. Keefe and Padilla (1987, p. 16) proposed that 'the acceptance of new cultural traits and the loss of traditional cultural traits varies from trait to trait'. For instance, the authors found that although it is true that some traits (e.g., first language ability) do diminish progressively from generation to generation, other traits (e.g., the extended family) actually seem to go stronger from the first to the fourth generation of Mexican American families. There is little research on differences between first and second generation Asians and African Caribbeans living in Britain (Ghuman, 2003; Modood et al., 1994; Robinson, 2003).

Cultural racism: Cultural racism is a relatively new form of racism and has been called 'modern racism' (McConahay, 1983), 'aversive racism' (Gaertner and Dovidio, 1986) and 'symbolic racism' (Sears, 1988). The root of 'modern racism' is in a continuing Eurocentric philosophy that values mainstream (dominant culture) beliefs and attitudes more highly than culturally diverse belief systems.

According to Fernando (1991, p. 18), 'racism affects our perceptions of culture and these assumptions are incorporated into the training of professionals'. In British society 'there is a hierarchy of cultures and those of "racial" minority groups are ranked very low indeed' (Ahmed, 1996, p. 123). White Western European religion, music, philosophy, law, politics, economics, morality, science and medicine are all considered to be the best in the world. Thus, 'references to black clients' cultures frequently reflect negative valuations rather than sensitivity' (Ahmed, 1996, p. 123). Gushue (1993) also notes that certain cultures (for example Northern European) are judged as more acceptable by the dominant culture than are others (e.g., African and Asian). Cultural racism includes the individual and institutional expression of the superiority of one race's cultural heritage (and concomitant value system) over that of other races. Therefore, the white majority value system summarized by Katz (1985) and elaborated upon in more recent texts (Pedersen, 1988; Ponterotto and Casas, 1991) serves as a foundation for cultural racism when it is perceived as the 'model' system, and when those individuals who possess alternative value systems are thought of by the white majority as being deficient in some way.

Limitations of Western developmental psychology

For many social scientists and psychologists, the word 'different', when applied to black people, became synonymous with 'deficient'. A main feature of Eurocentric psychology is the assumption among psychologists that people are alike in all important aspects. McLoyd (1991) notes the way this false universality is implied and maintained through the insistence by a great many psychological journals on the use of a European comparison group when doing research with African-American populations, in effect positioning the European-American comparison group as the standard of measurement. This comparative paradigm has been exacerbated by a heavy reliance on two theoretical models that have been used by psychologists to explain or describe differences among black and minority groups (Robinson, 1995). The inferiority model maintains that black people are intellectually, physically, and mentally inferior to white people – due to genetics/heredity (see Jensen, 1969). The deficit/deficiency model conceives of the 'culturally deprived' as those who lack adequate exposure to Eurocentric values, norms, customs, and lifestyles. Implicit in the concept of cultural deprivation, however, is the notion that the dominant white middle class culture established the normative standard.

In their attempt to explain what they considered to be 'universal human phenomena', European psychologists implicitly and explicitly began to establish a normative standard of behaviour against which all other cultural groups would be measured. According to Lamb (1992) Western social scientists have with a few recent exceptions, attempted to develop universally valid accounts of human development on the basis of studies that focused on only a narrow stratum of human existence.

What emerged as normal or abnormal was always in comparison to how closely a particular thought or behaviour paralleled that of white people. Hence, normality is established on a model of the middle class Caucasian male of European descent. The more one approximates this model in appearance, values and behaviour, the more 'normal' one is considered to be. The obvious advantage for Europeans is that such norms confirm their reality as *the* reality. But, the major problem with such normative assumptions for non-European people is the inevitable categorization of anyone unlike this model as 'deviant'. The result, as noted by various authors (Guthrie, 1998; Robinson, 1995; White and Parham, 1990) is often inferiority-based and deficit- and deficiency-oriented conclusions about the nature of black psychological functioning in general and human development in particular. The deficit model previously used in research of minority ethnic children contrasts sharply with the assumptions of the cross-cultural approach, which attempts to avoid ethnocentric evaluation of one group's practices and beliefs as being superior without considering their origins and functions from the perspective of the reality of that cultural group. It is only recently, and largely through the efforts of researchers with minority backgrounds, that deficit assumptions have been questioned in research on minority children. Rogoff and Morelli (1989) write that:

For many years researchers [in US and Britain] were intent on comparing the behaviour and skills of minority children with mainstream children without taking into consideration the cultural contexts in which minority and mainstream children develop. This approach involved 'deficit model' assumptions that mainstream skills and upbringing are normal and that variations observed with minorities are aberrations that produce deficits; intervention programs were designed to provide minority children with experiences to make up for their assumed deficits.

(1989, p. 346)

The field of developmental psychology is 'an ethnocentric one dominated by a Euro-American perspective' (Greenfield and Cocking, 1994, p. ix). According to Woodhead (1999), 'the vast majority of studies of early child development and education have been carried out in a very narrow socio-economic and cultural context – mainly in Europe and in North America. Yet, Europe only constitutes 12% of the world's population, North America a further 5% (Penn, 1998, cited in Woodhead, 1999, p. 9). The lack of attention to issues of race, ethnicity, and culture in developmental psychology has resulted in a literature on black children and their families that concentrates on explaining developmental deviations in comparison to white middle class populations rather than examining normative developmental processes and outcomes. Most psychological studies of child development tend not to use black people as respondents. This omission has been partly deliberate because it is considered that the marginal, devalued status of black people makes it unlikely that they will illuminate the processes of 'normal' development. In addition, differences in culture are considered likely to 'spoil' the results by introducing too many variables into studies. These factors often result in an over-representation of white, middle class mothers and children in psychological studies of child development. The converse of this omission from psychological studies when the 'normal' is being studied is an over-representation of black families when the pathological is being studied. White (1980) maintains that traditional psychology's use of an Anglo middle class frame of reference gives it a distorted view of the adaptive ability of black children and black families. The establishment and maintenance of white middle class child rearing patterns as the standard for normal development of intellectual, cognitive and social competencies not only obscures cultural differences in child rearing, but assumes that anything other than mainstream competencies are inferior. Some psychologists express little interest in trying to understand any culture other than their own. Wheeler and Reis (1988. p. 36) argue that 'It takes more intellectual resources than we have just to understand our own current culture . . . We just don't have time to read about [other] cultures'. Such sentiments are widespread among European American psychologists who represent the dominant white majority (Lonner, 1994; Marsumoto and Juang, 2005). Thus, the unwillingness of Western psychologists to acknowledge culture as central to the analysis and understanding of human development creates an atmosphere wherein the culture of the theorist becomes the lens through which the culture under study is viewed. A great many researchers (Nobles, 1986; Berry et al., 2002; Cole, 1995a; Greenfield and Cocking, 1994; Holdstock, 2000) have noted that theories are often tied to the theorist's perspective on human nature. As a result, theories are intimately connected to the theorist's worldview or his or her beliefs of how the world operates. As noted earlier, when the theorizing is done about a cultural group other than the one to which the theorist belongs, the result is often the imposition of some form of cultural bias. Woodhead (1999) argues that the

> social scientific lens needs to become more reflective, in order to problematise familiar child-rearing values and practices, ways of learning, thinking and conceptualising the self that are presumed to be normal or even natural . . . [however] 'reflexivity' remains an alien principle within much mainstream developmental psychology.
> (Woodhead, 1999, pp.12–3).

At the beginning of the 21st century, the mixture of voluntary and involuntary immigrants within countries such as Britain, US, and France 'has left physically identifiable subcultural groups termed *minorities* . . . [and] each minority group has its own cultural history and roots. These facts raise critical issues for understanding the development and socialization of minority children' (Greenfield and Cocking, 1994: X). Yet mainstream Euro-American psychology has not dealt extensively with immigration, perhaps because, like the study of culture (Shweder et al., 1982), it poses challenges to the search for universals in human behaviour and development. The relations between culture, socialization, and development are much more complex for minorities immersed in a dominant majority culture. Although the basic mechanisms for socialisation are the same for black and white children – reinforcement, modelling, identification and so forth – the transmittal sources and content may exhibit some subtle and some obvious differences for black children. The need for adaptive responses to social, economic and political barriers helps to shape the socialisation of black children (Harrison et al., 1990). Peters (1985) indicated that many black parents focused on racial barrier messages and emphasised learning to cope with and survive prejudice in a white-dominated society.

Toward a black perspective

The framework for developing a black perspective is based on the notion of common experiences that black people in Britain share. A black perspective in psychology is concerned with combating racist and stereotypic, weakness-dominated and inferiority-oriented conclusions about black people. This perspective is interested in the psychological well-being of black people and is critical of oppressive research paradigms and theoretical formulations that have a potentially oppressive effect on black people. Black psychologists (mainly in the US) have presented alternative perspectives on black child development (see e.g., Parham et al., 1999; Wilson, 1978). However, the research of black scholars, who have unique insights into the problems of minority children and adolescents, has largely been neglected by mainstream developmental psychology (Spencer et al., 1985). The training social workers receive is first 'in white middle class institutions, and second theoretically and culturally Eurocentric and American (i.e., US) in origin (Lago and Thompson, 1994, p. 210). Therefore, 'many white people are quite unable to cope with radical black perspectives and black people's pain and anger, specifically in relation to racism' (1994, p. 211). An understanding of the black frame of reference will enable social workers to come up with more accurate and comprehensive explanations of black child development.

Cross-cultural perspectives

Developmental psychology is an area that is perhaps more vulnerable to cultural influences than any other field of social sciences. As Nsamenang (1995) points out 'the cultural salience of children makes the study of child development open to the cultural guidance of the discipline in ways that are not possible in the case of other sciences that deal with subject matter which is less influenced by culturally mediated rules (Valsiner, 1987, cited in Nsamenang, 1995, p. 3). Recently a number of psychologists have begun to call for the inclusion of culturally centred as well as cross-cultural approaches to Western psychology (Cole, 1995a; Lum, 2003; Rogoff and Chavajay, 1995; Segall et al., 1998). Furthermore, there have been a number of articles noting the centrality race, culture, ethnicity, and importance of studying culture by psychological researchers (Betancourt and Lopez, 1993; Cole, 1984). Nevertheless, the dominant knowledge of current developmental psychology comes from Euro-American researchers studying the development of children from their own cultural experience.

Segall et al. (1990) define cross-cultural psychology as 'the scientific study of human behaviour and its transmission, taking into account the ways in which the behaviors are shaped and influenced by social and cultural forces' (1990, p. 1). The study of ethnic groups and minorities within culturally plural societies is just as much a part of cross-cultural psychology as the study of widely varying and geographically dispersed cultural groups.

Black psychology has also addressed the question of culture (see Baldwin, 1984; Boykin, 1994). Various authors (for e.g. Boykin, 1994; 1997; Nsamenang, 1995; Shade, 1991) have examined the effects of African and African American culture on the development of black children. For example, Nsamenang's (1995) research explores the effects of differing cultural contexts on the socialization of African children and Shade's (1991) research on African American social cognition argues empirically that cognitive style, in which people organize and understand their world, is culturally induced, further arguing that African Americans have a distinctive cognitive style that should be embraced, understood, and appreciated.

Berry et al. (1992) proposed three goals for the field of cross-cultural psychology: the first goal involves testing or extending the generalizability of existing theories and findings. Berry and Dasen (1974) referred to this as the 'transport and test goal' in which hypotheses and findings from one culture are transported to another so that their validity can be tested in other cultural settings or groups. For example, are the stages of cognitive development proposed by Jean Piaget specific to certain types of cultures, or are they universal? The second goal focuses on exploring other cultures in order to discover variations in behaviour that may not be part of one's own cultural experience. In other words, if findings cannot be generalized, what are the reasons for this, and are there behaviours unique to these other cultures? The third goal – which follows from the first two – is aimed at integrating findings in such a way as to generate a more universal psychology applicable to a wider range of cultural settings and societies.

Jahoda (1986), in an introduction to the special issue of the *International Journal of Behavioural Development*, called for a 'Cross-cultural developmental psychology . . . [which] is not just comparative [but] essentially is an outlook that takes culture seriously' and deplored the fact that 'theories and findings in developmental psychology originating in the First World tend to be disseminated to the Third World as gospel truth' (p. 417).

How can a cross-cultural perspective contribute to our understanding of human development? Gardiner (1994) has pointed to a number of important benefits. First, looking at behaviour from this perspective compels researchers to seriously reflect on the variety of ways in which their cultural beliefs and values affect the development of their theories and research designs. Second, increased awareness of cross-cultural findings provides an opportunity to extend or restrict the implications of research conducted in a single cultural group, most notably the United States and similar Western societies. Third, it reduces ethnocentrism – by looking at behaviours as they occur in another culture. It is important to note that the study of ethnic groups and minorities within culturally plural societies is just as much a part of cross-cultural psychology as the study of widely varying and geographically dispersed cultural groups.

One way of conceptualizing principles in cross-cultural studies is by using the analytical concepts of emics, etics, and theorics (Berry, 1969; Berry et al., 2002). Etics refer to aspects of life that appear to be consistent across different cultures; that is, etics refer to universal or pancultural truths or principles. Emics, in contrast, refer to aspects of life that appear to be different across cultures; emics, therefore, refer to truths or principles that are culture-specific (Berry, 1969). Etics that are assumed, but have not been demonstrated, to be true universals have been called imposed etics (Berry 1969, p. 124). Such etics are said to be usually only Euro-American emics indiscriminately, even ethnocentrically, imposed on the interpretation of behaviour in other cultures. A true etic, in contrast, is empirically and theoretically derived from the common features of a phenomenon under investigation in different cultures. Berry (1969, p. 124) called this a derived etic. Berry (1980, p. 13) defined theorics as 'theoretical concepts employed by social scientists to interpret and account for emic variation and etic constancies'. A cross-cultural psychology that relies solely or primarily on Euro-American concepts cannot be expected to achieve its stated aims. However, there is a paucity of theorizing with the use of concepts that are non-Western origin' (1980, p. 9).

Etic versus emic goals provides social workers with a theoretical framework for working with culturally diverse children and young people and adults. Poortinga (1997) states: 'Behavior is emic or culture specific, to the extent it can only be understood within the cultural context within which it occurs; it is etic, or universal, in as much as it is common to human beings independent of their culture' (p. 352). It follows that when a researcher or observer assumes that his or her own emic-etic distinction is true for all cultures, she/he is operating from an ethnocentric point of view and that cultural misunderstanding will result. For example, in the case of Erikson's theory, the development of autonomy and independence (the emic) 'fits' well with Western cultural values.

Ecological perspective

This approach allows us to clearly see and understand the connection between culture and development. The ecology of human development – defined by Bronfenbrenner (1979) – involves 'the scientific study of the progressive, mutual accommodation between an active, growing human being and the changing properties of the immediate settings in which the developing person lives, as this process is affected by relations between these settings, and by the larger contexts in which the settings are embedded' (1979, p. 21). Bronfenbrenner criticized traditional research carried out on children. He notes that 'much of contemporary developmental psychology is the science of the strange behaviors of children in strange situations with strange adults for the briefest possible periods of time' (1977, p. 513).

Bronfenbrenner divides the ecological environment into four levels – microsystem, mesosystem, exosystem, macrosystem. The microsystem represents the interactions between the child and his/her immediate environment (e.g., family) and resulting behaviours such as dependence or independence and cooperation or competition. Bronfenbrenner (1993) has expanded this definition to include 'a pattern of activities, roles, and interpersonal relations experienced by the developing person in a given face-to-face setting with particular physical, social, and symbolic features that invite, permit, or inhibit engagement in sustained, progressively more complex interaction with, and activity in the immediate environment' (p. 15). The second level, mesosystem, 'comprises the linkages and processes taking place between two or more settings containing the developing person (1993, p. 22). This is a system made up of two or more microsystems (e.g., home and nursery, nursery and school, or family and peer group). It is the mesosystem that links or ties together information, knowledge, and attitudes from one setting that help to shape behaviour or development in another setting. According to Bronfenbrenner, the exosystem 'comprises the linkages and processes taking place between two or more settings, at least one of which does not contain the developing person, but in which events occur that indirectly influence processes within the immediate setting in which the developing person lives' (1993, p. 22). Bronfenbrenner provides an example of the link between the home and a parent's workplace for the developing child. Other less formal settings might include the extended family (aunts, uncles, cousins) as well as friends and neighbours. The macrosystem is the final level. Bronfenbrenner notes that this level 'consists of the overarching pattern of micro-, meso-, and exosystems characteristic of a given culture, subculture, or other extended social structure, with particular reference to the . . . belief systems, resources, hazards, lifestyles, opportunity structures, life course options and patterns of social interchange that are embedded in such overarching systems' (1993, p. 25). The ecological perspective is particularly 'relevant in analyzing the impacts of poverty, discrimination, immigration, and social isolation on the psychosocial development and adjustment of minority children and youth' (Gibbs and Huang 2003, p. 6).

Although it is essential for social workers to have a basic understanding of people's cultural values, there is the ever-present danger of over-generalizing and stereotyping. Information about Asian and

African Caribbean cultural values should act as guidelines rather than absolutes. Belonging to a particular group may mean sharing common values and experiences; but, as noted above, individual members of a culture may vary greatly from the pattern that is typical within that culture (Robinson, 1998). It is critical for cross-cultural psychology to acknowledge the extent of individual differences within a given cultural or linguistic group. Thus, there may be generalizations to make about a group, in terms of beliefs, values, actions, but these generalizations cannot be expected to hold for all members of the group. Members of every group are shaped by culture, but also by acculturation, gender, age, income, education, etc. Recognizing intragroup differences is critical and helps avoid stereotyping. Race, gender and class inequalities all play a part in shaping dominant and minority groups' cultures, defining opportunities and moulding traditions (Ahmed et al., 1986; Gilroy, 1987; Mirza, 1992).

Conclusions

What are the implications of the above discussion for social work training, practice and policy?

The issues discussed in this book are offered as the initial steps towards the development of a conceptual framework for social work practice with minority children and adolescents. My intent in this book is to present a framework that is sensitive to a variety of ethnic and cultural groups. Social workers need to be offered choices about a child psychology that reflects the diverse cultures and upbringing of their clients. Social workers operate in a context of diversity, and forms of practice that do not reflect this are likely to undermine the importance of nondominant cultural patterns, beliefs and expectations. Practitioners' values may conflict with the values of minority ethnic groups. For example, many social work theories reflect Western, middle class values (e.g., individualism) that conflict with the 'familialism and group responsibility' (collectivism) valued by black people. An understanding of the dimension of an individualistic or independent (Western) versus a collective or interdependent orientation (Asian, African) will enable social workers to gain a better understanding of the cross-cultural roots of socialization practices in Asian and African Caribbean families. According to Sue and Sue (1999, p. 110)

To become a culturally skilled helper [practitioner], one must 1) be aware of one's own cultural heritage and of biases, values, and preconceived notions that can intrude in helping relationships, 2) acquire knowledge of culturally diverse groups that will pave the way for grasping the worldviews of culturally different clients, and 3) develop a range of intervention strategies and skills that are appropriate, relevant, and sensitive to diverse groups.

However, social workers must not let their assumptions about other cultures become so fixed that they expect all black clients from a particular culture to think or behave in the same way.

The book draws together research material and literature on black/minority child development from North America and Britain. It will be difficult to strike a careful balance between American and British literature, as there is a dearth of research/literature on the development of black children in British literature. Most of the existing research and literature in this area is US based. However, many of the findings are relevant to other non-white racial groups. The book identifies the appropriate elements within child psychology which are most relevant to social work students and practitioners working with black children.

There are limitations to the extent and depth an introductory text can cover. I prefer to cover some topics in relative depth, rather than write a catalogue. It is hoped that an understanding of child development from a cross-cultural, black, and ecological perspective will help social workers move away from a deficit model of black child development in which differences are seen as deficiencies (Robinson, 1995; 2001) and adopt 'an approach which acknowledges considerable racial, cultural and social diversity, and at the same time maintains an anti-discriminatory and anti-oppressive value base' (Boushel, 2000, p. 85). Social workers can work more effectively with black clients if they begin from their clients' points of strength. A strengths-coping perspective tends to describe black behaviour almost exclusively as positive adaptation and does not attempt to utilize a white cultural framework as a standard for all behavioural phenomena.

Chapter 2 discusses attachment theory and its relevance to children from different cultural groups. Chapter 3 discusses racial and ethnic identity development and acculturation in black adolescents. It examines eurocentric theories of identity development and discusses different racial/ethnic identity development models, including Cross's model of psychological nigrescence and Phinney's model of ethnic identity development. It also discusses Berry's model of acculturation and implications for social work practice. Chapter 4 examines the intellectual development of black children. It discusses Piaget's theory of cognitive development and intelligence as measured by IQ tests. Chapter 5 discusses cross-cultural perspectives in communication. Chapter 6 examines the racial/cultural influences on socialization practices in minority families.

Each chapter will include a section entitled 'Implications for social work practice' which will attempt to relate child development theory and research to social work practice. Finally, this book aims to contribute to the development of anti-racist and culturally sensitive social work practice with black children and adolescents in Britain.

2

Attachment Theory:
Cross-Cultural Perspectives

This chapter is not intended to be an exhaustive overview of attachment research (for a detailed review see, Bretherton and Waters, 1985; Parkes and Stevenson-Hinde, 1982). Instead, the aim of this chapter is to focus on one aspect of attachment that has sparked considerable research and debate in the past few years, the role of culture. More specifically, this chapter will examine the concept of attachment and its relevance in cross-cultural settings. It will also explore the implications for social work practice in multicultural Britain.

During the first year of life, children actively begin to explore their environment; their curiosity seems almost limitless. In order to ensure continued learning and growth, the caretaker must encourage this exploration. At the same time, the child must trust that the caretaker is nearby and provides a safe haven when needed. The emotional bond between child and caretakers that allows children to feel secure and to know to whom they can turn in threatening situations is known as attachment (Maccoby, 1980). Thus, attachment refers to the special bond that develops between the infant and caregiver. Attachment provides the child with emotional security. Once attachment is established, babies are distressed by separation from their mothers (called separation distress or anxiety). The studies on attachment in rhesus monkeys by the Harlows (Harlow and Harlow 1962) highlighted the importance of contact and physical comfort in the development of attachment.

Attachment behaviours

Seeking the contact and closeness of the parent or caregiver is one set of behaviours that indicate an attachment. Other attachment behaviours include the infants showing relief or joy upon reunion. Even if there is no physical contact the infant displays a clear preference for the caregiver by seeking eye contact or by being especially attentive to the sound of the mother's or father's voice. The parents would display a similar, though more subtle, set of attachment behaviours. Another characteristic of attachment behaviour is the extent to which the infant uses attachment figures as a secure base from which to explore the physical and social environment. Infants vary in the extent to which they use their parents as a secure base and source of comfort.

Bretherton (1992) has provided an excellent and thorough review of the origins and historical development of attachment theory and of the contributions of its principal architects – John Bowlby and Mary Ainsworth (cited in Bretherton 1992) for a more extensive discussion.

Attachment theory was first introduced in the 1960s by John Bowlby (1907–1990), a child psychiatrist. Bowlby's studies evolved from studies in the 1940s and 1950s of bonding behaviour in birds and mammals, which showed that bird and other animal babies did not develop normally when separated from their mothers. Around the same time, other studies were beginning to show the adverse effects of institutional care on human infants. In his own practice, Bowlby was observing anxiety, grief, and depression in children separated from their mothers when hospitalized – feelings that could not be explained by the then-prevalent concepts of psychoanalytic theory. From these studies and observations, Bowlby concluded that like other animals and birds, human infants too must have such bonding behaviours, that they too must be predisposed toward some sort of relational experience, and that with them too development could go awry if separated from their mothers. Thus began the theory of attachment and separation. Attachment theory was advanced by his colleague Mary Ainsworth in her studies of mother–infant bonding during the first year.

Bowlby (1969) detailed four phases occurring in the first few years of life during which the infant gradually directs more attention and efforts toward being physically close to his or her caregiver. In the first, pre-attachment phase (0–3 months), the infant appears to be interested in anyone. The primary caregiver is not distinguished from others. It is not until about two or three months of age that the infant discriminates the caregiver from other people. During the attachment-in-the-making phase (3–6 months of age), a unique relationship is forming between the baby and his or her primary caregiver. The infant smiles and vocalizes more frequently and intensely to the caregiver. Although the infant may be relatively receptive to strangers, the baby clearly is able to discriminate the mother figure. The clear-cut attachment phase emerges between 6–12 months of age. At this age the infant is able to get around by crawling, creeping, and walking. These motor skills allow the infant to actively seek out and become physically close to his or her parent. During this time infants also generally acquire object permanence (see Chapter 4), or in this case, person permanence (the infant can now keep someone in mind even when that person is absent). When the mother leaves the room, the infant is likely to show signs of distress or to protest by crying. This reaction is called separation distress and usually peaks in intensity around 12 months.

Stranger anxiety refers to the infant's general wariness of unfamiliar people. This type of wariness usually peaks in intensity around 8–10 months of age. According to Bowlby, the last phase is the goal-corrected partnership phase (12–24 months), which represents a more complex interplay of cognitive, social, and emotional behaviour.

In conclusion, Bowlby's (1969) evolutionary theory of attachment states that infants must have a preprogrammed, biological basis for becoming attached to their caregivers. This innate behavioural repertoire includes smiling and cooing to elicit physical attachment behaviours on the part of the mother. Bowlby argues that the attachment relationship between caregiver and child functioned as a survival strategy. Infants had a greater chance of survival if they remained close to the mother for comfort and protection.

Ainsworth's classification system of attachment

Ainsworth (1978) expanded upon Bowlby's primarily biological perspective through her now famous 'strange situation' experiments to study mother–infant attachment during the first year of life. These experiments involved observing children 12–18 months of age and their mothers in a series of separation and reunion sequences, in a laboratory situation and in their homes, several times over the course of a year. Ainsworth's experiments have been replicated by other researchers in different countries with different cultural groups. In the last three decades, attachment behaviours in infants, children, adolescents, and adults have been the subject of much research. In this research, four principal patterns of attachment and the family conditions that promote them have been identified. These are the secure, insecure-ambivalent/resistant, insecure-avoidant, and insecure disorganized/disoriented. These patterns begin to form in the first year of life, and barring a change in the attachment relationships or other outside intervention, they tend to persist through childhood, adolescence, and adulthood, and get played out in the individual's relationship with his/her own children.

Ainsworth and her colleagues (Ainsworth and Wittig, 1969) are credited with developing a standardized event (the strange situation) that makes it possible to observe the type of bond a child has with her primary caretaker. The Strange Situation procedure consists of eight standardized episodes (for a detailed account see Ainsworth, 1978). In the strange situation, a mother and child are placed together in a room equipped with toys. A stranger enters the room and sits quietly in a chair. The stranger begins a conversation with the caretaker and, after a while slowly approaches the child. The mother leaves the room while the stranger keeps interacting with the child. After a few minutes, the mother returns, re-unites with the child, and the stranger leaves the room. Another few minutes pass and the mother leaves the room again. Shortly thereafter, the stranger re-enters and tries to distract the child. Finally, the mother returns and re-unites with the child.

The child's responses are recorded at specific times during the situation. How close does the child stay to the mother during the initial period? How does she react when approached by a stranger in the presence of the mother? How distressed is the child when the mother leaves the room? How does she react when alone with the stranger? Is the child happy when reunited with the mother? Specific responses indicate the type of attachment the child has with the primary caretaker.

Ainsworth and her colleagues observed that children could be classified according to three categories of behaviour patterns when faced with the strange situation (Ainsworth, 1982). Children classified as *anxious/avoidant* will not pay much attention to whether the primary caretaker is absent or not. If they experience distress, they may turn to a stranger for comfort. On the mother's return, these children do not actively strive to reunite and be close. Children classified as *anxious/resistant* tend to stay close to their caretaker and become very distressed when she leaves the room. Even when comforted after the caretaker's return, these children will take a long time to settle down and remain anxious about the caretaker's whereabouts. Finally, *securely attached* children will be calm and not threatened by strangers in the presence of the caretaker. When the caretaker departs, the distressed child is unlikely to be comforted by a stranger. When the caretaker returns, the child is eager to re-unite and will settle down and relax very quickly.

According to Ainsworth et al. (1978), the securely attached infant uses the parent as a base of security in the strange situation. During the parent's absence and/or in the presence of the stranger the infant may or may not reduce play and exploration, and may or may not show signs of distress such as crying. Upon the parents return, though, securely attached babies generally make contact with their parents either by looking at and vocalizing to them or, in the case of those who have experienced distress, by seeking contact and comfort from them. The hallmark of securely attached infants is their ability to use their attachment figures to regain their source of security when stressed; this allows them to once again explore and play. The resistant, insecurely attached infant is more likely to seem anxious or distressed even when its parent is present in the room. This type of infant has trouble using the parent as a secure base for exploration. Upon reunion after separation, the infant, while seeking contact with the parent in the next moment, may resisit contact or act angry. The avoidant, insecure attachment pattern also reflects some difficulty between parent and child. The infant seems to ignore the parent much of the time and does not use the parent as a secure base for exploration. There is little distress or protest when the parent leaves, and the infant usually ignores the parent when she or he returns. This type of infant is as easily comforted by a stranger as by its parent.

According to Ainsworth (1978) the type of attachment an infant forms is influenced by the quality of the caregiver-child interaction. Caregivers who sensitively responded to their infants during the first year of life were likely to have securely attached infants. When the caregivers were insensitive, insecure relationships more often resulted. For the secure infant, the mother's high quality caregiving enabled the infant to form an internal working model of the self as worthy and competent and a model of others as responsive and dependable. Bowlby (1982) and Ainsworth (1982) concurred that these internal representations were essential to healthy personality development.

During the past two decades the Strange Situation procedure has been widely use by researchers in studying the development of individual differences in the quality of infant–adult attachments, and thus it has produced most of the empirical data in this area. The majority of attachment research has been conducted with middle class Euro-American families in the US. However, in recent years investigators in other countries – Germany, Holland, Israel, Japan and Sweden (Grossmann et al., 1981; Van Ijzendoorn and Kroonenberg, 1988; Sagi et al., 1985; Miyake et al., 1985; Lamb et al., 1982) have begun to employ the procedure.

Summary

Bowlby's (1969) evolutionary theory of attachment states that infants must have a preprogrammed, biological basis for becoming attached to their caregivers. He argues that the attachment relationship between caregiver and child functioned as a survival strategy. Ainsworth (1978) expanded upon Bowlby's primarily biological perspective through her 'strange situation' experiments to study mother–infant attachment during the first year of life. Four principal patterns of attachment have been classified. These are the secure, insecure-ambivalent/resistant, insecure-avoidant, and insecure-disorganized/disoriented. The type of attachment an infant forms is influenced by the quality of the caregiver–child interaction. Attachment research has been mainly conducted with middle class Euro-American families in the US.

Cross-cultural studies on attachment

Attachment theory was proposed as a universal theory of human development. If attachment is biologically based and adaptive in the evolutionary sense, as Bowlby (1969, 1982) asserted, then the major propositions in attachment theory should apply to all human beings in all times and places. The strange situation has been used in numerous cultures; by 12 months of age, infants universally display strong emotional attachments to their caregivers (Bretherton and

Waters, 1985). However, the quality and type of attachment seems to be influenced by the specific child rearing patterns predominate in the culture. Studies have shown that the Strange Situation attachment patterns occur in a wide variety of cultures (Lamb et al., 1982; Grosman et al., 1981; Miyake et al., 1985). Van Ijzendoorn and Kroonenberg (1988) summarized the distribution of the three attachment styles in eight different cultures (Germany, Great Britain, Netherlands, Sweden, Israel, Japan, China and United States). The authors found that the countries differed in the percentage of children falling into each of the attachment categories. The anxious/avoidant classification was relatively higher in West European countries and the anxious/resistant classification was relatively more prevalent in Japan and Israel.

Cole (1998) asks the question 'What are we to make of such variations?' (p. 21) He points out that:

> When interpretation is based on the distribution of types of attachment behaviours manifested in the Strange Situation alone, two lines of explanation are offered. The first assumes that the Strange Situation is a valid index of a universal form of emotional reaction that is distributed differently in different cultures. The second assumes that, although standardized, the Strange Situation is really a different situation in different cultural circumstances, in that it takes on different meanings for the participants. As LeVine and Miller (1990) point out, the assumption that the meaning of the Strange Situation is a culture-neutral and valid indicator of a universal form of relationship called attachment leads to the further assumption that the American pattern is a universal norm.
>
> (Cole, 1998, p. 21)

Several cross-cultural researchers have suggested that although a universal repertoire of attachment behaviours may exist among infants across cultures, the selection, shaping, and interpretation of these behaviours over time appear to be culturally patterned (Bretherton and Waters, 1985; Van Ijzendoorn 1990). Thus several scholars have suggested a move beyond 'the search for a so-called culture-free test . . . to [a] search for differences in outcomes in different cultures' (Van Ijzendoorn, 1990, p. 7). Or as Grossman and Grossman (1990) put it: 'The main issue is whether the different attachment strategies observed may be differentially adaptive in different cultures . . . It may well be that behaviour strategies are universal, but that the relevance for them may be culture-specific' (1990, p. 37). In a similar vein, Sagi (1990) notes that 'we can conclude that attachment theory is useful in the broader sense but always must be applied within the context of cultural idiosyncracies. Or, to state the case from a universalistic point of view, the repertoire of attachment behaviours is similar across countries, but the selection of these behaviours is culturally specific' (1990, p. 19).

Cross-cultural research on attachment relationships in Israel (Sagi et al., 1985A), Japan (Miyake et al., 1985), and Germany (Grossmann et al., 1981) suggests that aspects of attachment relationships are influenced by the cultural contexts. For example, Grossman et al. (1981) studied a group of families in northern Germany, and found that the majority of 12-month-old children were classifiable as insecurely attached to their mothers on the basis of videotaped strange situations. In particular, 49% were classified as insecure avoidant, almost double the proportion usually found in Euro-American samples. Observations of parent–child interactions within German homes, however, did not indicate that German mothers generally were insensitive to their children. Rather, these mothers endorsed a broader cultural belief system emphasizing independence; this system indicated that babies should be weaned from body contact with their mothers as soon as they became mobile. These cultural beliefs were translated into socialization practices that affected the mother–infant attachment relationships. For example, these mothers maintained a relatively large interpersonal distance from their children, they sometimes pushed their babies away, and they left them alone more often than US middle class mothers. German parents deliberately discourage their infants from clinging and becoming emotionally dependent because they value independence and obedience.

In Japan mothers are rarely separated from their infants; they spend much of their time talking to and touching their infants. Consequently, Japanese babies are more distressed by the presence of a stranger and separation from their mothers (Miyakeet al., 1985). Traditional Japanese mothers instill a strong sense of dependence in their young children by being available at all times (Miyake et al., 1985). As Japanese infants are rarely separated from their mothers, the separation during the Strange Situation may represent a highly unusual situation that may mean something different for Japanese infants and their mothers than for US infants and their mothers.

These two examples demonstrate that mother/caretakers bring their unique cultural beliefs about parenting to the relationship (Harkness and Super, 1996). Avoidance is also rarely observed in Strange Situations in Japan. From infancy on, Japanese children are socialized to maintain harmonious interpersonal interactions. Japanese citizens are expected to be very sensitive to others and to try and maintain harmony in personal relationships. Avoidant behaviour would be, at any age, considered rude. In preparing their children to live in a culture that values sensitivity and harmony, parents probably discourage their babies from ignoring caregivers or even turning the face away from a social partner. Ignoring the adult is certainly not likely to be interpreted or encouraged as a sign of healthy independence.

Of Israeli children that are raised on a kibbutz (collective farm), half display anxious ambivalent attachments and only a third appear to be securely attached (Sagi et al., 1985B). Sagi (1990) speculates that the high rate of insecurely attached children in the Israeli kibbutz may be a result of the specific child rearing arrangements. For example, caregivers in the kibbutz (metaplot) are often assigned to work with three or more infants during the day, while all of the infants are watched by a single caretaker at night (in kibbutzim with communal sleeping arrangements). Sagi argues that this 'multiple mothering' leads to inconsistencies in maternal behaviour and may result in different (possibly less secure) attachment patterns.

A study of attachment in China using the strange situation procedure has been conducted by Hu and Meng (1996). The distribution of attachment classifications in this Chinese sample was remarkably similar to the global distribution (Van Ijzendoorn and Kroonenberg, 1988). However, Hu and Meng (1996) questioned the validity of the avoidant category as an indication of insecure attachment. They noted that the avoidant infants did not show stranger anxiety, and they commented on the indifference the avoidant infants expressed toward their mothers at reunion. The researchers state that Chinese mothers emphasize early independence in their infants and, at the same time, stress their reliance on nonparental (usually the grandparent) caregivers. These factors, rather than an insecure relationship between the mother and her infant, may be responsible for findings of avoidant attachment. It may also be the case that subtle attachment behaviours (for instance, those that characterize avoidant relationships) are difficult even for well-trained coders to observe in infants from different cultures (Crittenden and Claussen, 2000).

One of the assumptions about the nature of attachment in Britain and US is that secure attachment is the ideal. The very term that Ainsworth and colleagues chose to describe this type of attachment, and the negative terms used to describe others, reflects this underlying bias. However, as noted above, cultures differ in their notion of 'ideal' attachment. Crittenden (2000) suggests that we should stop using value laden terms such as 'secure' and 'insecure' in describing the attachment relationship. Instead, she proposes that it may be more useful to describe the attachment relationship as 'adaptive' or 'maladaptive' to the specific context, which would take into consideration how cultures differ in the particular attachment strategy that may be most appropriate for that culture.

Some cross-cultural studies also challenge the notion that closeness to the mother is necessary for secure and healthy attachment. Indeed, this notion is prevalent in traditional theories of attachment based on research in the US. Studies involving an African tribe known as the Efe show a very different situation from that psychologists have come to accept as part of healthy attachment (Tronick et al., 1992). In the Efe tribe children enjoy multiple social relationships with other children and adults. However, particularly during the first year, the mother is involved in more than half of the child's social activities. This also means that children spend half of their time with individuals other than their mothers. For example, during the period when the mother works away from the camp, her child is left in the exclusive care of other adults or older children. Even when the mother is present, other family members, the children's peers, or other adults are continually engaged in social interactions with the child. In fact, the authors point out that at a given time about ten people are within sight or close hearing range of the child. The authors suggest that the children benefit from this setting in that they develop a multitude of social skills early in life; this leads to better adjustment in social situations later on.

Most of the literature on attachment patterns in different cultures suggests that attachment between infants and their caregivers is a universal phenomenon. There is also some evidence that the secure attachment relationship may be preferred in many different cultures (Posada et al., 1995). It does not, however, follow that the development of attachment is insensitive to culture-specific influences. If a cultural niche requires the suppression of negative emotions, infants may develop an avoidant attachment pattern to meet this cultural demand. The conceptual similarity of attachment security across diverging cultures does not mean that exactly the same infant attachment behaviours are considered to be indicative of secure or insecure attachment. In some cultures distal attachment behaviours may be stressed more than proximal behaviours or the other way round. For example, Gusii infants are accustomed to being greeted with a handshake instead of a hug by their mothers whereas Western infants look forward to 'more intimate' physical contact (Kermoian and Leiderman, 1986).

However, it is important to note that this is an ongoing debate. As stated earlier, researchers such as Crittenden (2000) argue that viewing attachment through the lens of being 'adaptive' and 'maladaptive' may be more useful than using the evaluative terms 'secure' and 'insecure'. She defines adaptive attachments as relationships that promote the maximum level of safety for the child within a specific cultural context. This would then allow us to define an 'optimal' relationship between infant and caregiver as one that may be achieved in different ways, under different circumstances, in different cultures.

In an article on African American-multiple caregiving, Jackson (1993) argues that 'attachments of African Americans should be studied with a focus on cultural practices of multiple caregiving and with an emic approach, in order to detect attachment phenomena inherent in the culture' (p. 87). Cross-cultural research has been using the etic approach more than the emic approach (Jackson, 1993; Van Ijzendoorn, 1990). As noted in Chapter 1, an etic refers to findings that appear to be consistent across different cultures; that is, an etic refers to a universal truth or principle. An emic, in contrast, refers to findings that appear to be different across cultures; an emic, therefore, refers to truths that are culture-specific. Thus, Jackson (1993) argues that 'misunderstanding of African American infant attachments is likely if evaluative standards derived from infant caregiving in traditional white middle class culture and an imposed etic approach are employed' (p. 87).

Substantial variation in the distribution of the three attachment classifications has been found among infants from differing regional and socio-economic populations within the same country

(Bretherton and Waters, 1985; Gardiner and Kosmitzki, 2005; Van Ijzendoorn and Kroonenberg, 1988). Harwood et al. (1995) carried out a study of mothers of infants of middle-income European American mothers, lower-income European American mothers, middle-income island Puerto Rican mothers, and lower-income island Puerto Rican mothers. The mothers were asked to comment on scenarios of toddlers' behaviours in the waiting room of a doctor's office (Harwood et al., 1995). Each scenario was a strange situation analogue and portrayed a child demonstrating behaviours associated with a different attachment classification – secure, insecure resistant, or insecure avoidant. Mothers' responses varied both with their socio-economic status and their culture. In discussing what they did or did not like about the toddlers' behaviours, European American mothers were more likely to discuss 'self-maximization', that is, self-confidence, independence, and development as an individual, and Puerto Rican mothers were more likely to discuss 'proper demeanor', that is, the child's manners, behaviour, cooperativeness, and acceptance by the larger community. However, within each cultural community, middle-income mothers were more likely to mention self-maximization, and lower-income mothers were more likely to mention proper demeanor (Harwood et al., 1995).

Summary

The Strange Situation attachment patterns occur in a wide variety of cultures. Although a universal repertoire of attachment behaviours may exist among infants across cultures, the selection, shaping, and interpretation of these behaviours over time appear to be culturally patterned. One of the assumptions about the nature of attachment in Britain and US is that secure attachment is ideal. Cultures differ on their notion of 'ideal' attachment and the meanings of different attachment behaviours. Studies have shown that similar behaviours in the strange situation may have very different meanings in different cultures. Viewing attachment through the lens of being 'adaptive' and 'maladaptive' may be more useful than using evaluative terms 'secure' and 'insecure'. This will take into consideration how cultures differ in the particular attachment strategy that may be most appropriate for that culture.

Implications for social work practice

Crawford and Walker (2003) state:

> Why is attachment theory important for social workers? The nature, form and development of relationships are crucial to social work practice. The assessment of these relationships will play a critical part in [social work] practice. Attachment theory provides part of a model of analysis in judging the quality of a relationship. This can be essential in knowing when to intervene, or even remove a child, where there are concerns in relation to attachment. . . . Social workers' skills in communication and observation will be essential in assessing and supporting the development of attachment behaviour . . . [the authors] recognize [that] children from different cultures . . . may experience their development in a different way from other children. The development and sustaining of attachment for babies and children is of critical importance and social work has a key role in assessing and supporting its development.
>
> (pp. 46–7)

Howe (1995, 1996, 1999) has written extensively on attachment theory and social work practice. However, there is a dearth of literature on attachment theory and social work practice with culturally different groups. As noted earlier, cultures differ on their notion of 'ideal' attachment and the meanings of different attachment behaviours. Thus, studies have shown that similar behaviours in the strange situation may have very different meanings in different cultures. For example, while Westerners may interpret anxious/resistant behaviour as 'clingy', Chinese parents may interpret it as 'bonded'.

In this situation, it is possible for social workers to mistakenly equate cultural characteristics with deficiencies or mistakenly define as a deficiency a characteristic that may actually represent a cultural difference. As noted in Chapter 1, for many psychologists, the word 'different' when applied to black people became synonymous with 'deficient' rather than simply different. The deficit model 'has entered social work practice as the conventional wisdom that guides the understanding of black families. It . . . shapes the style of social work that is carried out with black families' (Small, 1986, p. 279). Social workers need to move away from using a deficient model when working with black families. It is necessary for social workers to understand socially competent behaviour as it is conceived by the cultural group they are working with, in order not to mistakenly equate cultural characteristics with deficiencies.

Cross-cultural perspectives on attachment theory provides social workers with critical insights into the child's way of relating with others (patterns of relationships). Social workers need to be aware that notions about the quality of attachment and the processes by which it occurs are qualitative judgements made from the perspective of each culture. What is considered an optimal style of attachment may not necessarily be optimal across all cultures. Each culture has different but not necessarily better values than others. Furthermore, because nonparental caretaking is either the norm or a frequent form in most cultures (Weisner and Gallimore, 1977), examining the attachment network instead of focusing solely on dyads, as has traditionally been done, is of crucial importance (Van Ijzendoorn and Sagi, 1999).

Rashid (1996) points out that it is possible for social workers to 'evaluate the strength and nature of the attachment relationship between children and caregivers by using culturally specific notions like direct eye contact, for example, in settings where this might be regarded as culturally inappropriate' (p. 61). In African and Asian cultures, parents teach their children that looking an adult in the eye is a sign of disrespect (Byers and Byers, 1972). In contrast, white children are socialized to do just the opposite: looking away from a speaker is seen as disrespectful. Social workers need to understand that the meaning attributed to gaze behaviour in African and Asian cultures contrasts with the usual white attributions.

Daniel (1999) argues that:

> Attachment theory can be linked with the assumption that the traditional nuclear family provides a superior child-rearing environment . . . [which] can devalue cultural and ethnic variety in family structure, despite the evidence that children can develop successfully in many different family structures. The political and majority emphasis continues to be on a Western model of the nuclear family which is not the experience of many children.
>
> (p. 28)

For instance, as noted earlier, some cultures employ a system of multiple caregivers throughout the first few years of a child's life (Tronick et al., 1992). The child rearing remains the responsibility of a larger network of adult caregivers (Tronick et al., 1985). Fernandez (1991) questions 'the heavy emphasis on the mother (or surrogate)/child derived from Bowlby's work [which] makes little sense in cultures [Indian] where multiple carers are the norm' (p. 112). Social workers need to be aware that although extended families can differ in their composition, they have some things in common – for example, the sharing of emotional support and caregiving.

Sleeping arrangements influence early parent–child relationships and reflect cultural beliefs about infants' social development. The presence or absence of the caretaker during the night may even facilitate and reward a certain attachment style (e.g., anxious/resistant). This attachment style involves social behaviour patterns that are adaptive and desirable in certain cultures, since they tend to emphasize interdependence with others in a collectivist or group-oriented culture. Of the many different childrearing behaviours people of different cultures engage in, one of the most representative of cultural differences concerns sleeping arrangements. Characterizing sleep management as one of the earliest culturally determined parent–child interactions, Wolf and his colleagues (1996) suggest that their study may provide a useful framework for interpreting cross-cultural differences in the varying emphases placed on such behaviours as autonomy and dependence. While it is common practice among middle class families in US and Britain to put young infants in their own room to sleep (in part, to give them an early start down the road to independence), many mothers from African and Asian cultures view this custom as 'tantamount to child neglect' (Morelli et al., 1992, p. 608). Interdependence in some cultures (e.g., Japanese) can be attributable, at least in some measure, to the fact that Japanese children frequently sleep with their parents until the age of six or even, in some cases, to the beginning of puberty, when independent sleeping marks a culturally recognized change in one's developmental niche (Caudill and Plath, 1966, cited in LeVine et al., 1988). In a study of Indian Punjabi families in Britain, Dosanjh and Ghuman (1996) found that 'only one in five children sleep in their own bedrooms, the rest either share a bed or a bedroom' (p. 172). Similar findings were reported by Hackett and Hackett (1994) among Indian Gujaratis.

Singer (1998) notes that 'within attachment theory, the regulation of emotions fits neatly with Western culture, where a clear distinction is made between "inside" and "outside" the home, between "dependence" and "independence". A secure dependence on or attachment to the mother paves the basis from which the outside world can be explored, independently and autonomously' (p. 68). It is important to note that other cultures have very different ways of dealing with the need for dependence and independence.

According to Daniel et al. (1999) 'understanding several aspects of attachment relationships can guide social workers toward developmentally and culturally sensitive practice, as well as provide a foundation for recognizing problems in attachment relationships' (p. 27). Understanding universal aspects of attachment relationships, as well as the ways in which such relationships develop within particular social and cultural groups, provides a foundation for recognizing any problematic aspects of parent–child attachment relationships (Butler and Roberts, 2004).

Much more developmental research is needed to explore the context, meaning, and function of attachment behaviours in socially and culturally diverse families in Britain and United States. In the meantime, social workers must guard against making judgements based on limited information. An important strategy is to listen and learn from parents of diverse communities regarding the meaning and organization of attachment relationships in their particular social and cultural context.

Summary

Social workers need to be aware that notions about the quality of attachment and the processes by which it occurs are qualitative judgements made from the perspective of each culture. It is possible for social workers to mistakenly equate cultural characteristics with deficiencies or mistakenly define as a deficiency a characteristic that may actually represent a cultural difference. Cross-cultural perspectives on attachment theory provides social workers with critical insights into the child's way of relating with others. Some cultures use a system of multiple caregivers throughout the first few years of a child's life. Sleeping arrangements influence early parent–child relationships and reflect cultural beliefs about infants' social development. Cultures have different ways of dealing with the need for dependence and independence. Socialization goals differ across cultures.

Conclusions

More work still needs to be done to understand the attachment patterns in different cultures and the relationship between cultural milieu and attachment style. There is a lack of data from many countries. True et al. (2001) note that 'little systematic research has been conducted [on infant–mother attachment] outside Western or industrialized populations' (p. 1451).

The studies that do exist, however, are clear in suggesting that we cannot assume that what is seen most in Euro-American culture is best or most descriptive for all. Notions about the quality of attachment and the processes by which it occurs are qualitative judgements made from the perspective of each culture. What is considered an optimal style of attachment may not necessarily be optimal across all cultures. Each culture has different but not necessarily better values than others. Furthermore, because nonparental caretaking is either the norm or a frequent form in most cultures (Weisner and Gallimore, 1977), examining the attachment network instead of focusing solely on dyads, as has traditionally been done, is of crucial importance.

Jackson (1993) argues that there have been no studies on 'African Americans as a cultural group within American society, even though they have distinctive cultural practices with implications for the development of early attachments and they subsist in an ecological niche that differs markedly from that of white middle-class Americans' (p. 88). Jackson (1993) points out that in the US, 'African Americans are an overlooked cultural group who deserve the focused attention of investigators of infant attachment and early social-emotional development' (p. 88). In the US, very few published Strange Situation studies have used Hispanic, Asian, or other non-European American samples, and there is almost no data about whether the procedure is valid for these cultural groups (Jackson, 1993). The same is true in Britain with non-white populations. I would argue that there is a need for culture-specific studies of infant attachment of cultural groups (e.g., Asian and African Caribbean) in Britain.

3

Racial/Ethnic Identity Development

One of the primary tasks during adolescence is the self-conscious search for and development of one's identity (Marcia, 1980; Waterman, 1985). According to Waterman (1985), identity must be viewed as both a process and an outcome and 'refers to having a clearly delineated self-definition, a self-definition comprised of those goals, values, and beliefs that the person finds personally expressive, and to which he or she is unequivocally committed' (1985, p. 6). Waterman suggests that this development and subsequent commitment occurs in a variety of domains, including, but not limited to, the areas of career selection, political ideology, worldview, and the adoption of social and sex roles. Failure to establish identity commitments in these domains has particular psychological and social concomitants that can lead to role confusion, commitments to negative or dysfunctional roles, or both. One's identity and the attendant self-evaluation of that identity are most salient in the domains the individual considers to be most important (Waterman, 1985). Because race and ethnicity within Britain and US can have such a profound effect on personality development and psychological growth throughout the life span (Simpson and Yinger, 1985), the successful negotiation of one's racial or ethnic identity is crucial to the development of a functional self-concept and positive self-evaluations for black adolescents/ethnic minority youth (Cross, 1985; Phinney and Rotheram, 1987; Spencer, 1988).

The issue of cultural identification has particular relevance during adolescence when, as part of the identity formation process (Marcia et al., 1993), minority youths examine their ethnicity and its implications in their lives as they seek to establish a secure ethnic or racial identity (Helms, 1990; Montemayor et al., 2000; Phinney, 1989; 1990; 2000; 2001; Phinney 2000; Phinney et al., 2001;). In addition to examining their ethnicity, adolescents are likely to consider their role and position in the wider society. As they engage in this process, they are faced with the differing demands and possible conflicts among alternative cultural frames of reference, and the reality of minority status and discrimination (Fordham and Ogbu, 1986; Mendelberg, 1986).

Phinney and Kohatsu (1997) note that 'For adolescents of color, the successful transition to healthy functioning in adulthood requires the achievement of a secure sense of their ethnic and/or racial identity, in the face of stereotypical images of their group, cultural differences and conflicts, and restricted opportunities . . . this process, which is typically neither salient nor important for white adolescents, is of central importance to American [and British] adolescents from non-European backgrounds' (p. 420). According to Guernina (1995), 'Questions of identity dominate the concerns of adolescents, in particular ethnic minorities in the New Europe' (p. 52).

Although most of the theory and research is US based, many of the issues they raise are applicable to black groups in Britain. Two theoretical approaches to the study of black adolescents' racial and ethnic identity development are prominent: racial and ethnic identity formation theory and acculturation theory. The first approach has a more developmental focus, in that it looks at individual change and originally was based on ego identity formation theories. The second perspective is concerned with the extent to which ethnic identity is maintained when an ethnic minority group is in continuous contact with the dominant group. This chapter focuses on these approaches and implications for social work practice are explored.

Through the writings of Erik Erikson (1968) and James Marcia (1980) identity has become a popular theme in adolescent psychology. Erikson (1968) proposed a process whereby adolescents begin with an unclear sense of their identity, experience a 'crisis', and eventually achieve a clear sense of their identity. He felt that 'identity crisis' was normative to adolescence and young adulthood. Scholars 'no longer refer to this process as a "crisis". . . . Exploration better describes the typical adolescent's gradual, uneventful approach to identity formation' (Berk, 1998, p. 389). However, for some adolescents, 'identity development is traumatic and disturbing' (Berk, 1998, p. 389).

Erikson (1964) spoke of ethnic self-doubt and a pathological denial of one's roots as being seminal to Negro identity. He could not conceive that, for some individuals, their colour may actually be a source of pride. In an article, 'Memorandum on identity and Negro youth', he states: 'A lack of familiarity with the problem of Negro youth and with the actions by which Negro youth hopes to solve these problems is a marked deficiency in my life and work which cannot be accounted for by theoretical speculation' (1964, p. 41).

The development of identity, 'in an Eriksonian sense', has been minimally researched among minorities. However, Marcia (1966) provides a model useful in such research (Spencer and Dornbusch, 1990, p. 297). Marcia's (1966; 1993) identity status model has been a popular means of elaborating and refining Erikson's original theoretical notions on identity. Drawing upon Erikson's psychosocial definition of ego identity, Marcia proposed four approaches one might take in attempting to resolve (or not) meaningful identity-defining commitments to vocational, ideological, and relationship roles offered within one's larger social and cultural milieu.

According to Marcia, adolescents may move through four ego identity statuses that are based on the assumption that the development of an identity requires opportunities to explore and understand a variety of identity options and potential areas of commitment. An adolescent with a *diffused identity* has not yet committed to any particular roles. The diffused adolescent remains uninvolved in the identity search process. Failure to move beyond this status may likely result in a lack of identity resolution and developmental stagnation. The adolescent in the *moratorium identity* status reveals an individual who is struggling with his or her identity in an effort to make commitments to identity ideals. This status represents the normative developmental process for adolescents, and failure to move toward identity resolution is considered maladaptive. The adolescent with a *foreclosed identity* has adopted an identity based on a system of clearly defined goals and values, similar to the achieved identity youth. However, the commitments of the foreclosed adolescent tend to be prematurely based on the values and perspectives of parents or other authority figures and not acquired through the painstaking exploration process. Although representing a firm commitment to an identity, the foreclosed status is thought to be maladaptive because it does not reflect the individual's self-generated perspective. Finally, an individual who has developed *identity commitments* is thought to have reached the ideal status of an achieved identity. Adolescents who reach this level have apparently struggled and experimented with different roles and ideologies in hopes of discovering which ones best represent themselves. In the past three decades, numerous empirical studies, using Marcia's framework, have been conducted on identity development and on the relationship between ego identity development and emotional well-being (see reviews in Marcia, 1980 and Waterman, 1985).

Some definitions

Racial identity

Racial identity has been defined and studied using a wide range of theoretical approaches and research methods. Racial identities arise from the process of racialization (Miles, 1989, p. 73). Racialization occurs whenever 'race' is used to categorize individuals or explain behaviour. Since 'race' is not a biologically defensible phenomenon, racialization always involves an ideological process in which 'race' is given a status as an apparent truth. Thus, in this text, racial identity does not imply acceptance of 'race' as real, but acknowledges the social and political reality that people live in societies in which 'race' identities are attributed to them, and that these attributions have real consequences for their experiences of life. It is only appropriate to speak of racial identities because the processes of racialization have such potent power to shape people's perception of their shared world.

Racial identity is 'a) based on a sociopolitical model of oppression, b) based on a socially constructed definition of race, and c) concerned with how individuals abandon the effects of disenfranchisement and develop respectful attitudes toward their racial group' (Helms, 1995, p. 181).

Racial identity theories do not suppose that 'racial groups in the United States [and Britain] are biologically distinct, but rather suppose that they have endured different conditions of domination or oppression' (Helms, 1995, p. 181). Membership of these groups is determined by 'socially defined inclusion criteria (e.g., skin colour) that are commonly (mistakenly) considered to be racial in nature' (Helms, 1995, p. 181).

Gilroy argues that the tendency to reify racial identity as of unique importance to the individual 'reduces the complexity of self-image and personality formation in the black child to the single issue of race/colour' (1987, p. 66). This can result in the neglect of other important social identities, such as gender and social class (see Mama, 1995). The concept of racialization indicates the social construction of 'race' as a significant dimension in contemporary identities. But it cannot be an inclusive personal identity. Other variables, such as gender, age, class, sexual preference and nationality are some of the other important social identities. However, racial identity may predominate and be exclusively salient on occasions (Robinson, 1998). Some authors argue that issues of 'race' and ethnicity are highly salient for all minorities in American and British society throughout their life spans (Aries and Moorehead, 1989; Thomas, 1998).

Ethnic identity

Tajfel (1981) defines ethnic identity as 'that part of an individual's self-concept which derives from his knowledge of his membership of a social group (or groups) together with the value and emotional significance attached to that membership' (p. 255). 'Other definitions and interpretations of ethnicity include: self-identification; feelings of belongingness and commitment; and the sense of shared values and attitudes (see Phinney, 1990).

According to Phinney and Rotheram (1987) 'ethnic identity refers to one's sense of belonging to an ethnic group and the part of one's thinking, perceptions, feelings, and behaviour that is due to ethnic group membership' (1987, p. 13). Several subcategories have been identified that relate to ethnic identity including ethnic awareness, ethnic self-identification, ethnic preferences, ethnic attitudes, and ethnic behaviours (Phinney and Rotherham, 1987). Ethnic awareness refers to the knowledge one has of one's own group as well as other groups. This knowledge can include both factual and stereotypical information obtained from others and one's own experiences. Ethnic self-identity refers to 'the accurate and consistent use of an ethnic label, based on the perception and conception of themselves as belonging to an ethnic group' (Phinney and Rotheram, 1987, p. 17). Ethnic attitudes reflect the affective component of those views held about one's own group and other groups in the society at large. Ethnic attitudes are determined by the positive or negative experiences with which this ethnic knowledge is associated.

Ethnic identity 'a) concerns one's attachment to and sense of belonging to, and identification with one's ethnic group members (e.g., Japanese, Indian) and with one's ethnic culture; b) does not have a theoretical emphasis on oppression/racism; but c) may include the prejudices and cultural pressures that ethnic individuals experience when their ways of life come into conflict with those of the White dominant group' (Sodowsky et al., 1995, p. 182).

Self-esteem

The terms self-esteem and self-concept have often been used interchangeably. However, self-esteem (or self-worth) has been shown to be one component of self-concept (see, for example, Rosenberg, 1979). According to Mussen et al. 'Self-esteem is based on evaluations and judgements about one's perceived characteristics; self-concept does not imply positive or negative feelings about the self' (1984, p. 318). Rather, the self-concept is 'a set of ideas about oneself that is descriptive rather than judgemental' (Mussen, 1984, p. 356). For example, the fact that black children are aware that they are black is part of the self-concept but their evaluation of their racial characteristics is part of their self-esteem. Some authors define identity as a component of an individual's overall self-concept which involves the adoption of certain personal attitudes, feelings, characteristics, and behaviours (personal identity) and the identification with a larger group of people who share those characteristics (reference group orientation) (Robinson, 1995).

Black children and identity development: A brief overview

Concern about Black racial identity has a long history stemming, notably, from Kenneth and Mamie Clark's doll studies of colour preference in young black children (Clark and Clark, 1947). A vast amount of research in the United States has shown that black (African American) children may suffer from racial group identification difficulties due to the effects of discrimination and racism (see for example, Clark and Clark, 1940; Powell-Hopson,1985). The original studies of identity in black children were conducted in the late 1930s (Clark and Clark, 1940). These studies employed line drawings and photographs of black and white children to assess racial identity attitudes in black preschool children. Subsequently, the Clarks expanded the set of stimulus materials by using dolls and colouring tests (Clark and Clark, 1947). The Clark and Clark study was replicated by Powell-Hopson (1985) and by Gopaul-McNicol (1988), with similar findings to those of 50 years ago. That is, a majority of children in the Powell-Hopson and Hopson and in the Gopaul-McNicol studies indicated a preference for white dolls over black ones. Gopaul-McNichol (1988) presented black and white preschool children with black dolls and white dolls. The investigator asked the children questions such as 'Which dolls would you like to play with?' 'Which doll is rich, ugly, pretty?' Similar to research in the United States almost five decades earlier (Clark and Clark, 1947), most of the children chose the white doll in response to the positive questions. The author concludes that colonialism, along with the representation of blacks and whites in the media, has made a marked impact on attitudes toward and perceptions of ethnic groups in the West Indies.

Studies carried out in Britain with Asian and African Caribbean children have found that these children showed a preference for white experimental stimuli (Davey and Norburn, 1980; Milner, 1983). However, racial preference studies using doll tests have been criticized often for problems such as inconsistent and poor methodology (Banks, 1976), over-generalization of findings, and failing to consider the cognitive developmental state of their subjects (Spencer, 1982).

Grugeon and Woods' (1990) ethnographic study of primary schools in Britain identified a number of the effects of racism upon the self-images of South Asian children. Children were seen colouring themselves pink, describing themselves as having blue eyes and fair hair, they refused to go out into the sun in case they became brown(er), and avoided participation in minority ethnic festivals. In another study, Boulton and Smith (1992) reported that both Asian and White British children preferred to share various activities with, and had a more positive view of, unknown members of their own racial group compared with unknown members of other racial groups.

Summary

During adolescence the search for and development of one's identity is an important task. Two theoretical approaches to the study of black adolescents' racial and ethnic identity development are prominent: racial and ethnic identity formation theory and acculturation theory. The first approach has a more developmental focus, in that it looks at individual change and originally was based on ego identity formation theories. The second perspective is concerned with the extent to which ethnic identity is maintained when an ethnic minority group is in continuous contact with the dominant group.

Theoretical approaches that relate to adolescent racial/ethnic identity development

Racial identity development models

Several models of Black racial identity development and transformation were introduced in the United States in the early 1970s. Each hypothesized that identity development was characterized by movement across a series of sequential stages and that it was influenced by an individual's reaction to social and environmental pressures and circumstances (Cross, 1971, 1978; Thomas, 1971). Perhaps the best known and most widely researched model of black identity development is Cross's (1971, 1978, 1980) model of psychological nigrescence – which refers to the process of developing a black identity – where black is defined as a psychological connection with one's racial group rather than mere identification of the colour of one's skin. The nigrescence approach studies black identity in adolescents and adults.

Cross's model is useful as it enables us to understand the problems of black identity confusion and to examine, at a detailed level, what happens to a person during identity change. If a black person, as Baldwin (1984) asserts, is exposed to an environment which is unsupportive, denigrating, oppressive and even hostile, and if affirmation and validation of one's existence is lacking or nonexistent, then a negative sense of self is a likely outcome with the models of nigrescence serving as an appropriate explanation of the resolution process that an individual will be likely to experience.

Cross suggests that the development of a black person's racial identity is often characterized by his/her movement through a five-stage process, the transformation from pre-encounter to internalization.

1. Pre-encounter. In the first stage the person is likely to view the world from a white frame of reference (eurocentric). The black person accepts a 'white' view of self, other black people and the world. The person has accepted a deracinated frame of reference, and because their reference point is usually a white normative standard, they develop attitudes that are pro-white and anti-black. The person will also deny that racism exists. Cross et al. stress that this stage 'is in evidence across social class' (Cross et al., 1991, p. 323). Cross (1995) refers to this stage as one where the conditions for transformation and change are ripe. He suggests that at the center of the pre-encounter mentality is both an assimilation-integration philosophy that is linked to an attempt to secure a place in the socio-economic mainstream, but motivated by a desperate attempt to insulate themselves from the implications of being black.

2. In the second stage, 'encounter', some shocking or social event makes the person receptive to new views of being black and of the world. The person's eurocentric thinking is upset by an encounter with racial prejudice which precipitates an intense search for black identity. For example, a black person who views his or her 'race' as not important and wishes to be viewed and accepted as a 'human being' is denied access to living in an exclusive neighbourhood because of skin colour. Encounter experiences usually involve multiple emotional traumas that are so powerful that they begin to weaken and break down the person's previous identity resolution. The encounter stage appears to involve two steps: first, experiencing and personalizing the event when the person realizes that his or her old frame of reference is inappropriate and begins to explore aspects of a new identity; the second step is portrayed by Cross et al. (1991, p. 324) as 'a testing phase during which the individual [first] cautiously tries to validate his/her new perceptions', then definitively decides to develop a black identity.

Consequently, when the person absorbs enough information and receives enough social support to conclude that: a) the old identity seems inappropriate and b) the proposed new identity is highly attractive, the person starts an obsessive and extremely motivated search for black identity. At the end of the second stage the person is not depicted as having obtained the new identity, but as having made the decision to start the journey towards the new identity. The person feels less internally secure and seeks authentication through external validation.

Parham (1989) has argued that the vulnerability to examine one's attitudes and beliefs about race will be influenced by the degree of psychological defensiveness present at the time of each encounter. If the degree of defensiveness is low, then the probability of change is increased. If, however, the degree of defensiveness is high, then many more encounter experiences may be necessary in order for a person to challenge his or her Eurocentric beliefs and attitudes.

3. Immersion-emersion. 'This stage encompasses the most sensational aspects of black identity development' (Cross, 1971, p. 20). This is the period of transition in which the person struggles to destroy all vestiges of the 'old' perspective. This occurs simultaneously with an intense concern to clarify the personal implications of the new-found black identity (Cross, 1978). An emotional period ensues where the person glorifies anything black and attempts to purge him or herself of their former worldview and old behaviour. The old self is regarded in pejorative terms, but the person is unfamiliar with the new self, for that is what he/she hopes to become: 'thus the person is forced to erect simplistic, glorified, highly romantic and speculative images of what he or she assumes the new self will be like' (Cross et al., 1991, p. 325). The person begins to immerse him or herself into total blackness. He/she attaches him/herself to black culture and at the same time withdraws from interactions with white people. The person tends to denigrate white people and white culture, thus exhibiting anti-white attitudes. Cross et al., 1991 (p. 325) state: 'Since the new black identity is something yet to be achieved, the Stage 3 person is generally anxious about how to demonstrate to others that he/she is becoming the right kind of black person'. Hence, the demonstration of one's blackness is prominent – for example, black clothes and hairstyles, linguistic style, attending all-black functions, reading black literature. The person does not feel secure about their

blackness. They can be vicious in attacks on aspects of the old self that appear in others or themselves, and may even appear bizarre in their affirmation of the new self. The potential personal chaos of this stage is generally tempered by the social support a person gains through group activities. The groups joined during this period are 'counterculture institutions', which have rituals, obligations and reward systems that nurture and reward the developing identity, while inhibiting the efficacy of the 'old identity'. Although the initial part of Stage 3 involves total immersion and personal withdrawal into blackness, the latter part of this stage represents emergence from the reactionary, 'either-or' and racist aspects of the immersion experience. The person's emotions begin to level off, and psychological defensiveness is replaced by affective and cognitive openness. This allows the person to be more critical in his/her analysis of what it means to be black. The strengths, weakness, and over-simplifications of blackness can now be sorted out as the person's degree of ego-involvement diminishes and her/his sense of perspective expands. The person begins to feel in greater control and the most difficult period of nigrescence comes to an end.

4. Internalization. In this stage, the person focuses on things other than themselves and their ethnic or racial group. They achieve an inner security and self-confidence with their blackness. They feel more relaxed, more at ease with self. The person's thinking reflects a shift from how friends see them (am I black enough?) towards confidence in personal standards of blackness. The person also exhibits a psychological openness and a decline in strong anti-white feelings. The person still uses 'blacks as a primary reference group, [but] moves towards a pluralistic and nonracist perspective' (Cross, 1991, p. 326). Thus: 'As internalization and incorporation increase, attitudes toward White people become less hostile, or at least realistically contained, and pro-Black attitudes become more expansive, open and less defensive' (Cross, 1971, p. 24).

5. The previous stage and this stage, internalization-commitment, are characterized by positive self-esteem, ideological flexibility, and openness about one's blackness. In the fifth stage the person finds activities and commitments to express his/her new identity. Cross (1985, p. 86) contends that:

Implicit in the distinction between 'internalization' and 'internalization-commitment' is the proposition that in order for Black identity change to have 'lasting political significance', the 'self' (me or 'I') must become or continue to be involved in the resolution of problems shared by the 'group' (we).

Cross sees the person in stage five – internalization-commitment – as the new 'ideal', that is, psychologically healthy black person. They have made their new pro-black identity and values their own. They have a 'calm, secure demeanor' characterized by 'ideological flexibility, psychological openness and self-confidence about one's blackness' (Cross, 1980, p. 86). Blacks are a primary reference group, but the person has lost his/her prejudices about 'race', sex, age and social class. He/she also struggles to translate his/her values into behaviour that will benefit the black community. According to Cross et al. (1991, p. 328):

> For the person who has reached Stage 4 and beyond, the internalized black identity tends to perform three dynamic functions: to defend and protect a person from psychological insults, and where possible to warn of impending psychological attacks that stem from having to live in a racist society; to provide social anchorage and meaning to one's existence by establishing black people as a primary reference group; to serve as a point of departure for gaining awareness about, and completing transactions with, the broader world of which blackness is but a part.

Cross (1995, p. 113) maintains that 'the successful resolution of one's racial identity conflicts makes it possible for the person to shift attention to other identity concerns such as religion, gender and sexual preference, career development [and] social class'.

In summary, the research suggests that:

1. Many black people have a predominantly positive racial identity, with perhaps a minority having a negative identity.
2. Black identity has links to behaviour.
3. Black identity can have links to other attitudes and personality characteristics.

It should be noted that Cross's (1978) model has a specific history

(Mama, 1995), and that it outlines a specific case of what the present author would argue are generic psychological processes. This theoretical tool illuminates our understanding of the potential dynamics of identity negotiation. There is an extensive empirical literature that confirms Cross's model of black identity development (see Cross, 1971; 1991; 1995; Hall et al., 1972). According to Mama (1995): 'Most of the research that has involved testing for the plausibility of Cross's model offers support for it' (Mama, 1995, p. 60). However, readers need to be aware of some possible limitations of Cross's model.

Thus, 'while the theory of nigrescence [Cross's model] may provide a useful description of the development of black identity' (Mama, 1995, p. 162), the model does not adequately address issues of class, age or gender. However, Cross maintains that 'the successful resolution of one's racial identity conflicts makes it possible for the person to shift attention to other identity concerns such as religion, gender and sexual preference, career development [and] social class' (Cross, 1995, p. 113).

Parham's lifespan nigrescence model

Perhaps the most important theoretical advance in the field of nigrescence is Parham's application of a lifespan perspective to the study of nigrescence. In Cross's model nigrescence was regarded as a 'one-time event' in the person's life cycle.

Parham's (1989) proposed that identity development may recycle throughout adulthood. Some people might have completed the nigrescence cycle at an early stage in the life cycle – for example, in adolescence or adulthood – but they may find that the challenges unique to a later phase in the life cycle – for example, middle age or late adulthood – may bring about a recycling through some of the stages. From Parham's perspective, recycling does not mean the person reverts to the old (Pre-encounter) identity and then traverses all the stages. Rather he/she is inclined to believe that the challenge or trauma acts as an encounter episode – which exposes small or giant gaps in the person's thinking about blackness, and the person recycles in order to fill such gaps. Thus depending upon the nature of the challenge or new encounter, recycling may mean anything from a mild 'refocusing experience' to one involving full-fledged immersion-emersion and internalization episodes.

Parham presents a life-cycle nigrescence model based on a modification of the Cross model. Parham is concerned to identify the earliest phase of the life cycle at which a person is capable of experiencing nigrescence. He argues that the 'manifestations of Black identity [during childhood] may be a reflection of externalized parental attitudes or societal stereotypes that a youngster has incorporated rather than a crystallized personal identity' (Parham, 1989, p. 95). Accordingly, he proposes that it is during adolescence and early adulthood that a person might first experience nigrescence, and after this first experience, the likelihood of experiencing nigrescence is present for the rest of a person's life. Parham's model assumes that there is a qualitative difference between the nigrescence experience at adolescence or in early adulthood than in, say, middle or late adulthood, because:

> A Black person's frame of reference is potentially influenced by his or her life stage and the developmental tasks associated with that period of life . . . [and] within the context of normal development, racial identity is a phenomenon which is subject to continuous change during the life cycle.
>
> (Parham, 1989, p. 196)

A person's racial identity development does not have to begin with a pro-white/anti-black viewpoint (pre-encounter stage). This assertion represents a significant departure from the traditional nigrescence models presented by Cross, Jackson, and Thomas, which implicitly or explicitly suggest that one's racial identity development begins with a pro-white/anti-black frame of reference or worldview. Parham speculates, for example, that if a young adolescent is exposed to and indoctrinated with parental and societal messages that are very pro-black in orientation, the personal identity and reference group orientation initially developed by that youngster might be pro-black as well. Parham (1989) is also clear in his assertion that African American cultural identity is an entity independent of socially oppressive phenomena. This independent identity notion provides a critical extension of the original nigrescence theories that initially conceptualized black identity and the affirmation of oneself as an African American as only a reaction to the oppressive conditions of white American racism.

Parham proposes three different ways in which people deal with their racial identity as they advance through life: stagnation, stage-wise linear progression and recycling (see Parham, 1989 for detailed review). According to Mama (1995, p. 62), 'the most important advance Parham makes is that he puts forward a theory of the black person as a dynamic subject . . . it is a theory of subjectivity that moves some way beyond the linear stage models of black identity development'. However, Parham does not address the 'possibility that multiple stages (or positions) may co-exist within (or be available to) a given moment' (Mama, 1995, p. 62).

It is important to note that racial identity attitudes are not fixed but are subject to change throughout the lifespan (Parham, 1989). The lifespan perspective is 'a balanced view that recognizes great complexity in human change and the factors that underlie it. It assumes that development is multidimensional and multidirectional as well as highly plastic' (Berk, 1998, p. 39). In extending Cross's nigrescence model, Parham (1989) has proposed that, within the context of normal development, racial identity development is a phenomenon that is subject to continuous change during one's lifetime. Parham's model assumes that there is a qualitative difference between the nigrescence experience at adolescence or in early adulthood and that in, say, middle or late adulthood because: 'A black person's frame of reference is potentially influenced by his or her life stage and the developmental tasks associated with that period of life . . . [and] within the context of normal development, racial identity is a phenomenon which is subject to continuous change during the life cycle' (Parham, 1989, p. 196). Carter (1995) argues that racial identity development is a life long process that begins in childhood. However, as children approach puberty and social and peer relationships take on increasing importance, race and racial identity become particularly salient.

More recently, Cross (1991, 1995; Cross et al., 1998) has proposed revisions in the conceptualizations of nigrescence. His recent descriptions of the stages depict a more diverse set of attitudes and behaviours associated with the different stages than he originally described. Cross (1991; Cross et al., 1998) has recognized that the original definitions of the pre-encounter and internalization stages may have been limited by their focus on single dimensions in each stage. In the case of the pre-encounter stage, he now posits a continuum of racial attitudes that extend from low salience, to race neutral, to anti-black. Thus, a person with pre-encounter attitudes may acknowledge his or her blackness while believing that it has little importance or meaning in their life (low salience). He/she value things 'other than their blackness, such as their religion, their lifestyle, their social status, or their profession' (Cross, 1995, p. 98); or he or she may express strong anti-black sentiments as a way of denigrating the culture and distancing themselves from other African Americans who are perceived to be 'too Black' for their personal comfort. Thus, not all black people place race and black culture at the center of their identity (Cross and Fhagen-Smith, 1996). For some, social identity or reference group orientation may be grounded in religious ideas or the fact that they are gay or lesbian, whereas for others, race, ethnicity, and black culture are at the core of their existence (Cross, 1991). According to Cross et al. (1998) low salience identities (LS) refer to black social identities or reference-group orientations that accord only minor significance to race and African American culture in determining what is, and is not, important in one's everyday life; *high salience* identities (HS) characterize black social identities for which race and African culture are of central significance. Adolescence is the period during which a broad range of LS and HS social identities come to fruition. It is also the point at which LS identities may be changed by a nigrescence conversion (Cross, 1991; Cross et al., 1998).

With regard to the internalization stage, Cross (1995, 2001) now takes the position that an individual's resolution of internalized attitudes will also vary, for example, from a monocultural focus (nationalistic) to one that is more multicultural in orientation. In either case, as with the pre-encounter stage, it is important to remember that the nigresecence process does not evolve into a single ideological stance. Rather, there is a multitude of ways in which one's cultural pride and internalized identity may be expressed.

The five stages of black identity development, however, remain the same. Cross also notes that the immersion-emersion stage can result in regression, fixation or stagnation instead of continued identity development. Regression refers to those people 'whose overall experience is negative and thus non-reinforcing of growth toward the new identity [and therefore] may become disappointed and choose to reject Blackness' (Cross, 1991, p. 208). Some people can become fixated at this stage due to extreme and negative encounters with white racists. Thus: 'Individuals who experience painful perceptions and confrontations will be overwhelmed with hate for white people and fixated at stage 3' (p. 208). Finally, dropping out of any involvement with black issues is another response to the immersion-emersion stage. Some people might drop out because they wish to 'move on to what they perceive as more important issues in life' (p. 209). These people tend to label their experience as their 'ethnicity phase'. Cross has noted that this often occurs with African American college students.

There are multiple ways in which black identity operates or functions in one's daily life. The five key identity operations for conducting a functional analysis of black identity include: buffering; bonding; bridging; code-switching, and individualism (Cross, 1991; Cross et al., 1995). The buffering function refers to those ideas, attitudes, feelings, and behaviours that accord psychological protection and self-defence against everyday encounters with racism. The person either anticipates that which might be avoided or employs a buffer to blunt the sting and pain arising from an unavoidable or unsuspecting racist encounter. HS African Americans tend to recognize potential racist encounters in everyday American life and consider the development and constant refinement of the buffering mechanism to be crucial to their psychological integrity. Conversely, LS African Americans stress a colour-blind perspective and tend to see less racism in everyday American life.

The bonding function addresses the degree to which the person derives meaning and support from an affiliation with or attachment to black people and black culture. HS African Americans place importance to their attachment to black people and black culture. LS African Americans tend to exhibit less attachment and affiliation to black culture.

The bridging function refers to those competencies, attitudes, and behaviours that make it possible for a black person to immerse himself or herself in another group's experience, absent of any need to suppress one's sense of blackness. The person moves back and forth between black culture and the ways of knowing, acting, thinking, and feeling that constitute a non-black worldview. During these bridging transactions, no demands are made on either party to deny his or her cultural frame of reference.

Some HS African Americans who embrace a black nationalist or Afrocentric perspective may not place much value in bridging, preferring to concentrate their time and energy on black (in-group) tasks and problems. Some HS African Americans, who are as comfortable by that which makes them American as that which makes them black (biculturality) or who relish sharing experiences with a range of other groups (multiculturality), are more likely to use the bridging function. LS African Americans may have experiences across racial and cultural divides, not out of a sense of cultural or ethnic bridging, but because their colour blind philosophy makes out-group friendships and experiences possible.

The buffering, bonding, and bridging functions of black identity have been identified by Cross (1991) as well as Cross et al. (1995). Cross et al. (1995) extended the list to include codeswitching and individualism. The codeswitching function allows a person to temporarily accommodate to the norms and regulations of a group, organization, school, or workplace. Finally, individualism is the expression of one's unique personality.

Although Cross's identity development model has been developed with African American samples in the USA, it is argued by various authors (for example, Maximé, 1986, 1993; Phinney, 1990; Robinson, 2000; Sue and Sue, 1990, 1999) that other minority groups share similar processes of development. For instance, Sue and Sue (1990, p. 95) indicate that: 'Earlier writers (Berry, 1965, cited in Sue and Sue, 1990; Stonequist, 1937) have observed that minority groups share similar patterns of adjustment to cultural oppression. In the past several decades, [in the USA] Asian Americans, Hispanics, and American Indians have experienced sociopolitical identity trans-formations so that a "Third World consciousness" has emerged with a cultural oppression as the common unifying force'. Sue and Sue (1999, p. 124) point out that 'early models of racial identity devel-opment all incorporated the effects of racism and prejudice (oppres-sion) upon the identity transformation of their victims'.

In Britain, Robinson (2000) compared the racial identity atti-tudes and self-esteem of African Caribbean adolescents in residential care in a city in the West Midlands and a group of African Caribbean adolescents living with their own families and attending a multi-racial school in the city. Both respondents in residential care and the comparison group primarily endorsed positive racial attitudes. Self-esteem and racial identity attitudes were positively related. Residential care staff found Cross's model extremely useful in thera-peutic work with African Caribbean children.

Scholars have found that the formation of a sense of black racial identity is an important element in the psychological development of black adolescents and young adults (Parham and Helms, 1985a).

In a more recent study, Shorter-Gooden and Washington (1996) explored the personal salience of the following identity domains: race, gender, sexual orientation, relationships, career, religious beliefs and political beliefs in late adolescent African American women. In keeping with the literature on African American adolescents and young adults (Parham and Helms, 1985a, 1985b; Parham, 1989; Phinney, 1989), racial identity was a salient and central aspect of these women's self-definition. 'Race', more than any other area, was a source of self-definition for these women. Fujino and King (1994) speculate that women of colour may develop a sense of racial identity first and a sense of gender identity later.

Pre-encounter attitudes have been reported to be related to a preference for white counsellors (Parham and Helms, 1981; Tuckwell, 2002), high anxiety (Carter, 1991; Parham and Helms, 1985a), low self-regard, and low self-esteem (Parham and Helms, 1985a; Pyant and Yanico, 1991). Carter (1991) found that pre-encounter attitudes were related to more psychological dysfunction. Pyant and Yanico (1991) report that high pre-encounter attitudes were related to low scores on a measure of psychological well-being and high scores on the Beck Depression scale (Beck et al., 1961). High levels of pre-encounter attitudes seem to be associated with a low level of racial awareness and some psychological distress, as well as preferences for interaction with white people.

Encounter attitudes for college students were associated with low anxiety, high self-actualization, high self-regard, and a preference for black counsellors (Parham and Helms, 1981; Parham and Helms, 1985b). Pyant and Yanico (1991) found that non-college students' encounter attitudes were predictive of low psychological well-being, low self-esteem, and higher depression scores. Parham and Helms (1985a) found that immersion attitudes were associated with low self-actualizing tendencies, low self-regard, and high anxiety and hostility. Carter (1991) reports that immersion-emersion attitudes were characterized by 'cultural paranoia' or a hypersensitivity to feelings, attitudes, and behaviours motivated by racism.

More recently, theories have evolved such that more emphasis is placed on racial identity as an aspect of an individual's psychological make-up in a race-based society (Carter, 1995; Cross et al., 1998; Helms, 1990; Helms and Piper, 1994). It is apparent from the growing body of theoretical activity that racial identity is becoming a major theoretical and empirical model in psychology.

Ethnic identity formation/development

Since the 1970s, racial, ethnic, or minority identity theories have been introduced to include other visible racial/ethnic groups. The term 'visible racial-ethnic' applies to African American, Asian, Indian, and Latino Americanos; it identifies them as members of both racial and ethnic groups who are recognized by skin-colour, physical features, and/or language. Ethnic or racial or cultural identity models have been proposed for Asians, Hispanics (Berry, 1980), and minorities in general (Atkinson et al., 1989; Phinney, 1990)

Atkinson et al. (1979, 1989, 1993) proposed the Minority Identity Development (MID) model, which is intended to describe the issues of identity development common to members of all groups in United States and Britain who are politically and/or socially oppressed. The MID model is anchored in the belief that all minority groups experience the common force of oppression (Atkinson et al., 1989). In their model, Atkinson and colleagues proposed that the search for a positive racial-cultural identity involves progression through five stages: conformity; dissonance; resistance; introspection; awareness. In content, the stages are similar to those of racial identity development, as discussed above, and to Asian identity models (Sue and Sue, 1990).

Phinney (1989) views the process of ethnic identity development as a progression through a series of stages. The model proposed by Phinney (1989) is congruent with the racial and ethnic identity development models discussed above (i.e., Atkinson et al., 1983; Cross, 1978). This congruence is based on the fact that Phinney's model is rooted in the ego identity development literature by sharing the idea that an achieved identity occurs through stages and is the result of a crisis, an awakening, and/or an encounter, which leads to a period of exploration or experimentation, and finally to a commitment or incorporation of one's ethnicity. Apart from focusing mainly on adolescents, Phinney's model differs from the others by reducing the number of stages contained in the model.

Phinney's (1989) model of ethnic identity development in adolescents is therefore made up of three stages. The first stage is known as unexamined ethnic identity (i.e., individuals at this stage are not in the process of exploring ethnicity). This may be accompanied by lack of interest or concern with the subject (diffusion) or by attitudes about one's ethnicity that are derived from others (foreclosure).

These attitudes 'may be either positive or negative, depending on one's socialization experiences' (Phinney, 1989, p. 38).Phinney holds that the diffused and foreclosed statuses from Marcia are similar to each other. With foreclosure, individuals either have accepted the ethnic attitudes or identification of their parents or they have accepted the majority culture's values and attitudes, whereas in the diffuse status, the adolescent may not have been exposed to ethnic identity issues. In both the diffuse and foreclosed states, the adolescent has not examined his or her ethnic identity and is therefore in Phinney's 'unexamined' first stage. In the second stage, ethnic identity search (moratorium), individuals are involved in exploring and seeking to understand the meaning of ethnicity for themselves. Phinney (1989) reported experiences similar to those described by Atkinson and colleagues (1983) as 'a growing awareness that not all cultural values of the dominant group are beneficial to him/her' (1983, p. 37). This exploration may be triggered by a significant 'awakening' experience around their ethnicity that often is followed by an 'intense process of immersion in one's own culture through activities such as reading, talking to people, going to ethnic museums, and participating actively in cultural events' (pp. 502–3). Through this process, Phinney argued, individuals come to a deeper understanding of what their ethnic identity means to them. This culminates in the third stage of ethnic identity development, the achievement or internalization of ethnic identity. Individuals at this stage are characterized by a clear and confident sense of their own ethnicity. Phinney (1989) found that subjects at this stage had come to terms with negative stereotypes and conflicting values. For example, a Mexican American female stated, 'People put me down because I am Mexican, but I don't care any more. I can accept myself more' (1989, p. 44).Thus, there is 'evidence of exploration, accompanied by a clear, secure understanding and acceptance of one's own ethnicity' (Phinney 1989, p. 38).

The ideal outcome of the identity process is an achieved identity. Individuals with an achieved ego identity have resolved uncertainties about their future direction and have made commitments that will guide future action (Marcia, 1980). In the area of ethnicity, identity achievement corresponds to acceptance and internalization of one's ethnicity. Writers from diverse backgrounds have described the sense of ethnic identity achievement as follows: 'Following this period of cultural and political consciousness . . . individuals develop a deeper sense of belonging to the group . . . When the person finally comes to feel at one with the group, the internalization process has been completed, and ethnic identity established' (Arce, 1981, p. 186).

Phinney suggested that the encounter and exploration stages may not be separate stages but actually only one stage. This suggestion is based on the research with 10th-grade minority youth in which she found little evidence of any specific event or series of events that were emotionally intense or disruptive. According to Phinney (1993):

> Some subjects mentioned what sounded like encounter experiences, such as name calling and discrimination, but these did not necessarily lead to rethinking of the issues. It may be that an encounter experience is evident when individuals look back at the process of their own search, but that is not clear at the time it happens. Therefore, it may be more useful in empirical studies to consider encounter and exploration as a single stage.
>
> (p. 69)

In several studies, Phinney (1989) found that adolescents with an achieved ethnic identity show better psychological adjustment and higher self-esteem (Phinney and Alipuria, 1990). Phinney (1992) concludes that 'the concept of ethnic identity is meaningful for young adolescents, and that it is related in theoretically meaningful ways to other dimensions of the adolescents' experience . . . It remains to be demonstrated how ethnic identity is related to the wider experience of adolescents, for example their ethnic socialization, the ethnic context in which they live, and the attitudes of the community toward a particular group' (Phinney, 1992, p. 8).

Thus, in work that provides a theoretical bridge between the Erikson/Marcia ego identity framework and the black racial identity model, Phinney and her associates have made similar findings: for African American adolescents, and perhaps especially for black girls, ethnic/racial identity is a very salient aspect of identity (Phinney and Alipuria, 1990), and is related to psychological well-being (Phinney, 1989).

More recent studies (Phinney and Alipuria, 1990; Phinney and Devich-Navarro, 1997; Phinney, 2000) also present empirical evidence for a model of ethnic identity development that is consistent with Marcia's (1966) model of model of ego identity and with the ethnic identity models cited. Phinney's (1990) review of generational differences in ethnic identity emphasized a general decline in ethnic group identification in later generations. However, studies cited by Phinney (1990), that involved Asian Americans contradicted this trend. In reference to a study of Chinese Americans by Ting-Toomey (1981), Phinney (1990) pointed out that change in ethnic identity may involve a more 'cyclical process', whereby ethnicity becomes more important, especially by the third- or fourth-generation descendants of immigrants.

Phinney (1992) devised a scale, the Multigroup Ethnic Identity Measure (MEIM), to measure ethnic identity. Considerable research has been carried out using Phinney's model (e.g., Martinez and Dukes, 1997).

Critique of stage models

Stage theories of ethnic identity development have been criticized by some researchers as being too linear and not recognizing the multi-dimensional nature of ethnic identity (e.g., Yeh and Huang, 1996). Many stage theories fail to capture the complexity and uniqueness of the ethnic minority experience. For example, the stage model for minority identity development proposed by Atkinson et al. (1983) has received scrutiny and criticism from the psychology field. Jones (1991) argues that this model is too linear; there is no explanation of what factors contribute to or promote progression on to the next stage. This model also does not fully acknowledge the dominant society's role in the continuing cycle of racism in the United States and Britain (Helms, 1986). Furthermore, Jones (1991) argues that the model of ethnic identity development proposed by Atkinson et al. (1983) places the blame of racism on the victim – suggesting and encouraging change in the ethnic group – and not on the majority group's attitudes and behaviours. A final criticism of ethnic identity development models is that there are few majority group identity models, thus placing emphasis on minority group differences. Because US and British society includes various cultural groups and influences, theories should emphasize cultural similarities as well as differences.

However, the conceptual models that have been proposed in the literature are useful in understanding the experiences of black and minority adolescents in US and Britain (Sue and Sue, 2003).

Summary

The best known and most widely researched model of black identity development is Cross's model of psychological nigrescence – which refers to the process of developing a black identity – where black is defined as a psychological connection with one's racial group rather than mere identification of the colour of one's skin. The development of a black person's racial identity is often characterized by his/her movement through a five-stage process: pre-encounter; encounter; immersion-emersion; internalization; internalization-commitment. The nigrescence approach studies black identity in adolescence and adults. Parham (1989) presents a life-cycle nigrescence model based on a modification of the Cross model. More recently, Cross (1995; Cross et al., 1998) has proposed revisions in the conceptualizations of nigrescence. His recent descriptions of the stages depict a more diverse set of attitudes and behaviours associated with the different stages than he originally described.

Other racial, ethnic or minority identity models include Atkinson et al.'s (1989, 1993) Minority Identity Development (MID) model and Phinney's (1989) ethnic identity development model. Phinney (1989) views the process of ethnic identity development as a progression through a series of stages: unexamined ethnic identity; diffusion; foreclosure. Adolescents with an achieved ethnic identity show better psychological adjustment and higher self-esteem (Phinney and Alipuria, 1990).

Stage theories of ethnic identity development have been criticized by some researchers as being too linear and not recognizing the multidimensional nature of ethnic identity. However, the models are useful in understanding the experiences of black and minority adolescents in Britain.

Acculturation

The second theoretical framework, acculturation theory, is similar to the models discussed earlier (Cross, 1978; Atkinson et al., 1983; and Phinney, 1989) in its emphasis on a conflict model of ethnic identity. Both theories assume there will be an apparent conflict for ethnic minorities because of being part of two different cultural systems – the minority group to which they belong and the majority or dominant group. However, acculturation theorists (e.g., Berry,

1990) argue that 'acculturation may be a more complex and multi-dimensional concept, so that a simple stage model will hardly do justice to the process whereby an individual comes to terms with his or her ethnic identity' (Coleman and Hendry, 1999, p. 65). Ethnic identity is an aspect of acculturation that is concerned with how individuals feel about or relate to their own ethnic group as part of the larger majority or dominant society. Acculturation theory, then, is concerned with the extent to which ethnic identity is maintained when an ethnic group is in continuous contact with the dominant group (Phinney, 1990).

Phinney (1999) points out that:

> Within multicultural industrialized nations, issues of cultural contact and the resulting identity conflicts are most obvious among immigrants and the children of immigrants, who on a daily basis face exposure to differing cultural expectations. Children of immigrants are confronted with the task of constructing an identity by selecting or combining elements from their culture of origin and from the new culture in which they are growing up.
>
> (p. 27).

The term acculturation originated in anthropology. The classical definition of acculturation was presented by Redfield, Linton and Herskovits: 'Acculturation comprehends those phenomena which result when groups of individuals having different cultures come into continuous first-hand contact with subsequent changes in the original culture patterns of either or both groups' (1936, p. 146).

The concept of psychology of acculturation was introduced by Graves (1967). It refers to changes in an individual who is a partic-ipant in a culture contact situation, being influenced both directly by the external culture, and by the changing culture of which the individual is a member. The main reason for keeping these two levels distinct is that not every individual enters into, or participates and changes in the same way. This literature has been extensively reviewed by Berry (1997), Liebkind and Jasinskaja-Lahti (2000), and Ward (1996; Ward, 2001). Garcia et al. (1995) write that 'the process of acculturation is important not only for immigrants but also for any individual who for historic, economic, political, linguis-tic, and/or religious reasons is exposed or expected to adapt to a new cultural environment' (p. 199).

While acculturation is a neutral term in principle (that is, change may take place in either or both groups), in practice acculturation tends to induce more change in the immigrant group. There are vast individual differences in how people attempt to deal with acculturative change (Berry, 1997). These strategies (termed acculturation strategies) have three aspects: their preferences ('acculturation attitudes'; see Berry et al., 1989); how much change they actually undergo ('behavioural shifts'; see Berry, 1980); and how much of a problem these changes are for them (the phenomenon of 'acculturative stress'; see Berry et al., 1987).

Berry (1990) has suggested that the acculturation strategies of ethnic minority groups can best be described in terms of two independent dimensions: a) retention of one's cultural traditions, and b) establishment and maintenance of relationships with the larger society. When these two central dimensions are considered simultaneously, a conceptual framework is generated which posits four acculturation strategies.

Acculturation strategies involve: assimilation, integration, separation and marginalization. If individuals do not wish to maintain their cultural identity and seek daily interaction with other cultures, then the assimilation strategy is defined. In contrast, when non-dominant persons place a value on holding onto their original culture, and at the same time wish to avoid interaction with others, then the separation alternative is defined. When this mode of acculturation is pursued by the dominant group with respect to the non-dominant group, then the term separation is the appropriate one. When there is an interest in both maintaining one's original culture, and in daily interactions with other groups, integration is the option; here, there is some degree of cultural integrity maintained, while at the same time moving to participate as an integral part of the larger social network. Finally, when there is little possibility or interest in cultural maintenance, and little interest in relations with others then marginalization is defined. Attitudes towards these four alternatives, and actual behaviours exhibiting them, together constitute an individual's acculturation strategy. Substantial evidence now exists showing that individuals who pursue the integration strategy have the most positive adaptation, while those who are marginalized by the process of acculturation are least well adapted; assimilation and separation lie in between, one or the other being the more successful depending on the group and their situation (Berry and Sam, 1997; Ward, 2001).

This presentation of attitudinal positions is based on the assumption that immigrants have the freedom to choose how they want to engage in intercultural relations. However, this is not always the case (Berry, 1974). For example, a mutual accommodation is required for integration to be attained, involving the acceptance by both dominant and non-dominant group of the right of all groups to live as culturally different peoples within the same society. This strategy requires immigrants to adopt the basic values of the nation society, while at the same time the national society must be prepared to adapt national institutions (e.g., education, health, justice, employment) to better meet the needs of all groups now living together in the larger plural society.

Berry's model is more useful than a linear, one-dimensional model. However, a 'major shortcoming of [Berry's] model is that it underplays the significance of the attitudes, values and the zeitgeist of the receiving society. The decision to integrate or not to integrate does not entirely rest on the immigrants and their descendants but also – perhaps more so – on the reaction of the host society' (Ghuman, 1999, p. 27). Phinney and Devich-Navarro (1997) argue that 'The attitudes of the larger society toward the ethnic group are clearly an important influence on the extent to which individuals feel bicultural' (cited in LaFromboise et al., 1993, p. 26) The authors note that 'a determining factor in one's cultural identification appears to be the individual's perception of society; to feel bicultural, one must see the larger society as inclusive' (p. 26). In addition, 'Both racial identity theory (Helms, 1990) and studies of cultural or ethnic identity (Arce, 1981; Phinney, 1989, 1993) suggest that individuals need to explore and become secure in their own cultural background as part of the process of accepting other groups and the larger society' (Phinney and Devich-Navarro (1997, p. 28).

There is little empirical evidence about how individuals from ethnic minority groups in Britain think about and handle their relationship with the two cultures in which they live. Very little empirical work using Berry's acculturation model has been conducted in Britain. It helps us to explore the adaptation strategies of minority groups living in Britain (Ghuman, 1999; Robinson, 2003).

In Britain, studies of young Asian people have shown that most young people prefer the integration mode of adaptation (Ghuman, 1997; Hutnik, 1991; Robinson, 2003; Robinson, 2006; Stopes-Roe and Cochrane, 1990). Ghuman (1997) found differences within the

Asian group. For instance, Hindu young people were more in favour of taking up English values and ways of life than Muslims. Sikh young people came somewhere in-between Hindus and Muslims as judged by their performance on the scale.

Studies of Asians in Britain (e.g., Anwar, 1978; Robinson, 2003; Shaw, 1988; 2000) indicate that first generation Asians employed 'separation' as a mode of working and living in Britain. In another study, Stopes-Roe and Cochrane (1990) concluded their discussion of the personal identity of first and second generation Indians and Pakistanis by noting that the first generation 'felt primarily 'Indian' or 'Pakistani' as the case might be, rather than British, whereas 43% of young people identified as British' (p. 198). However, the authors also found that three-quarters of this group felt that there were differences between themselves and the white British. This could be attributed to the 'cultural customs which the young Asians valued' (p. 199). However, the respondents in Stopes-Roe and Cochrane's study were only given two choices – British or Indian/Pakistani. They were not given the option of indicating a bicultural or hyphenated identity.

Ghuman (1999) found that the majority of young Asian adolescents in his study preferred integration to other strategies of adaptation (for example, assimilation, marginalization and separation) Thus, the majority of young Asians were bicultural and bilingual. They defined their personal identity in a 'hyphenated way' (for example, British-Asian). However, 'this has not changed the fact that they continue to suffer racial abuse both in and out of school and have mixed feelings about whether they belong [in Britain]' (Ghuman, 2003, p. 130).

In a recent study undertaken as part of the International Comparative Study of Ethnocultural Youth, Robinson (2003) found that the acculturation attitude most favoured by Indian and African Caribbean adolescents was Berry's integration strategy and marginalization was least favoured by all groups. However, the separation strategy was most favoured by Pakistani adolescents. Ethnic identity scores were high for all groups and was positively related to life satisfaction for all ethnic groups. Majority identity was important for Indians and African Caribbeans but ethnic identity was more important than majority identity for all groups. There was a significant relationship between high ethnic identity scores and psychological adaptation as measured by mastery and life satisfaction (Robinson, 2003; 2006).

In a qualitative study of ethnic identities of first and second generation Asians and African Caribbeans, Modood et al. (1994) found that several young Asians used hyphenated labels (for example, 'Pakistani-British') to describe their identity. The authors conclude that 'most of the Asian second generation wanted to retain some core heritage, some amalgam of family cohesion, religion and language, probably in an adapted form, but did not expect this to mean segregated social lives, for they lived and wanted to live in an ethnically mixed way' (p. 110). Thus, Asians who saw themselves in terms of a bicultural or hyphenated identity did not think that there was an inevitable conflict between the two sides of their identity. However, a minority of second generation Asians 'felt alienated from British culture which they perceived as hostile to their family-centred and religious values' (p. 119).

Most first generation identified with their specific ethnic or religious identity rather than with a pan-Asian ethnicity or British nationality. Similar trends were also found by Anwar, 1998. For a majority of Asians religion was the main basis for their ethnic identity (Anwar, 1998). However, there were differences between Asian groups. For example, almost three-quarters of Muslims thought religion was very important for the way they lived their life, compared with less than half of Hindus and Sikhs saying this. Similar trends for young Asians were also found in Modood's (1994) study and Robinson's (2003) study.

Modood (1994) found that both first and second generation African Caribbean respondents used the term black as an identifying label. Indeed, 'for some second generation respondents 'Black' referred to all who suffered racism and thus included South Asians' (p. 117). Second generation respondents were more likely than first to express the notion of a shared 'black' identity between themselves and South Asians living in Britain, e.g., 'we are all 'of colour' (p. 85). The respondents 'were more likely to recognize the basis for solidarity with South Asians out of a common colonial history, the experience of racism and youth culture' (Modood 1994, p. 87). Although most of the African Caribbeans in Modood's study had a strong sense of social and cultural commonality with the white British, they found it difficult to lay claim to be British. For this group 'racism rather than any sense of distinctive ethnic heritage was seen as an obstacle to feelings of unity with the white British majority' (p. 118).

Summary ▐▬▬▬▬▬▬▬▬▬▬▬▬▬▬▬▬▬▬▬▬▬▬▬

Acculturation theory is concerned with the extent to which ethnic identity is maintained when an ethnic group is in continuous contact with the dominant group. Berry's model is more useful than a linear, one-dimensional model. According to Berry (1990) acculturation strategies involve: assimilation, integration, separation and marginalization. Individuals who pursue the integration strategy have the most positive adaptation, while those who are marginalized by the process of acculturation are least well adapted; assimilation and separation lie in between, one or the other being the more successful depending on the group and their situation (Berry and Sam, 1997). Studies of Asians in Britain indicate that first generation Asians employed 'separation' as a mode of working and living in Britain. Most second generation Indians prefer the integration mode of adaptation. Robinson (2003) found that the acculturation attitude most favoured by Indian and African Caribbean adolescents was Berry's integration strategy and marginalization was least favoured by all groups. However, the separation strategy was most favoured by Pakistani adolescents. The separation strategy was also most favoured by first generation respondents.

Mixed parentage children and young people

This section will explore issues related to working with children and young people of mixed parentage. The terms 'mixed parentage'; 'mixed race' 'dual heritage' 'biracial' are often used to describe first generation offspring of parents of different 'races'. They most typically describe individuals of black and white racial heritage (Sebring, 1985) but are not limited to this combination. In this section the terms will refer to individuals one of whose parents is African Caribbean or Asian (Indian, Pakistani, Bangladeshi) and the other white European.

Identity formation is 'crucial for ethnic minority [mixed parentage] children who face many disparagements to self-esteem from the external world' (Bagley, 1993, p. 72). As children of mixed parentage increase in the population (see Census, 2001), many will manage to achieve truly integrated identities, while others will experience chronic identity conflicts. This latter group will pose a growing challenge to social work professionals in the 21st century.

The topic of racial/ethnic identity in mixed parentage children has received increasing attention in recent years (e.g. Root, 1992; Tizard and Phoenix, 1993; 2003). This interest has been spurred by demographic trends that indicate a rapid increase in the mixed-parentage population and by the acknowledgement that there is little well-defined research and theory in the area. According to Berrington (1995), more than one in five of all ethnic minority children in Britain under the age of 4 years are of mixed parentage. The size of the ethnic minority population was 4.6 million in 2001 or 7.9% of the total population of the United Kingdom. Of the ethnic minority population 15% described their ethnic origin as mixed and about a third of this group were from white and black Caribbean backgrounds (Census, 2001). The experiences of these mixed parentage children will vary, reflecting differences in their class, education and family cultures.

Reviews of the limited research in Britain suggest that few children seemed to experience their situation 'as a painful clash of loyalties between black and white' (Wilson, 1987; Tizard and Phoenix, 1993; 2003). In Tizard and Phoenix's (1993) study most of the children had high self-esteem and positive identities. They found that 'a mixed identity was as likely to be positive as a black identity' (1993, p. 174) and that 'wanting to be white was the major indicator of a problematic identity for mixed parentage adolescents' (Tizard and Phoenix, 1993, p. 162). Tizard and Phoenix (2003) reported that children were as likely to identify themselves as 'mixed' as they were 'black': Even if they were seen as black by others, they experienced themselves as 'mixed'. They note that black self-identification among children of mixed parentage tends to correlate with the degree of politicization on issues of 'race' and racism. Their study also found that despite majority 'white' orientations in terms of friendships, racialized conflict situations produced strong black identifications.

There are some mixed-parentage children whose experiences give cause for concern. These are the children who are up to two-and-a-half times more likely than other children to enter care (Bebbington and Miles, 1989). Recent studies of the placement of black children with permanent families found almost twice as many mixed-parentage children as children with two African Caribbean parents (Barn, 1990; Charles et al., 1992). Studies have shown that some mixed-parentage adolescents in local authority care exhibit identity confusion and low self-esteem (Banks, 1992; Maximé, 1993; Barn et al., 1997). Researchers have often conjectured that mixed-parentage children are at risk for developing a variety of problems (Stonequist, 1937; Porterfield, 1978). Potential problems include cultural and racial identification issues, lowered self-esteem, difficulties in dealing with conflicting cultural demands, and feeling marginal in two cultures. A long-held notion is that mixed parentage individuals who are the offspring of one white parent and one black parent, should identify with only one racial/ethnic group, specifically with the group of the black parent (Root, 1996). Some authors (Small, 1986; Maxime, 1993) argue that mixed-parentage children and youngsters should be classified as black and that they should see themselves as so. The argument is that society sees them as black and they will be better off if that is their self-perceived identity. This tendency is related to the 'one-drop rule', whereby a person with any amount of black racial heritage would be designated as black. Indeed, in some United States studies, 'mixed white and Afro-American children are regarded as black, and not studied separately' (Tizard and Phoenix, 1989, p. 431). Today, most researchers (see Root, 1996) argue that the one-drop solution is not a useful way to categorize mixed-parentage people. They propose the creation of a category for mixed-parentage people that acknowledges them as separate and distinct from black and white people.

Although mixed-parentage children and youngsters encounter the problems faced by most minorities, they must also figure out how to reconcile the heritages of both parents in a society that categorizes individuals into single groups. Thus, if a person wants to achieve a positive biracial identity, he or she has to take in and value both racial parts of himself or herself. However, the development of a healthy biracial identity 'means not only accepting and valuing both [black and white] heritages and being comfortable in both the minority and majority community, but having the flexibility to accept that others may identify them as minority, majority or biracial' (Pinderhughes, 1995, p. 81). Wilson (1987) writes 'it seems to me desirable that mixed race children accept both sides of their dual heritage, provided that in doing so they do not lose sight of the fact that white society sees them as black and metes out to them the same degree of disadvantage that it does to all black people' (p. vii).

Carter (1995) argues that 'a person who is biracial should become grounded in the devalued [black] racial group as a foundation for facilitating the merger of the two racial groups. This is particularly true for racial groups in the United States [and Britain]' (1995, p. 120). According to Carter 'when one has first developed a positive Black identity and uses the Black identity as a foundation, it allows incorporation of the White aspect of identity' (1995, p. 120). In a study of racial identity attitudes of mixed-parentage (African Caribbean/white) adolescents in Britain, Fatimilehin (1999) used the RIAS-B scale (Parham and Helms, 1981) to investigate the attitude of these youngsters to their black heritage. Fatimilehin (1999) found that older teenagers were more likely to have positive racial identity attitudes and a positive relationship was found between racial identity attitudes and self-esteem. However, monoracial models of minority identity development do not address all the issues facing mixed-parentage adolescents. For example, Cross's (1978, 1991) model includes rejection of the minority culture followed by rejection of the majority culture and does not include the possibility of integrating more than one racial/ethnic group identity into one's sense of self. Various authors (e.g., Poston, 1990) have, therefore, argued that there is a need to develop models of biracial identity development.

Several models of biracial identity development have been proposed (e.g., Jacobs, 1992; Kerwin and Ponterotto, 1995; Poston, 1990; Root, 1992). These authors questioned the applicability of monoracial identity models to those of biracial heritage. Many of these frameworks demonstrate a similar hierarchy of stages that begin with initial learning about race and ethnicity differences, move to the struggle to find an identity but feeling pressured to choose only one group, and finally end in achievement of some level of biracial identity where both cultures are accepted and integrated into the person's overall identity. Root (1992) is the exception here. She describes four different paths that individuals can choose, all of which can lead to a positive biracial existence. Her possible outcomes include choosing the identity assigned by others, identifying with both racial groups, choosing one racial group over the others, and identifying with a new, biracial or multiracial group. Although Root (1992) describes how an individual can be successful with any of these choices, her model, like many of the others, implies that the latter of the solutions is possibly the most beneficial. All of these models differ from Stonequist's (1937) early deficit conceptualization of biracial individuals who suffer marginalized existences because they never live fully in either culture of their background. In an article that reviewed the theories about mixed parentage identity formation. Kerwin and Ponterotto (1995) outlined the following myths regarding mixed parentage children: the stereotype that biracial children are marginal persons; the myth that mixed parentage individuals must choose to identify with only one group; that mixed parentage children do not want to discuss their racial identity. Important variables to consider with these children are that they may choose one group over the other at different stages of their life (Poston, 1990) and that these choices are often influenced by their social and family situation and exposure, the composition and nature of their peer group, their participation in cultural activities, their physical appearance and language facility, inter-group tolerance, and their self-esteem (Kerwin and Ponterotto, 1995; Stephan, 1992).

Refugees

The experiences of refugees differ from those of economic immigrants (Hodes, 2000). There are similarities and differences between the experiences of refugees and economic immigrants. Both groups may experience discrimination and exclusion, poverty and social isolation on arrival in the UK. However, economic immigrants may have planned their destination and journey, and will be able to maintain links with their relatives and communities in their countries of origin and make return visits (Hodes, 2000). On the other hand, refugees may be leaving communities and societies that have been destroyed by organized violence or the threat of it. Refugees may also experience detention and dispersal, which may increase social isolation, economic hardship and unemployment. Jones (2001) highlights the conflict between the Children Act 1989 and immigration legislation and policy, especially the use of detention centres. Jones (2001, p. 258) argues that 'the social work profession singularly failed to provide critical scrutiny on the status and relationship of immigration and child care law and the erosion of children's rights'.

The number of refugee children arriving in the UK is rising annually (Woodcock, 2003). Over the last decade, there has been an increase in the number of unaccompanied asylum seeking children receiving child welfare services. The vulnerability of refugee children has legal, emotional and practical aspects (Woodcock, 2003). Thus, 'legally, children who are asylum seekers have far fewer rights than indigenous children . . . [also] they will have been exposed to a range of emotional events, which may include massive loss, disruption, fear and huge, unexpected changes. . . . they will [also] face practical difficulties with schooling and problems with health-care provision' (Woodcock, 2003, p. 264–65). An understanding of these issues will enable social workers to conceptualize some of the underlying reasons that make refugee children more vulnerable. Research on social work practice with unaccompanied asylum-seeking children is limited (Kohli and Mather, 2003)

Implications for social work practice

The Children Act 1989 (Section 22(5)) stipulates that care workers should have regard to the racial, religious, cultural and linguistic needs of children. In order to do this, social workers and social work educators need to recognize intra-racial and intra-ethnic differences in racial identity attitudes and ethnic identity development; and acculturation strategies and their implications for social work practice.

Black children are severely disproportionately represented in care, being twice as likely to enter care as white children, and are as likely as white children to be made subject to a care order even where the initial admission was voluntary (Rowe et al., 1989; Barn, 1993). The research undertaken by Barn (1993) indicated that 78% of young people placed in children's homes were between the ages of 13 and 18, while only 22% were between the ages of 6 and 12 (Barn, 1993). In this important though relatively small study of the care careers of black children in an inner city local authority social services department, Barn (1993) found that 'black families and children [compared to white families and children] underwent a qualitatively different and inferior experience in their dealings with the social services' (1993, p. 123). Black children's experiences in residential institutions were dependent on the nature and location of these institutions. Thus, children placed in their own locality and in residential homes with both black and white workers were able to maintain a healthy sense of their racial and ethnic identity, as well as good links with their family and community (Barn, 1993; 2002). Children's homes in rural settings with mainly white workers, on the other hand, were 'alienating for black children and did little to meet their emotional and psychological needs' (Barn et al., 1997, p. 9). This could be due to the children's lack of contact with their family and community, as well as to the lack of black workers in the residential homes. In a study of social services provision for black children and families in three different local authorities, Barn et al. (1997) found evidence of some very good work being conducted on identity issues by black residential staff in children's homes in a local authority in the West Midlands. Ince (1998) notes that when black members of staff are present in residential homes, the young people feel more supported.

The overt and covert racism experienced by black children in residential institutions was highlighted by the *Black and In Care* (1984) report. In a recent in-depth qualitative study of ten young black people's experience of long-term care (residential and foster) in two local authorities in Britain, Ince (1998) found that 'the presence of racism (institutional and personal) within the care system restricted the development of a positive black identity. As a result, many young people's needs – racial and cultural – remained unmet, creating a sense of powerlessness' (1998, p. 82). Ince (1998) considers that many of 'the experiences recorded in [her] study echo those in previous ones' (1998, p. 91).

Mehra (2002) cites the case of an Asian boy called Gurvinder, who was in local authority care for four years. The following case illustrates the identity problems black adolescents can face while they are in care:

> Gurvinder did not have any input of Asian culture and there were no provisions . . . to expose him to Sikh religion, Asian food or to maintain any contact with the Asian community or his own family . . . to be accepted by his co-residents and social workers, he was doing his utmost to become a white child . . . He stated: I am British. My name is Gary. I don't like Pakis'.
>
> (p. 258)

Mehra (2002) explored Gurvinder's feelings about his identity with him and eventually he 'was successfully rehabilitated with his family' (p. 259).

Coombe (1994) argues that there needs to be a greater awareness of the effects of racism on black children in residential care. It is therefore essential that social workers working with black children and adolescents ensure that racial issues and implications are not overlooked. Children and adolescents need to develop a positive identity, including a positive racial identity (Maximé, 1993; Robinson, 1995; 2000; Ince, 1998).

An understanding of Cross's and Phinney's model should sensitise social workers to the role that oppression plays in a black individual's development. Maximé (1993) has used Cross's model in the understanding of identity confusion in black children and adolescents in residential, transracially fostered and adoptive care settings. It was clearly apparent from Robinson's (2000) study of racial identity development and self-esteem among African Caribbean adolescents in residential care in a city in the West Midlands that residential care staff found Cross's model extremely useful in therapeutic work with African Caribbean youngsters (Robinson, 2000).

Exploring racial and ethnic identity attitudes of adolescents in residential care is, and remains, a vital part of adolescent personality development theory.

Robinson's (2000) research on racial identity attitudes of black adolescents in residential care highlights the importance of studying the racial identity attitudes of young black people in residential care, building on work such as that by Maximé (1986) in using racial identity theories to understand the identity confusion of black adolescents in residential care. Although the study indicated that pre-encounter attitudes were not widely endorsed by either the residential or the school sample, residential staff need to be aware that an individual holding pre-encounter attitudes may have yet to experience the sort of encounter that will catch them off guard. Maximé (1986, 1993) cites several examples of children in local authority care experiencing encounters that shattered the appropriateness of their current identity and worldview. Individuals in the pre-encounter stage are, according to Cross (1995), 'sitting ducks' for an encounter that may cause them to rethink their positions on blackness. As noted earlier, the immersion-emersion stage encompasses the most sensational aspects of black identity development. The individual at this stage tends to denigrate white people and white culture, exhibiting generally anti-white attitudes. This could be 'painful for white residential workers who suddenly find themselves "under attack" verbally and emotionally' (Maximé, 1993, p. 178). Black adolescents at the immersion-emersion stage are usually suspicious and hostile toward white professionals. They are likely to regard their own psychological problems as products of oppression and racism. A white care worker or fieldworker will be viewed by the black service user as 'a symbol of the oppressive Establishment' (Sue and Sue, 1999, p. 122). Black adolescents in the immersion-emersion stage will constantly test the sincerity and openness of the white care worker and be likely to share their problems only with a black worker. However, they may also be anxious that the black practitioner will not meet their own standards of blackness since the black worker's education, training, authority and status all depend on participation in the white world.

Many service providers assume that a black staff member is a better therapeutic match for a black service user than a white practitioner. Yet such an assumption seems questionable if, for example, the black care worker has pre-encounter attitudes where, as noted earlier, racial identity attitudes toward blackness are negative and white culture and society are seen as the ideal. Similarly, a black worker at the encounter stage may have confused feelings when working with a black client. Thus an individual's stage of racial identity may have a greater impact on the counselling/therapeutic process than does 'race' *per se* (see Carter, 1995; Robinson, 1998).

Guernina (1995) points out that 'Ethnic minority youth are subject to particular stresses such as cultural alienation, racial discrimination, inter and intra group conflicts. If these persist they will have adverse psychological effects on adjustment and health in general' (p. 54). In a small qualitative study of the care experiences of young black people, Ince (1998) found that all the participants 'reported racism at school and within their care setting, having limited or no help from carers or professionals to help with the stress and negative feelings left in the wake of racist behaviour' (p. 46). Social workers need to assess the impact of prejudice and discriminatory practices on the self-image, self-esteem, and identity of young black people and must also be cognizant of their own prejudices. Frequently, a social worker's prejudices, which may be subtle, can interfere with the relationship.

Social workers need to take an active approach in helping black children build positive self-images of themselves. A number of workbooks have been published by Maximé (1987) to help social workers. The aim of one workbook 'Black Like Me' is 'to assist and enhance in the development of a positive and secure black identity' (Maximé 1987, p. 2). Another workbook (Maximé 1991), intended for black and white children, describes the contributions black people have made in various fields – for example, medicine, mathematics, technology, arts, sports, etc. In Thoburn et al.'s (2000) study one black young man placed with black foster parents 'was very positive about the way in which they had helped him to feel good about himself as a black person' (p. 135). The following is a quote from this young person: 'The foster parents introduced me to some books like Martin Luther King and Malcolm X. So they set me on the road to learning about my blackness . . . I think I would have been confused if I'd gone to a white foster family' (p. 135).

It is valuable to show children the contributions black people have made to art, music and science (Banks, 2003). However, the child must first 'begin to develop an acceptance of self before being able to identify with another' (p. 167).

Guernina (1995) notes that 'The highest problems on the agenda in Nafsiyat [intercultural therapy center] are related to social identity crises. They are mainly related to the adolescents' awareness of not being fully accepted by the majority culture' (p. 53). The following case study cited by Guernina (1995) illustrates some of the issues raised in this chapter:

Ahmed was 19 years old when referred for therapy by his GP. His parents are Pakistani, he speaks both Urdu and English very well. He feels at home in both cultures. He goes back to Pakistan very often and perceives himself as the ambassador of his [adopted] country, Britain. He defends the British way of life. When he is in Britain he feels more Pakistani and defends Pakistan. Ahmed came for therapy to make sense of the pains and the confusion he was struggling with, such as coping with the victimization and humiliation he gets from his peers by being Black European. He feels pained by the daily comments people make, such as: 'When are you going back to your country?', 'You speak good English for Pakistani', 'How did your parents get a good job in this country?', 'When do you finish your studies and go back to your country?' Very often, Ahmed is taken for an overseas student: 'I always pretend that I am in Britain studying. . . . I always feel accepted as a foreign student but not as a British citizen.' He stresses finding it difficult to interact with people who are rigid and insensitive to other cultures: 'The more racist people are against me the more drawn I feel towards my parents' family and the culture of my ancestors because I feel threatened'.

(p. 54)

In counselling sessions with Ahmed, Guernina (1995) explores the issues raised by Ahmed including how he is affected by institutional and cultural racism as well as issues related to his identity and his level of acculturation. Guernina (1995) notes that:

> The themes which are expressed in therapy and counseling by ethnic minority adolescents are related to painful experiences concerning their physical features (skin colour) and about the disintegration of the self within different cultural systems . . . [and] most adolescents who seek counseling have the deep desire to find strength that would help them challenge oppression without fragmentation of the self.
>
> (p. 55)

Social workers need to be aware of the above issues when working with black adolescents in residential and foster care. According to Guernina (1995) 'In a transcultural approach, the over-riding therapeutic process is the awareness of the client's negative feelings that reflect an internalization of the mainstream cultural attitudes towards ethnic minorities' (p. 55). Some minority ethnic adolescents 'suffer from losing their roots, they feel grief over the separation from their parents' history, their language and culture. They find that the opportunities are not given to them to rediscover their parents' past' (Guernina 1995, p. 55). In Nafsiyat these issues are given space, are identified and valued.

As noted earlier, acculturation research (Berry, 1997; Berry and Sam, 1997) documents the stress that results when one cultural group comes in contact with another. Adolescents who are members of second or later generations in Britain and US are likely to be well acquainted with the mainstream culture, but may face conflicting demands due to differences between mainstream values and those of their ethnic culture. The issue they must resolve is the way to combine these competing identities; that is, the extent to which they identify with their ethnic culture and also with the larger society. The issue may be problematic for several reasons, including pressures both from within their ethnic group and from the mainstream culture.

Of greatest practical importance for social workers is the question of how ethnic and majority identities and the resulting identity categories are related to the adaptation of minorities and immigrants. Berry's (1990) acculturation model proposes that immigrants adopting an integration strategy show better psychological adaptation than those favouring the other acculturation orientations (for e.g., assimilation). In Britain, Robinson (2003) found that the integration strategy related positively and significantly with life satisfaction for minority ethnic adolescents. Because of the importance of one's ethnic identity as a defining characteristic of minority and immigrant group members (Phinney, 1990), pressures to assimilate and give up one's sense of ethnicity may result in anger, depression, and, in some cases, violence.

Canino and Spurlock (2000) state that: 'For many minority and immigrant children the process of acculturation is studded with stressors. This is especially so when they are not fully rooted in either culture. The children struggle over appropriate behaviour and values as they try to adhere to two, sometimes contrasting, sets of standards' (p. 16). Social workers need to be aware that integration, that is, simultaneous ethnic retention and adaptation to the new society, is the most adaptive mode of acculturation and the most conducive to immigrant and minority adolescents' well-being, whereas marginalization is the worst (Berry, 1997; Berry et al., 1987; Berry and Sam, 1997).

Adolescents vary in the extent to which they find this issue problematic and in the ways they deal with it (Berry and Sam, 1997). Some seem to resolve the conflicts between ethnic and mainstream culture and achieve a bicultural identity. Others choose to identify solely with their ethnic culture and remain separated from the wider society. Still others may not find a satisfactory identity with either group and become marginalized.

Dominelli (2002, p. 55) notes that 'failure to respond to identity issues adequately is currently exemplified in the work that is being done with children of mixed parentage or heritage'. It is important for social workers and carers to 'acknowledge the importance of all aspects of ethnicity and their role in promoting a strong sense of self-identity and positive self-image [in mixed-parentage children and young people']' (Sinclair and Hai, 2002, p. 34).

Many researchers stress that it is important for children of mixed-parentage to learn to cope as black people or people of colour, because, as noted earlier, white British or American society is ultimately going to categorize them as such (Ladner, 1977; Shackford, 1984; Maximé, 1993). Thus, while mixed-parentage children and adolescents may declare themselves as biracial, they must also develop strategies for coping with social resistance or questions about their racial group membership (Root, 1992).

In 2001, the Department of Health published the National Statistics on the Ethnicity of Children Looked after and on the Child Protection Register (Department of Health, 2001). In England, 18% of children in public care are from ethnic minority groups and of these 36% are of mixed heritage. In England, 16% of children on the Child Protection Register were from minority ethnic groups and 35% of this group were of mixed heritage.

The increase in the number of mixed parentage children in care poses a new set of challenges for social workers. It will be necessary for social workers to expand their knowledge in this area through continued education, workshops and in-service training. Social workers need to be aware of their own opinions and biases about interracial marriages, racial identity of biracial persons, and their own personal identity, and be aware of internalized racial and ethnic stereotypes. Gibbs (2003, p. 320) argues that 'the central issue for the clinician [social worker] to assess in evaluating biracial adolescents is their underlying attitudes toward their dual racial/ethnic heritage . . . Typically, the racially mixed teens seen by clinicians [social workers] express ambivalent feelings toward racial/ethnic backgrounds of both parents, alternatively denigrating and praising the perceived attributes of both groups'. However, Gibbs and Huang (2003, p. 320) emphasizes that: 'clinicians [social workers] should not assume that psychological or behavioural problems presented by biracial adolescents are necessarily responses to conflicts over their ethnic identity . . . adolescents of all races may experience emotional distress because of normative developmental and social experiences, interpersonal relationships . . . and a host of other causes'.

In a small scale study of children of mixed-heritage in need in Islington, Sinclair and Hai (2002, p. 33) found that 'the quality of information on children's background needs to be improved; more detail is needed on . . . all aspects of ethnicity – 'race', culture, religion and language'. Social workers need to ensure that 'Carers are adequately prepared and supported in helping children develop and sustain a positive self image and to understand their full ethnic background' (Sinclair and Hai, 2002, p. 33). The young people in Sinclair and Hai's (2002) study indicated a positive awareness of their ethnicity. However, there was still recognition that this did give rise to particular needs: about accepting all aspects of their heritage, especially from an absent parent; and about addressing racism, sometimes from within the family. The authors report that both social workers and carers were active in addressing these needs, for example 'by trying to maintain some "quality" contact with the different aspects of the child's background, through engagement with the local "ethnic" communities . . . and using of cultural activities to foster positive contact' (p. 34).

Prevatt-Goldstein and Spencer (2000) suggest the following principles for social workers finding suitable placements for mixed parentage children: 'ensuring that the child . . . develops those heritages that are most minimized or devalued [and] ensuring that the valuing and reflection of these heritages does not diminish the promotion of, or access to, other identities of the child' (p. 14).

Transracial placements

The practice of transracial adoption is a controversial area of social work practice (for a full discussion, see Bagley, 1993; Kirton, 2000; Small, 1986). How transracial adoption affects a child's psychological well-being and sense of identity is important. Investigators continue to disagree on what is best. Some have found no impact on a child's well-being and sense of identity (Bagley, 1993; Vroegh, 1997), but others have reported varying consequences (for e.g., Scarr and Weinberg, 1983). Maxime argued that 'black children growing up in white families fail to develop a positive black identity. Instead, they suffer identity confusion and develop a negative self-concept, believing or wishing that they were white, and harbouring negative attitudes towards black people' (Maximé, 1986, p. 101). *Adoption Now: Messages from Research* (Department of Health, 1999) concludes that: 'The grounds for matching black with black may lie . . . most notably in the nurturing of a black identity and in defence against racism' (p. 10). Phoenix (1999) argues that ' "debates" on "transracial adoption" cannot, usefully, be settled in favour of one "side" or the other. . . . Yet enough is currently known to indicate that, for practice to be anti-discriminatory, and to take the plurality and complexity of racialized identities seriously, adoption decisions have to be informed by understandings that childhood is racialized' (p. 76).

In a study of the care experiences of young black people, Ince (1998) highlights the impact of transracial placements on young black people's racial identity. She found that five of the young people, in her sample of ten, perceived themselves to be white while growing up in care. These young people showed a resistance to 'mixing' with black people and held negative views about them due to a lack of racial/cultural input from white foster and adoptive parents, and from social services, and a lack of contact with black people (Ince, 1998). Indeed, one young person states: 'I ended up being racist against black people, 'cause I used to live with white foster people and I think they were racist' (Ince, 1998, p. 79). Thoburn et al. (2000) found that 'the race of the parents has an important bearing on how they fulfil the specific parenting tasks of helping children develop a positive racial and cultural identity, and confronting racism . . . The task is particularly difficult and complex when young people have been socialized into thinking of themselves as white and have absorbed racist attitudes from previous carers or relatives' (p. 206).

In a survey of local authority provision for black and minority ethnic children and their families, Richards and Ince (2000) found that 'black children [were] still being placed in white families with totally inadequate support and where basic needs are not being met' (p. 63). Goldstein and Spencer (2000) point out that other authors (e.g., Kirton and Woodger, 1999 and Howe and Feast, 2000) also cite examples of adoption and foster placements with white parents/carers where the needs relating to ethnic identity and self-esteem of black children were not addressed. Kirton (2000) notes that 'there is substantial consensus around the view that black children must deal with negative social imagery and hostility and that the solidarity provided by a mixture of family, peer group and community is important in helping them do so' (p. 64).

Small (1986) asserts that 'unless they are very carefully trained, white families cannot provide black children with the skills and "survival techniques" they need for coping in a racist society' (Small 1986, p. 85). In a study of permanent family placement for children of ethnic minority origin, Thoburn et al. (2000) found that 'whilst some white families can successfully parent children who are of a different ethnic origin from themselves, they have extra obstacles to surmount in ensuring that the young people have a positive sense of themselves as members of a particular ethnic group' (p. 159).

Some authors (for example, Prevatt-Goldstein and Spencer, 2000; Ince, 1998; Maximé, 1993; Robinson, 2000) prefer same-race placements. Goldstein and Spencer (2000) argue that for a black child placement should be with a black family that reflects his/her ethnicity and that placements with white families should 'remain exceptional' (p. 17). However, if social workers have to place black children in white homes, they must ensure that transracial adoptees be raised in racially aware contexts. In such a context: 'the family acknowledges and accepts the child's race. The families usually live in racially diverse neighbourhoods, and the children attend integrated schools. Typically, adoptees are familiarized and even actively involved with their birth cultures. Adoptees raised in such a context are more likely to develop positive racial attitudes' (Kallgren and Caudill, 1993, p. 552). Rushton and Minnis (2000) carried out a review of the outcome of transracial placements and concluded that where transracial placements are the only option, then support and training should be provided for the substitute families. In addition, consideration needs to be given to placing children in multi-ethnic communities (Rushton and Minnis 2000). Barn (1993) found that children placed in residential homes, which were located in multiracial and multicultural areas had a positive racial and ethnic identity as a result of regular contact with their own community. Thoburn et al. (2000) report that 'some white families can successfully parent black children and those of other ethnicity, [and] that the optimum environment for them to do this is one where there are many role models, including some in high status occupations, who are of the same ethnic origin' (p. 207). Thoburn et al. (2000) conclude from their interview data that 'the requirement in the Children Act 1989 to seek to place children with parents who can meet their identified needs as individuals, and who are of a similar cultural and ethnic background, provides a sound basis for policy' (p. 206).

Much more must be written, researched, and published in order that all of us may better understand what experiences are necessary and therefore should be provided to every black child and adult in order to facilitate the development of a positive racial, ethnic and bicultural identity. Maintenance of a strong ethnic identity is generally related to psychological well-being among members of acculturating groups (Liebkind and Jasinskaja-Lahti, 2000); Nesdale et al.,

1997; Phinney and Devich-Navarro, 1997). Social workers have still much work ahead in the area of fostering healthy, positive, self-images in black children and adolescents.

Conclusions

Most black and mixed-parentage people in Britain 'possess the survival skills necessary for the development of a positive racial identity . . . [but there are those] who experience difficulty in maintaining a positive sense of racial identity' (Maximé, 1986). Some black and mixed-parentage children and adolescents in residential, transracially fostered and adoptive care settings show racial identity confusion. In particular, social care workers are likely to encounter young people with negative attitudes about their colour (Maximé, 1986, 1993). Thus, the need for greater participation by social care workers and educators in the promotion of racial pride and self-acceptance in black children and adolescents is still urgent today. Exploring racial identity attitudes of black and mixed parentage adolescents in Britain is a vital part of adolescent personality development theory.

4

Cognitive Development:
Cross-Cultural Perspectives

Introduction

Cognitive development is an area in psychology that is concerned with the study of how thinking skills develop over time. Cognition includes the psychology of thinking, what we usually call intelligence. Theories of cognitive development have traditionally focused on the period from infancy to adulthood. One theory has dominated this field during the latter half of the 20th century, and that is Piaget's stage theory of cognitive development. The testing approach (intelligence tests) is more concerned with cognitive products than the process of development. This approach attempts to 'measure behaviours that reflect mental development and arrive at scores that predict future performance such as later intelligence, school achievement and adult vocational success' (Berk, 2001, p. 158). In Britain and the US, the term intelligence is used to refer to a number of different abilities, skills, talents, and knowledge, generally all referring to people's mental or cognitive abilities.

This chapter will discuss cognitive development as studied by Piaget and the testing approach to intelligence. It discusses cross-cultural research in these areas and implications for social work practice.

Piaget's theory of cognitive development

Piaget based his theory of cognitive development on observations of Swiss children. He found that these children of various ages tended to solve problems quite differently. To explain these differences, Piaget (1952a) proposed that children progress through four stages

82

as they grow from infancy into adolescence. According to Piaget, these stages of development are not entities in themselves but serve as points of reference for understanding the course of development. Nor are they absolute; they are a prescription for what could be achieved. The actual rate and degree of completion vary with each individual, depending on the individual's biology, culture, and the nature of stimuli in his environment.

Piaget theorized that individuals learn by actively constructing their own cognitive world. To Piaget, development is a dynamic process that results from an individual's ability to adapt thinking to meet the demands of an ever-changing environment and, as a result, to formulate new ideas.

According to Piaget, mental development occurs via the mechanism of adaptation that characterizes any biological organism. Adaptation occurs via the twin processes of assimilation and accommodation. Assimilation is the transformation of the external world in such a way as to make it an integral part of oneself. This refers to taking in new knowledge and experiences (stimuli) from the environment and fusing them into the pre-existing structures of the mind – the knowledge, intelligence, and the preconceived notions. Accommodation is the stretching of the pre-existing structures in different directions and modifying them in such a way as to permit fusion of new information that could not be assimilated otherwise. That is, it is the altering of preconceived notions to interpret an event or experience in a new way.

In terms of Bronfenbrenner's (1979) ecological systems approach, these cognitive processes can be said to begin in the family (microsystem); gradually extend to increasingly complex situations that arise in the neighbourhood, at day care, or at school (mesosystem); and eventually, as the individual moves into adolescence and adulthood, operate in the workplace (exosystem) and the culture at large (macrosystem).

The four stages identified by Piaget are as follows:

Sensorimotor stage. This stage typically ranges from birth to about 2 years of age. The most important achievement of this stage is the acquisition of object permanency; that is, knowing that objects exist even when they cannot be seen. Early in this stage, children appear to assume that when a toy or other object is hidden (for example, when a ball rolls under a sofa) it ceases to exist. Later in this stage, children will search under the sofa for the lost ball, demonstrating that they have come to understand that objects exist continuously. Other cognitive developments also typically occur during this stage that have implications for later cognitive development and enculturation. Among these are such skills as deferred imitation, language acquisition, and mental imagery. Imitation and imagery are important cognitive components of observational learning, and language skills are necessary to ensure proper communication of verbal socialization processes.

Thus in this first major period of cognitive development, substructures for cognition develop via the repetitive, rhythmic exercise of sensori-motor structures – vision (looking), hearing (listening), prehension (grasping) ingesting (sucking), vocalization (crying) and the general limb movement. Intelligence develops via action; the child learns by doing. Initially the child's universe is entirely centred on his/her own body and action. In the course of the first 18 months, a kind of general decentering process occurs whereby the child comes to regard himself as an object among others in a universe that is made up of permanent objects. He/she learns that an object does not cease to exist when it disappears, and he learns where it does go.

Pre-operational stage. This stage ranges from about 2 to 6 or 7 years of age. Piaget defines this stage in terms of five characteristics: conservation, centration, irreversibility, egocentrism, and animism. Conservation is the awareness (or in this stage, the lack of such awareness) that physical quantities remain the same regardless of whether they change shape or appearance. Centration is the tendency to focus on a single aspect of a problem. Irreversibility is the inability to imagine 'undoing' a process. Egocentrism is the inability to step into another's shoes and understand the other person's point of view. Animism is the belief that all things, including inanimate objects, are alive.

At this stage, the child is beginning to take a greater interest in objects and people around him/her. He knows the world only as he sees it, and he sees it from his own point of view. This is the age of curiosity. Preschoolers are always questioning and investigating new things, looking for explanations of why things are the way they are. They can focus on only one idea at a time. For example, a mother can only be a mother; she cannot also be a wife, a sister, a daughter, or have any other role simultaneously. A big red ball can be either big or red. It is difficult to comprehend both qualities of the ball at the same time. Children at this age do not have the faculty of conservation – the ability to retain in memory the characteristics (shape, size, weight, colour) of an object encountered in the past, which is not in view presently. Piaget's experiments with glasses of different sizes are commonly used to illustrate this concept. The same amount of liquid is poured into a tall, thin glass and a short, wide glass. When asked which glass has more liquid, the two-year old will invariably point to the tall glass. The level of the liquid is higher, so, in the thinking of the child, it must be more.

Stage of intuitive thought (4–7 years) For children between the ages of 4 and 7, widening social contacts reduce egocentricity and increase social participation. Children begin to use words to express their thoughts and feelings. They begin to grasp the concept of numbers and the notion of reversibility, that what can go up can also go down, numbers that can be added can also be subtracted. Symbolic play becomes the most important developmental phenomenon. It is through symbolic play that the child assimilates new experiences. Thinking is based more on intuition than on reason or logic. Thus, this period is characterized by development of language, use of symbols, and egocentric thinking (e.g., failure to distinguish between one's own point of view and that of another individual).

Concrete operations stage. This stage lasts from about 6 or 7 years until about 11 years of age. During this stage, children acquire new thinking skills to work with actual objects and events. They are able to imagine undoing an action, and they can focus on more than one feature of a problem. Children also begin to understand that there are different points of view from their own. This new awareness helps children master the principle of conservation. A child in the concrete operations stage will understand that six apples, regardless of how they are grouped or spaced, still add up to six apples and that the amount of clay does not change as a lump is moulded into different shapes. This ability is not present in the pre-operational stage. However, instead of thinking a problem through, children in this stage tend to rely on trial-and-error strategies.

For a child around the age of 7, concepts of numbers, time, space, and speed begin to coalesce. The child begins to understand the concepts of multiplication and division. She/he can now group things with like characteristics (classification) and arrange them according to increasing or decreasing size (seriation). She/he also discovers the notion of conservation. Now when asked which glass has more liquid, she/he can see that it is the same amount of liquid, regardless of the shape of the glass.

Formal operations stage. This stage extends from around 11 years of age through adulthood. During this stage, individuals develop the ability to think logically about abstract concepts. These might include such concepts as peace, freedom, and justice. Individuals also become more systematic and thoughtful in their approach to problem solving.

As the child enters the age of pre-adolescence, new substructures of abstract thought, reason, and logic begin to evolve. The nature of thought, therefore, changes. While the child thinks largely in terms of the present, the here-and-now, the adolescent can think beyond the present, beyond his/her own experiences and belief systems, to the future. While still egocentric, the adolescent can hear and see things from perspectives other than his/her own. He/she can now comprehend geometric and proportional relationships, the concepts of relativity, probability, and chance, and think in terms of the hypothetical. He/she forms notions, ideas, and concepts about everything from the past through the present into the future; his conceptual world becomes full of ideas and theories regarding himself, life, society – what is, what ought to be, what could be. Values regarding morality, religion, social justice, and social ideals may be questioned, re-examined, and re-formed, in agreement with or in opposition to family and culture – depending also on social factors such as socialization and cultural transmission. These new substructures of abstract thought, reason, and logic make the adolescent capable of reflective thinking.

The transition from one stage to another is often gradual, as children develop new abilities alongside earlier ways of thinking. Thus, the behaviour of some children may represent a 'blend' of two stages during periods when the children are in a state of transition from one stage to another.

Piaget and Inhelder (1969) maintained that all children go through the same stages in mastering conservation of the different characteristics of objects. However, children do not achieve conservation of all characteristics at the same time. Piaget believed that children in all cultures learn to conserve different quantitative characteristics in the same invariant order, although the rate at which they acquire the concepts may vary as a function of specific experiences (e.g., whether they have attended school or had experience with physical objects). Thus, conservation of number is achieved before quantity, and conservation of quantity occurs before weight conservation, which precedes volume conservation. Although Piaget provided age ranges for these stages, he recognized that the exact age at which a particular child enters a specified stage could be significantly affected by the child's physical, cognitive or cultural experiences (Piaget et al., 1974).

According to Dasen (1994) there are hardly any 'orthodox' Piagetians left nowadays. However the basic Piagetian ideas continue to be influential in education as well as psychology. His theory was established on very small samples. The influence of cultural factors has been studied particularly at the concrete and formal operational stages of development (Dasen and Heron 1981; Woodhead 1999).

Summary

Piaget based his theory of cognitive development on observations of Swiss children. Piaget (1952a) proposed that children progress through four stages as they grow from infancy into adolescence. These stages are: sensorimotor stage; pre-operational stage; concrete operations stage; and formal operations stage. Basic Piagetian ideas continue to be influential in education as well as psychology.

Cross-cultural perspectives on Piaget's stage theory

While there is no doubt that Piaget's theory has had a significant impact on the study and understanding of cognitive development in mainstream Western psychology, his ideas have been challenged (Owusu-Bempah and Howitt, 2000; Woodhead, 1999). Owusu-Bempah and Howitt (2000) argue that 'Piagetian tests cannot be applied in cultures outside the Western world without implying Eurocentrism, the cultural superiority of the West. For example, cross-cultural studies using Piagetian tests suggest that Western European children undergo a more rapid cognitive development than their African peers (Berry and Dasen, 1974), even though in the first two years of life, they lag significantly behind African infants of their age group' (p. 116).

Piaget drew for his theories on interviews with and observations of those around him in middle-class Geneva, especially with his own well-educated children. Kelly (1977) and Lancy (1983) revealed the culture-bound nature of much Piagetian theory. They found that most Papua New Guinean children 'failed to develop' according to Piagetian structures and timetables. The authors showed that the increasingly sophisticated and efficient information-processing strategies, posited in the theory, were of little use in societies that contained, in fact, relatively little information (Lancy, 1983). Lancy argued that people tend not to progress inevitably to a stage of thinking reminiscent of the rational scientist (e.g., the formal operations of Inhelder and Piaget, 1958).

Owusu-Bempah and Howitt (2000) argue that 'the assumption that Piaget's grand theory is race- and culture-free and so poses a challenge to biological racism and ethnocentrism is illusory, if not false . . . such claims only help us to deny the culture specificity of psychology as a whole' (p. 116). Piaget's theory of cognitive development has often been criticized. It inspired a wealth of cross-cultural research on cognitive development (Dasen, 1977; Gardiner and Kosmitzki, 2005). In the following section, I will review this research.

However, it is important to bear in mind that 'because much cross-cultural psychology was carried out within the confines of a universalist paradigm, it made limited impact in relativising conceptions of child development' (Woodhead, 1999, p. 8).

Cross-cultural variations in conservation skills

Cross-cultural research using Piagetian tasks has not uniformly supported the view that all children acquire conservation skills in the same sequence or at a similar age (Dasen, 1977). Most of the studies in support of Piaget's theory have been done on children living in industrialized and relatively literate cultures. When children living in non-Western non-industrialized cultures are tested on conservation tasks, they generally lag behind children from industrialized countries by about a year (Dasen, 1977). For example, Nigerian children were found to achieve conservation by age eight (Price-Williams et al., 1961). In some studies the lag is a significant one; Greenfield (1966) tested Senegalese children on a series of conservation tests and found that most had not achieved conservation by the age of 11 or 12. The meaning of this developmental lag has been the subject of much debate, most of which has focused on the testing procedures used to assess concrete operational skills. Woodhead

(1999) states that 'predictably . . . European populations and those who had experienced European type schooling [showed] higher levels of competence [in Piagetian tasks]' (p. 8).

Owusu-Bempah and Howitt (2000) note that 'there are methodological difficulties involved in the cross-cultural application of Piaget's theory of cognitive development. A number of researchers have reported difficulties in setting up experiments in a way which their participants found relevant' (p. 117). Piaget interviewed children during the assessments and, depending on their answers, asked other questions to determine whether the children understood the concept being tested. When non-indigenous researchers test children on the Piagetian tasks, children do not do as well as children who are tested by someone from their own culture and in their own language (Nyiti, 1982). Also, children living in non-Western cultures may find the idea of testing in itself to be strange and unfamiliar; they may be uncertain about how they should respond, or the meaning of their performance to the 'foreign' tester.

When children are trained to do conservation tasks, their performance improves (Dasen, 1994). Dasen (1994) found that with Australian Aboriginal children the 'relative rate of cognitive development in different domains, such as space and quantification, reflects what is highly valued, and also what is needed, what is adaptive' (p. 147).

Sensorimotor stage

Of all Piaget's periods, the sensorimotor (occurring during infancy) has been the least studied from a cross-cultural perspective. A major reason is that observation methods and data-collecting techniques based on Piagetian concepts have only recently been standardized (Cole, 1995b). According to Dasen, the first cross-cultural study of sensorimotor intelligence, using a scale developed by Corman and Escalona (1969), was conducted in Zambia (Goldberg, 1972). In general, while minor differences in behaviour were noted – a slight advance for African infants over American (and other whites) at six months and a slight lag at nine and twelve months, Goldberg's findings tend to support Piaget's observations. Another study in the Ivory Coast Dasen et al. (1978), suggested that African infants are advanced in their development of object permanency and other object-related cognitive behaviours.

In an early review of the cross-cultural literature, Dasen and Heron (1981) recognized that differences in the ages at which the substages of the sensorimotor are attained do occur. However, they go on to stress that 'in emphasizing these cultural differences, we may overlook the amazing commonality reported by all these studies: in fact, the qualitative characteristics of sensorimotor development remain nearly identical in all infants studied so far, despite vast differences in their cultural environments' (p. 305). Werner (1979), however, concluded that 'even in the first stage of cognitive development, that of sensorimotor intelligence, culture seems to influence the rate of development to some extent, although admittedly, the similarity of structure and process is more striking than the differences. Content seems to have little relevance to the activation of sensorimotor schemata' (p. 216).

Formal operations

Piaget's theory assumes that the scientific reasoning associated with formal operations is the universal end point of cognitive development. In other words, Piaget assumed that the thinking most valued in Swiss and other Western societies (in formal operations) was the yardstick by which other cultures should be judged. Piaget considered scientific reasoning to be the ultimate achievement. His stage theory, therefore, is designed to retrace the steps by which people arrive at scientific thinking. Indeed, this perspective with regard to the ultimate end point of cognitive competence has been widely accepted within Euro-American psychology.

Piaget's stage of formal operations also has been studied cross-culturally, and it is the view of some researchers that individuals in many societies never achieve this type of thinking (Byrnes, 1988; Shea, 1985). For example, in studies carried out among adolescents in New Guinea, no subjects perfomed at the formal operational level (Kelly, 1977). Similarly, few adolescents showed formal operational thought when tested in Rwanda (Laurendeau-Bendavid, 1977). On the other hand, among Chinese children exposed to the British education system in Hong Kong, formal operational performance was found to be equal to or better than the performance of American or European children (Goodnow and Bethon, 1966). Based on these and similar findings, Piaget (1972) proposed that development of formal operational thinking is influenced by experience as well as by culture (Rogoff and Chavajay, 1995). These examples provide added impetus for considering the ecological setting in understanding why behaviour, including cognitive activity, is expressed as it is. For example, Cole and Cole (1996) point out that 'a lawyer might think in a formal manner about law cases but not when sorting the laundry' (p. 674). As evidence, they cite a study by Retschitzki (1989) showing that when African men and older boys play a popular board game involving the capture of seeds from opponents, they make use of complex rules, complicated offensive and defensive moves, and skilled calculations. Their strategies in playing this game made use of the types of logical thinking usually attributed to formal operations.

Shea (1985) has suggested that formal operational thinking (i.e., scientific reasoning) may not be valued in all cultures. Dasen (1994) also noted that 'hypothetico-deductive scientific reasoning, Piaget's ... "formal stage" is not necessarily what is most valued in every community, not even within Western societies. In fact, the development of formal reasoning (as strictly defined by Piaget) seems to be strongly dependent on secondary schooling' (p. 149). Dasen (1994) argues that 'some form of highly abstract reasoning occurs everywhere, but possibly taking different forms or cognitive styles. Recent research in Cote d'Ivoire by Tape Goze suggests that the abstract reasoning valued in the African worldview is "experiential", symbolic, global, inductive, analogical, end oriented, and seeks to answer the question "why", as opposed to formal reasoning, which is experimental, analytical, deductive, ... and asks "how"' (p. 149). Dasen (1994) found that among the Baoule of Cote d'Ivoire 'the superordinate concept of intelligence referred to both "technological" aspects (cognitive alacrity) and "social" aspects (cooperative social responsibility)' (p. 149). In the Baoule parental belief system about the goals of child development and education, the social aspects were clearly more valued than the technological ones. Cognitive skills are valued only if they are used for the good of the social group, not for individual promotion.

It is important to carefully evaluate the meaning of cross-cultural studies of Piaget's stage of formal operations. In some cultures very few people are able to complete fourth-stage Piagetian tasks (Mishra, 2001). Does this mean entire cultures are suspended at a lower stage of cognitive development? To answer this question, we must first be able to show that Piagetian tasks are a culturally appropriate way of measuring an advanced stage of cognitive development. As noted above, such tests may not be meaningful in other cultures. Besides the issue of cultural appropriateness, there is also the issue of what is being tested. People who have not attended high school or college in a Westernized school system perform very poorly on tests of formal operations (Laurendeau-Bendavid, 1977; Shea, 1985). This again raises the question of the degree to which Piagetian tasks depend on previous knowledge and cultural values rather than cognitive skills. It is also important to note that cognitive development is complicated, and it is unlikely that such tasks can capture all of its complexity.

Woodhead (1999) writes that 'whether children have access to Western style schooling appeared to be one of the most significant variables affecting their performance in Piagetian experiments. . . . One interpretation was that the environment and teaching offered by schools extends not only to the teaching of essential skills . . . but also promotes general cognitive abilities' (p. 10). Woodhead (1999) argues that: 'Development' is about the acquisition of particular cultural skills and tools that are adaptive to a particular socio-economic context and historical epoch, not about a once-for-all universal process' (p. 10).

It is also important to remember that there are considerable within-cultural differences in cognitive development. These within-culture differences make it extremely difficult to draw valid conclusions or inferences about differences in cognitive development between cultures (Modgil and Modgil, 1976).

Given the fact that large numbers of people are unable to complete Piagetian tasks of formal operations, it has not been possible to demonstrate the universality of the fourth stage of Piaget's theory of cognitive development. It is possible that most adults possess the potential to complete Piagetian tasks but fail to do so because they lack either the motivation or knowledge of how to demonstrate such ability. To successfully demonstrate success on a task purporting to measure some aspect of cognitive ability or intelligence, it is crucial that the test-taker and the test-maker agree on what is being assessed. Cultural differences in the desired end points of cognitive development as well as cultural differences in definitions of intelligence contribute to this dilemma. Goodnow (1990) concludes that Piagetian theory can be effectively applied to the conservation of weight, amount, and volume. However, she goes on to say that 'if one's goal is to go beyond these domains – to construct an account of cognitive development that cuts across many domains or that takes place in everyday life – then classical Piagetian theory will certainly need some additions' (pp. 277–8). I will conclude this section with a quote from Woodhead (1999, p. 12):

> the developmental endpoint that has traditionally anchored cognitive developmental theories –skill in academic activities such as formal operational reasoning and scientific, mathematical, and literate practices – is one valuable goal of development, but one that is tied to its contexts and culture, as is any other goal or endpoint of development valued by a community . . . consequently, it is not possible to take western expectations about children's development as an inviolable standard against which to judge other childhoods.

Summary

Piaget's theory of cognitive development has been challenged by several authors. They have revealed the culture-bound nature of much Piagetian theory. Cross-cultural research has shown differences in conservation skills. Children living in non-Western cultures may find the idea of testing in itself to be strange and unfamiliar. It is important to note that Piaget's tasks which originate in Europe and are based on European studies with European children favours European populations as showing higher levels of competence, especially those who had experienced European-style schooling. It is important to evaluate the meaning of cross-cultural studies of Piaget's stage of formal operations. People who have attended high school or college in a Westernized school system perform very poorly on tests of formal operations. This raises the question of the degree to which Piagetian tasks depend on previous knowledge and cultural values rather than cognitive skills. Finally, it is important to note that there are cultural differences in the desired end points of cognitive development as well as cultural differences in definitions of intelligence.

Other theories of cognitive development

While Piaget's theory is the most influential in US and Britain, it is important to note that it is only one of many stage theories proposed by social scientists in the West. In the past few years, a great deal of attention has been directed to the social context of children's development of cognitive skills (e.g., Rogoff, 1990; Rogoff and Morelli, 1989; Rogoff and Tudge, 1989). Much of this attention stems from Vygotsky's (1978) sociocultural theories, especially his notion about the zone of proximal development (ZPD), which represents the difference between what a child can do with adult guidance and what he/she is able to do independently. According to Vygotsky, children's future independent performance is largely dependent upon the types of guidance provided by the adult in the ZPD. Adults create the zone and mediate the process of learning by providing guidance that reflects cultural values. As noted in the above section, Piaget's position was that cognitive development is largely an individual accomplishment, directed and shaped, in part, by the environment. However, he has said little about the importance of the social context in learning. This view was challenged by Vygotsky (see Vygotsky 1978 for detailed review).

Intelligence as measured by IQ

Spearman (1927) and Thurstone (1938) developed what are known as factor theories of intelligence. These theories view intelligence as a general concept comprised of many subcomponents, or factors, which include verbal or spatial comprehension, word fluency, perceptual speed, etc. Guilford (1985) built on factor theories to describe intelligence using three dimensions – operation, content, and product – each of which has separate components. Through various combinations of these three dimensions, Guilford suggests that intelligence is actually composed of upwards of 150 separate factors (see Guilford, 1985 for detailed review).

Spearman (1927) also proposed a 'general' intelligence representing overall mental ability. The general intelligence approach is one of the earliest approaches to the study of cognition. This approach is based on the idea of a unitary cognitive competence called 'general ability', which is evidenced by a set of positive correlations among performances on a number of cognitive tasks such as verbal, spatial, numerical, and so forth (Spearman, 1927). There is a belief in the existence of a general central cognitive processor that accounts for varying levels of intelligence across individuals in a population. The measurement and meaning of 'general ability' has come under considerable scrutiny in the past several decades (Burg and Belmont,

1990). In cross-cultural studies of intelligence, the existence of more specialized factors (e.g., verbal, mathematical, and conceptual reasoning) besides 'g' has been demonstrated (Burg and Belmont, 1990; Vernon, 1969).

While traditional thinking and reasoning abilities have dominated views of intelligence in the past, in recent years psychologists have begun to turn their attention to other aspects of the mind as part of intelligence. For example, Sternberg (1985) has proposed a theory of intelligence that is based on the existence of three separate 'subtheories' of intelligence: contextual, experiential, and componential intelligence. Contextual intelligence refers to an individual's ability to adapt to the environment, solving problems in specific situations. Experiential intelligence refers to the ability to formulate new ideas and combine unrelated facts. Componential intelligence refers to the ability to think abstractly, process information, and determine what needs to be done. Sternberg's theory focuses more on the processes that underlie thought than on specific thought outcomes. Because intelligence is defined as process rather than outcome, it has the potential for application across cultures.

Despite the fact that inclusion of these various types of intelligence has added a new dimension of diversity to definitions of intelligence, traditional mainstream definitions of intelligence still tend to centre around cognitive and mental capabilities concerning verbal and mathematical skills.

Intelligence in a cross-cultural context

When considering intelligence in a cross-cultural context, the first thing we need to take into account is the fact that many languages have no word that corresponds to the Euro-American idea of intelligence. Definitions of intelligence often reflect cultural values. The closest Mandarin equivalent, for instance, is a Chinese character that means 'good brain and talented'. Chinese people often associate this with traits such as imitation, effort, and social responsibility (Keats, 1981). Such traits do not constitute important elements of the concept of intelligence for most people in the West. African cultures provide a number of examples. The Baganda of East Africa use the word 'obugezi' to refer to a combination of mental and social skills that make a person steady, cautious, and friendly (Wober, 1975). The Djerma-Songhai in West Africa use the term akkal, which has an even broader meaning – a combination of intelligence, know-how, and social skills (Wober, 1975). Still another society, the Baoule, uses the term 'n'gloele', which describes children who are not only mentally alert but also willing to volunteer their services without being asked (Dasen, 1984).

Because of the enormous differences in the ways cultures define intelligence, it is difficult to make valid comparisons of the notion of intelligence from one society to another. That is, different cultures value different traits, which comprise their notion of 'intelligence'. Consequently, there are divergent opinions across cultures concerning which traits are useful in predicting future important behaviours, especially because different cultures value different future behaviours. People in different cultures not only disagree about the very nature of what intelligence is but also have very different attitudes about the proper way to demonstrate their abilities. In Western (US and British) society, individuals are typically rewarded for displaying knowledge and skills. This same behaviour may be considered improper, arrogant, or rude in societies that stress personal relationships, cooperation, and modesty (Matsumoto and Juang, 2004). In Uganda, Wober (1975) found that 'intelligence' referred to shared knowledge and wisdom, and in particular the way an individual acted to the benefit of his or her community. In Zambia, Serpell (1977) found that adults labelled children who were obedient, who could be trusted to follow instructions, and who had respect for their elders' as being intelligent. These descriptions of intelligence place far more importance on social behaviour and responsibility, than do the traditional Western descriptions of intelligence.

Much cross-cultural research on intelligence has focused on the issue of testing within multicultural societies where cultural minorities are evaluated with tests designed for a dominant culture. Cross-cultural research extends not only to cultures in different countries but also to subcultures within Western society. In the next section, I will examine some of the problems involved in defining and measuring intelligence within multicultural societies.

Cultural influences on the measurement of intelligence

Intelligence tests were first developed in the early 1900s for the purpose of identifying mentally retarded children (Binet and Simon,

1905). Intelligence tests provided a way to distinguish children in need of special education from those whose schoolwork suffered for other reasons. In the years that followed, intelligence tests came into widespread use in public schools and other government programmes in US and Britain.

But not everyone benefited from the new tests of intelligence. Because such tests relied at least in part on verbal performance and cultural knowledge, immigrants who spoke English poorly and came from different cultural backgrounds were at a disadvantage.

Jensen (1969) claims that blacks, as a group, tend to score significantly less (about 15 IQ points) than whites on intelligence tests. Jensen (1969, 1980, 1981) argues that differences in IQ scores between different societies and ethnic groups are mainly hereditary or innate. He conducted studies examining differences between African and European Americans and found that African Americans scored lower on IQ tests than European Americans. Jensen argues that about 80% of a person's intelligence is inherited and suggests that the gap between the scores of European Americans and ethnic minorities in US is due to biological differences.

The research and writing about black-white differences in intelligence has generated a great deal of controversy (see Williams and Mitchell, 1981). Hilliard (1981) described intelligence testing as having questionable validity and purpose and no practical application to instruction. One of the most widely used tests for the measurement of children's intelligence, the Wechsler Intelligence Scale for Children-Revised (WISC-R), is considered to be an extremely biased and limited test by many black educators and psychologists (Hilliard, 1987). As there are numerous definitions of intelligence, 'each test developer makes a subjective decision about what "intelligence" will mean for his test' (Williams and Mitchell, 1991, p. 194).

If a test is made specifically for a particular group one would expect members of that group to score higher on the test than members from out-groups. Most standardized IQ (intelligence quotient) tests in use today are culture-specific in that they are comprised of items and validated against responses taken from the specific culture of the white middle class. Hence, persons belonging to other socio-economic classes and other racial groups tend to make responses that deviate from the identified norm. Wilson (1978, p. 134) asserts that: 'the "intelligence" determined by IQ tests is the "intelligence" which may be defined as the degree to which an individual has assimilated and accommodated, i.e., adapted, himself [herself] to a certain set of values, standards, attitudes, ways of verbalizing, ways of thinking, ways of perceiving and other ways of behaving that a particular culture, subculture or individual evaluates as important to the maintenance and advancement of its way of life'. He argues that 'the principal function and purpose of IQ tests is to "objectively" justify, maintain and advance the white middle class life and cognitive style' (p. 135).

It appears that 'the minority individual is being judged by a test which is based on an experience which he [or she] has not been allowed to have and which gives no credibility to his [or her] actual experiences' (Williams and Mitchell, 1991, p. 194). There is a debate surrounding the interpretation of test scores of groups who do not belong to the dominant culture. Ogbu (1994, p. 369) argues that 'IQ tests measure only a set of cognitive skills functional in Western middle-class culture . . . These skills are not universally valued, nor equally functional; other cultures require and stimulate the development and use of other cognitive skills for coping with their environments'.

The debate about population differences in general intelligence has been fuelled more recently by two volumes that claim a substantial genetic basis for intelligence (Herrnstein and Murray, 1994; Rushton, 1995). Rushton has proposed a theory in sociobiology whereby Asians, Caucasians, and Africans, as a result of evolution, may be hierarchically ranked such that Mongoloids> Caucasoids>Negroids. Rushton's conclusions have been challenged by various authors (Fairchild, 1991). For example, Fairchild (1991) argues that 'Rushton's sociobiology of racial differences is unscientific in its assumptions and interpretations, and therefore may properly be regarded as scientific racism' (Fairchild, 1991, p. 112). According to Darling-Hammond et al. (1995), the bell curve hypothesis proposed rests primarily on the presumptions that intelligence is inherited and distributed unequally across groups, that intelligence is represented by a single measure of cognitive ability that predicts life success, and that intelligence is only minimally affected by environmental factors.

Summary

When considering intelligence in a cross-cultural context, we need to take into account the fact that many languages have no word that corresponds to the Euro-American idea of intelligence. Definitions of intelligence often reflect cultural values. Because of the enormous differences in the ways cultures define intelligence, it is difficult to make valid comparisons of the notion of intelligence from one society to another. Much cross-cultural research on intelligence has focused on the issue of testing within multicultural societies where cultural minorities are evaluated with tests designed for a dominant culture. The research and writing about black-white differences in intelligence has generated a great deal of controversy. Most standardized IQ (intelligence quotient) tests in use today are culture-specific in that they are comprised of items and validated against responses taken from the specific culture of the white middle class. There is a debate surrounding the interpretation of test scores of groups who do not belong to the dominant culture.

Implications for social work practice

Daniel et al. (1999) list the following implications for practice from Piaget's work of cognitive development. The authors note that social workers:

> should expect to see children actively trying to work out how the world they live in works and it is a cause for concern if they are not doing so; initially in the school years children's ability to grasp abstract concepts is limited, therefore explanations for what is happening to them need to be couched in concrete terms; if children are not able to assimilate new ideas and concepts their thought processes may be disorganized and unpredictable. Similarly, if they are unable to accommodate their thought patterns to new ideas and concepts their thinking could be rigid and unchanging; if a child's thought processes seem unusual it may be helpful to try and see the world from their own viewpoint and work out what their logic is.
>
> (p. 209)

For example, 'some children whose cognitive skills are limited have great difficulty with understanding concepts of family relationships

. . . to help children understand where they fit in a family network it could be helpful to draw simple family diagrams, or use dolls' (p. 210). However, Daniel et al. (1999) do not discuss cross-cultural implications for working with children from different cultures. We need to question whether the above quote applies to minority ethnic children. Cross-cultural research on Piaget's theory has shown differences within the stages and has questioned whether abstract, scientific reasoning is the ultimate end point of cognitive development. However, cross-cultural research, has also shown considerable cultural similarities, as well as differences, in the manner by which people progress through the various stages of cognitive development. These similarities have to do with the nature of the stages through which people progress in developing their abstract reasoning skills and in the general age ranges associated with each of the stages.

Piaget's theory of cognitive theory was used by educators and parents to understand what the child was able to do at different ages. Woodhead (1999, p. 5) writes that 'Piaget's universal stages in individual development-from sensori-motor action to autonomous logical thinking – was highly influential in shaping beliefs about primary education practice during the 1960s and 1970s'. While Piaget's theory has 'been heavily disputed, [its] power has been in offering an authoritative account of what it means to be a child and what is appropriate in terms of . . . education. While they may have been offered as scientific theories, the function they have served is as pedagogies of child care and education' (p. 5). However, it is important to note that Piaget's 'European-originated tasks, based on studies with European children . . . favoured European populations as showing higher levels of competence, especially those who had experienced European-style schooling' (p. 131).

As noted earlier, Piaget's cognitive developmental theory has been the focus of many cross-cultural research studies since the mid 1970s. Of particular interest to schooling have been those studies carried out on concrete and formal operational thinking. Tasks devised to explore conservation, simple logic and spatial thinking when applied to different cultures have shown that, in some instances, there may be a completed lack of concrete reasoning. This is because the context in which the members of a culture operate does not seem to need this type of thinking. However, Dasen (1982) has shown that with training, children can think in concrete terms if the opportunity arises. This means that cultural differences often show up as differentials in terms of performance rather than a lack of competence.

Cole and Scribner (1977) have argued that the application of Piagetian tasks to adults often assigns them to a type of child like status, and that applying value judgements to whether they should or should not reach a certain status needs to be avoided, as there are strong eco-cultural reasons for the way adults and indeed children in some cultures perform. However, the role of training (which is closely related to schooling), appears important in changing a certain status in the level of concrete operational thinking, and so the implications for educators and other professionals are significant for improving learning and teaching. That is, instruction strategies could include specific intervention schedules that would enhance a child's understanding of number, or substance conservation, or act as a preparation for children to solve problems using deductive and hypothetico-deductive reasoning.

Keats (1982), comparing formal operational thinking in Australian students with ethnic Malay, Indian and Chinese Malaysians, found that 'on a proportionality training session, what differences existed between and within the groups were due to performance factors rather than being related to competence' (p. 65). Educators and social workers should be careful about using situations that are not culturally suitable for non schooled children, otherwise they will draw the wrong conclusions about children's performance and their competency to carry out cognitive tasks. However, this caution also extends to those children attending school and who come from different cultural backgrounds. Thus, Canino and Spurlock (2000) argue that 'In determining the level of formal operational thinking (mainly dominated by pedagogies which emphasise analytical and experimental thinking styles), it is important that the teachers [and social workers] are aware of the emic dimension to thinking styles that reflect cross-cultural forms of analysis and interpretation, when solving formal operational problems' (p. 23).

The over-representation of ethnic and culturally different children in special education classes has been partially attributed to 'the indiscriminate use of psychological tests, especially IQ tests' (Cummins, 1984, p. 1). The IQ test has legitimized the labelling of many minority/black children as 'mentally retarded' and their resulting placement in special education classes. Schools are the largest consumers of intelligence tests.

The belief that intelligence has an underlying biological or genetic substrate implies the notion of 'deficit', whereas the cultural viewpoint suggests the notion of 'difference'. Early explanations for lower academic and intellectual functioning among black children referred to 'genetic deficits' in the black population.

Teachers have poor expectations linked to attitudes/perceptions about low intelligence. Intelligence testing has become equated with academic aptitude. As noted earlier, at its earliest inception, IQ tests were designed to assess school performance. Binet and Simon (1916) developed one of the earliest tests that was based on materials and problems that would be relevant to school activities (Lewontin et al., 1984). Over time, IQ tests have become associated with a much broader definition that has resulted in many of the concerns raised regarding racial/ethnic differences. In particular, IQ has been equated with 'potential'. IQ tests measure what a person has learned (Kaufman, 1990). Kaufman indicated that the content of intelligence tests is based on information that is learned in a particular cultural context (e.g., home, school, community). The IQ test is in many ways a measure of 'past learning' (p. 25). The abilities tapped by traditional measures have not changed dramatically for decades.

Ivey (2003, p. 22–3) states that: 'The controversies concerning innate intelligence demonstrate how psychological testing has been used as a political tool by which white groups could enforce their dominant position in the social hierarchy, while black populations were consigned to lower positions'. Since the notion of intelligence as a neutral, objective phenomenon has been disputed (Chaplin, 1975), intelligence tests serve only to reinforce the self-perpetuating nature of social and educational systems. There continues to be a resurgence of studies from time to time that affirm intellectual differences on grounds of race. This is evident in studies by Hernstein and Murray (1994), Jensen (1981).

In Britain, IQ tests were widely used in schools for selecting children for grammar schools. These tests 'were seen as a measure of innate ability' (Tuckwell, 2002, p. 22). A study of African Caribbean children aged 5 years by the Birmingham local education authority found that they 'were twice as likely as 5 year olds from other ethnic groups to be classed as above average, against national norms, in numeracy tests. . . . [However] 'by the time they reach 16 years of age, they were four times more likely to be excluded from secondary school and considerably less likely to get five or more GCSE passes at grades A to C' (Dwivedi, 20023, p. 203).

Indeed, Coard (1971) suggested that the 'British school system [was] contributing to the disadvantages experienced by many black children because of the Eurocentric curriculum, as well as white teachers' low expectations of black pupils' (cited in Tuckwell, 2002, p. 22). In a book entitled *How the West Indian Child is made educationally subnormal in the British school system*, Coard (1971) argues that teachers' attitudes and expectations towards African Caribbean children caused them to underestimate the ability of all black children.

Asian and African Caribbeans experience negative interactions with the teachers in the classroom. Teachers hold stereotypes about both Asian and African Caribbean children. Asian children are perceived as weak in the English language and African Caribbean children, especially boys, are seen as disruptive (Wright, 1992).

Social workers need to be aware that 'black children [are] often viewed negatively by white teachers in terms of their behaviour and academic potential, and [are] frequently stereotyped as "good at sport" and "good at music"' (Tuckwell, 2002, p. 23). The majority of teachers operate in a system, which continue 'to reinforce the dominant position of white children and the disadvantage of many black children' (p. 23). Tuckwell (2002) notes that from her own experience in schools,

> there did not appear to be many white teachers who fully understood how the educational system, together with discrimination in employment, housing and criminal justice, contributed to black underachievement. . . . There seemed to be few white teachers who appreciated the extreme concern of many African Caribbean parents about their children's progress, or were aware of the supplementary schools organized by black groups in the community to improve literacy and to teach black children about black leaders such as Marcus Garvey and Malcolm X.
>
> (p. 24).

As noted earlier, a review of the major issues involved in testing black children reveals two general models – a 'deficit' and a 'difference' model. The deficit approach assumes that black people are deficient when compared to whites in some measurable trait called intelligence, and that this deficiency is due to genetic or cultural factors or both. Majors (2001, p. 53) points out that 'as many in Western countries view IQ and intelligence as genetic, stable, trait like, and immalleable, belonging to a group with a stigma of intellectual inferiority is a daunting prospect'. The deficit approach has reinforced stereotypes that characterized black people as inferior, and has maintained the comparatively low teacher expectations that produce academic underachievement. The deficit hypothesis leads to compensatory education, a 'remedial' approach that implies a forceful assimilation to the dominant norms. The difference hypothesis, on the other hand, will lead to building on existing strengths, and provide the necessary skills without a derogatory value judgement on their absence. Social workers and teachers need to understand that if some pupils have problems, it may be not because they have some deficit, but because the school is not meeting their needs. Maybe the school still has a monocultural philosophy.

The tendency to rely on stereotypes to ease the difficulty of interacting with the unfamiliar is very strong for all people. It is easier to draw on preconceptions when in doubt than it is to make the effort to seek out and know individuals. The following case study cited by Arnold (1997), which was given to white social workers in a training seminar illustrates the stereotypes social workers have about Asians and African Caribbean young people:

> A 14-year old black girl was referred for assessment with complaints by teachers of persistent truancy. On the occasions when she attended, she was very disruptive, talking incessantly and interrupting the teacher, refusing to pay attention to any instruction, and encouraging her peers to join in her escapades. Her parents had admitted that they were unable to control her difficult behaviour at home and were afraid that she would influence her younger siblings. [Social workers' responses to this case study were] If West Indian, perhaps her parents were too strict; If Indian or Pakistani, perhaps parents were arranging a marriage for her. However, the responses of the social workers to the same case study but with a white adolescent were: 'Adolescent acting out'; 'Struggling for independence and resenting the responsibility of looking after her younger siblings'
>
> (Arnold, 1997, p. 157)

Social workers 'felt that they had been influenced by the client being black, in responding to an image of black children as inevitable failures at school' (Arnold, 1997, p. 158–9). Social work models have tended to pathologize black families and encourage practitioners to perceive the families as being the 'problem'. Consequently, social work intervention focuses almost exclusively on client's weaknesses, inabilities, and inadequacies. Social workers need to mobilize the strengths and competence in black families. Emphasis on strengths and competencies must replace attention to pathology and deficiency. Other challenges for social workers include resisting poor teacher expectations and stereotyping of black pupils.

Black children (particularly black males) are up to 15 times more likely to be excluded from school than their white counterparts (Osler, 1998). Children in local authority care are at greater risk of permanent exclusion from school (Firth, 1995). This is partly due to schools and social workers having low expectations of children in care and this can contribute to underachievement and failure (Okitikpi, 1999). Majors argues that 'many of these exclusions occur because of a lack of cultural awareness, miscommunication, racism and negative stereotyping . . . [and] because the culture of Black pupils is (in most instances) so different from that of their teachers, teachers often misunderstand, ignore, or discount Black children's language, non-verbal cues, learning styles and worldview' (Majors, 2001, p. 2). Majors (2001, p. 3) also notes that black pupils have reported that 'they have observed differential treatment with regard, among other things, to teacher bullying (e.g., harassment, over-monitoring) discipline, length of punishment, the choice of who is to speak in class, and how they are communicated with'. The high levels of exclusion among Black children has affected their academic performance (Gillborn and Gipps, 1996; Majors, 2001).

A study was carried out by the Office for Standards in Education (OFSTED) and Social Services Inspectorate (SSI) (Department of Health/OFSTED, 1995) into the education of children in care. The majority of the children of school age missed school regularly and few of the children in care achieved any qualifications. In addition, the study found that social workers and teachers did not give sufficient priority to the educational progress of children in care and teacher contact with social workers was also unsatisfactory. Also, a great number of these children were black. Okitikpi (1999) argues that 'there is very little discussion about how the educational needs of black children can best be met whilst they are still in care to help raise their level of educational attainment. He argues that there is a need for 'closer partnership between teachers and social workers; setting homework; worker/carer's involvement with homework; supplementary schools; religion; extracurricular activities' (p. 107). I agree with Okitikpi's arguments. It is important for social workers to show interest in all aspects of black children's school life. Social workers need to maintain close links with the school and need to prioritize continuity of schooling and school for academic and social reasons. It is important that professionals and caregivers working with children in need appreciate the academic, social and developmental importance of a positive school experience. Parents and teachers should work in partnership in supporting children in school and more specifically in avoiding exclusions. There is also a need for social workers to have an awareness of the range of supplementary educational provisions (Saturday or evening schools) available within the locality where the black child is residing.

German (2002, p. 209) argues that 'despite the inquiries that have been initiated, despite the recommendations, despite the adoption of policies, the provision of training and the availability of positive learning resources, the same struggle is being waged and the same battles fought by countless black families who feel that their children are being disadvantaged by the schools they attend and by teacher attitudes and classroom practices'.

To conclude, social workers need to note that: 'Failure to take seriously the long-term future needs of black children in care would result in a group of children who have no stake in the country or in the community . . . it is imperative that their education needs are given the highest priority' (Okitikpi, 1999, p. 124).

5

Communication: Cross-Cultural Perspectives

Introduction

This chapter will address from a psychological point of view issues relating to intercultural communication with black children and adolescents and their families. An understanding of cultural differences in communication will enable social workers to communicate effectively with black children and adolescents.

According to (Samovar and Porter, 2002, p. 46) 'intercultural communication is communication between people whose cultural perceptions and symbol systems are distinct enough to alter the communication event'. Intercultural communication, therefore, 'entails the investigation of those elements of culture that most influence interaction when members of two different cultures come together in an interpersonal setting' (Samovar and Porter, 2002, p. 46). My usage of the term 'intercultural communication' parallels that of Samovar and Porter's definition. Interethnic communication is a form of intercultural communication (Samovar and Porter, 2002). Interethnic communication describes 'differences in communication between members of [ethnic] groups who are all members of the same nation-state' (Lustig and Koester, 1993, p. 60). Similarly, in this chapter, communication between African Caribbeans/Asians and white British people is referred to as interethnic communication. The chapter will examine conceptual ways of understanding the processes involved and will apply the practical implications of this thinking to social work practice. It discusses the role of language in intercultural communication. In particular it focuses on bilingualism and the relationship between language and ethnic identity.

This chapter will examine some of the culture-bound values of black people and their relationship to interethnic communication. It will explore the significance of nonverbal behaviours among black children and young people and social workers. The meanings we interpret from nonverbal behaviours are culturally conditioned. The differences in nonverbal behaviour among cultures can cause breakdowns in intercultural communication (Barna, 1994; Matsumoto and Juang, 2004). The importance of nonverbal communication in interethnic settings is significant because the lack of trust between ethnic communities has caused interethnic communicators to reject the values of verbal communication and to search for nonverbal cues as indicators of real meanings and response in interethnic communication situations. Finally, implications for social work with black children, adolescents and their families are discussed.

Bilingualism and intercultural communication

Bilingualism is a far more common phenomenon than many monolingual native speakers imagine. Over 70% of the world's population speaks more than one language (Siraj-Blatchford, 1994). Thus it is as natural to grow up speaking more than one language as it is to grow up speaking only one language.

In Britain English is the major language, but children are exposed to other languages. Some children (e.g., Indian) are exposed to several languages and can selectively respond in each language, e.g., a child may respond to father in English and in Hindi or Urdu to his/her mother. Research has shown that 'bilingual children who acquired their second language from an early age were more flexible in their use of labels for words (Oren, 1981)' (cited in Gormly and Brodzinsky, 1997, p. 192).

Bilingualism is the ability to understand and make oneself understood in two or more languages. Research (Skutnabb-Kangas, 1981; Kesslar and Quinn, 1987; Milne and Clarke, 1993) has shown the positive benefits of bilingualism. Some of the advantages identified in these studies are: increased self-esteem, positive identity and attitudes towards language learning, cognitive flexibility, increased problem-solving. Research has shown that encouraging children to become bilingual can contribute to their cognitive flexibility (Milne and Clarke, 1993).

For young children entering a new language environment, the

continued use of the home language is important for social and personal development (see Baker, 1995). According to Keats (1997) 'For some children learning two languages may also add to their sense of self-esteem and help them learn about their cultural heritage' (p. 192).

In a study of the development of bilingualism among Punjabis living in Britain, Dosanjh and Ghuman (1996) found that English was increasingly becoming the first language of the Punjabi homes. A significantly higher proportion of the third-generation children used English with their mothers, fathers and siblings compared with the second-generation counterparts. Ghuman (1999) notes that 'there has been a shift in the languages spoken at home; most of the second generation families are bilingual and their British-born children increasingly use English as their first language' (p. 30). Robinson (2003) found that the majority of second generation Indians and Pakistanis were able to speak one or more of these languages – Punjabi, Hindi or Urdu – and used these languages to communicate with their parents and grand-parents. They used English with their siblings. However, the majority of the young people were unable to read or write in these languages.

According to Dosanjh and Ghuman (1996) 'the present organization of nurseries and schools does not take serious account of the arguments advanced by very many academics (see Baker, 1995; Tomlinson, 1984), who argue that there should be a degree of continuity between home and school life in order to achieve an all –round social and intellectual development of children' (p. 116). Most of the mothers in Ghuman's sample were in favour of teaching their community language, whether it be Punjabi or Hindi or Urdu and were intending to send their children to a community school (Dosanjh and Ghuman, 1996). It is clear that Asians would like to preserve their mother tongues as they see this as an integral part of their ethnic and cultural identity. Hylton (1997) states that 'it is widely recognised that mother tongue transference of traditions to children occurs commonly in South Asian households, and also to some extent through Creole [black English] within African Caribbean households' (p. 8).

Modood et al. (1997) found that an overwhelming majority of Asians spoke a non-European language and a majority of them were also able to write it. Interesting findings from the survey relate to age; these showed that while nearly all the younger generation

16–34 year olds still sometimes use a community language in talking to family members older than themselves, only about half of Indians and African Asians, six out of ten Pakistanis and a high 85% of Bangladeshis in this age group used an Asian language with family members of their own age group (Modood et al., 1997). Within the family circle, the continued use of the first language is important for strengthening the bond between parents and children and for communicating effectively with older family members and parents (Robinson, 2003).

There are indications that, while many Asian children are able to speak their mother tongue or community languages, they are not in the same way proficient in reading and writing these languages (Anwar, 1998; Modood et al., 1997; Robinson, 2003). However, for access to religious and cultural literature in Asian languages, reading is important. Therefore, in Asian communities, many supplementary schools or classes are arranged to teach Asians not only their religion and religious practice, but also their community or heritage languages. Such provision is generally attached to mosques, gurdwara and temples. These classes are held either after school hours or at weekends. However, many Asian parents and young people would like such a provision as part of the school curriculum (Dosanjh and Ghuman, 1996; Drury, 1991). There is a widespread feeling among Asians that their religions and languages are not treated by the educational system in the same way as European languages such as French, German, etc.

People make a positive or negative evaluation about the language that others use. Generally speaking there is a pecking order among languages that is usually buttressed and supported by the prevailing political order. In Britain, 'there is a temptation to disparage others' language forms as deficient. [But] as with the concept of culture, others language forms are different, not deficient' (Lago and Thompson, 1996, p. 56). Since many Western societies place such a high premium on the use of English, it is a short step to conclude that minorities are inferior, lack awareness, or lack conceptual thinking powers. On the other hand, those who speak English are evaluated according to their various accents and dialects.

The use of standard English to communicate with one another may unfairly discriminate against those from a bilingual background. Not only is this seen in the educational system, but also in the social work interview. The bilingual background of many Asians may lead to much misunderstanding. When clients have to communicate in a language that is not their native language, important aspects of experience may be left out. As discussed earlier, Asians are likely to come from a collectivistic, family-oriented culture. However, the English language 'is more limited in defining family relationships when compared with languages from family-centred cultures' (d'Ardenne and Mahtani, 1990, p. 67). For example, in Hindi, there are four different words for 'aunt' and four different words for 'uncle' (Rack, 1982). Thus, 'in counselling [or interviewing] a client from this family-centred culture, the counselor [or social worker] working only in English is limited in her understanding of the subtlety of family relationships' (d'Ardenne and Mahtani, 1990, p. 67). According to Sue et al. (1992), 'promoting bilingualism rather than monolingualism should be a major goal to the provision of mental health [and social] services: it is an expression of personal freedom and pluralism' (p. 79).

Language and identity expression

One major function of language is the expression of identity (Giles et al., 1977). Keats (1997) argues that 'for many ethnic minorities the [ethnic] language is regarded as perhaps the most evidence of their cultural identity and is used to preserve the culture in the midst of external pressures to conform to the demands of the majority culture' (p. 22).

Giles and Johnson (1981) contend that language is vital to any group's identity and is particularly salient for ethnic groups. Giles et al. (1977) developed ethnolinguistic identity theory to explain how members of language communities maintain their linguistic distinctiveness, and how and when language strategies are used. Other authors (for example Jenkins, 1982; Smitherman-Donaldson, 1985) have related specific language and dialect to identities. Jenkins (1982) notes that within the African American community there are linguistic markers of identity, and members of the group are often catalogued by their language characteristics.

Social identity theory assumes that individuals seek positive social identities in intergroup encounters. Social identity is 'that part of an individual's self-concept which derives from his [or her] knowledge of his [or her] membership in a social group (or groups) together with the value and emotional significance attached to that membership'

(Tajfel, 1978, p. 63). That part of the self-concept not accounted for by social identity is personal identity. Language is a vital aspect of the social identity of any group, particularly ethnolinguistic groups (see Giles and Johnson, 1981 for a detailed review).

The basic tenets of ethnolinguistic identity theory revolve around techniques and processes for maintaining distinctiveness that include a variety of speech and nonverbal markers (e.g., vocabulary, slang, posture, gesture, discourse styles, accent) that create 'psycholinguistic distinctiveness' (Giles and Coupland, 1991). People use linguistic distinctiveness strategies when they identify strongly with their own group and are insecure about other groups (Giles and Johnson, 1981).

The following example cited by Giles and Coupland (1991) illustrates within group differences in language attitudes and behaviours among Indians living in Leicester, whose community language is Gujerati. One older respondent stated: 'If I didn't speak Gujerati, I would feel drowned . . . I would suffocate if I didn't speak Gujerati. If an Indian tries to speak to me in English I always ask "can't you speak Gujerati?". If he can't I feel distant from him' (Giles and Coupland, 1991, p. 104). However, a younger respondent stated: 'I was at a polytechnic in London and a year passed before I spoke any Gujerati. Even when I met a Gujerati from Leicester, we got to know each other in English and wouldn't dream of speaking anything else' (Giles and Coupland, 1991, p. 104). Ethnolinguistic identity theory takes into account between-group and within-group differences in language and ethnic attitudes. The theory enables us to analyze who uses which language strategy, when and for what purposes. For instance, in the examples cited above, the first respondent may identify herself as a 'Gujerati', while the second would probably self-identify as 'British'.

A Creole language or dialect, referred to as black English, has been identified as a distinctive language characteristic of black (African American and African Caribbean) culture (King and James, 1983; Labov, 1982). There is a tendency among some authors to describe black English as a deviant or deficient form of mainstream or standard English (Smitherman, 1977; Smitherman-Donaldson, 1988). Viewing black English as a dialect stems from a Eurocentric perspective that describes only what is 'missing' and what is grammatically 'incorrect'. Therefore, we need to use the term black English rather than black dialect to indicate the language form.

Black English is now recognized as a legitimate form with a unique and logical syntax, semantic system and grammar (Stewart, 1970; Smitherman, 1977; Jenkins, 1982; Smitherman-Donaldson, 1988) that varies in its forms depending upon which African language influenced it and in which region it was developed (Smitherman, 1977).

The Caribbean-based Creole, or Patois as it is often called, is an important feature among African Caribbean youth. In order to understand the importance of Creole, it is important to appreciate the nature of the relationship between the black (African Caribbean) community and the dominant white society. Racial and ethnic hostility expressed in racist language employed by the white dominant society can result in hostile feelings on the part of the oppressed group. The use of Creole among African Caribbean people can be seen as a reaction to the values and standards of the dominant culture. It is a means of expression that serves both to express hostile reactions and to preserve the integrity of the group. It enables African Caribbeans to communicate with each other while maintaining secrecy from the white dominant society. Wong (1986, p. 105) notes that Patois and Creole are languages that developed because they were 'necessary for intra-community communication that excluded others. The language became at once a source of pride as well as a barrier behind which the community survived'.

Creole, as a source of strength and pride, functions as a means of maintaining the identity and group solidarity of the African Caribbean community. The language or dialect people select thus reinforces their social identities. It enables black people to fight the inherent racism in British society (Wong, 1986). African Caribbean teenagers use Creole to establish in-group identity and to act aggressively (Hewitt, 1986). For example, among some group arguments produce increased use of Jamaican pronunciations. Teenagers seem to equate strength and assertiveness with Creole and use it strategically with authority figures such as police, teachers and social workers. Where there is a power differential, Creole use takes on political and cultural significance because it denotes assertiveness and group identity.

The adoption of Creole by many African Caribbean adolescents is also a reaction against standard English, which is seen by many as militating against African Caribbean people. Racist attitudes to any language spoken by African Caribbean people, as well as the racist overtones and nuances of the English language itself, have contributed to the adoption of Creole by many second generation young African Caribbean people (Wong, 1986). For many African Caribbean adolescents, 'Patois is a powerful social and political mantle which . . . becomes an aggressive and proud assertion of "racial" and class identities' (Wong, 1986, p. 119). Thus, the acquisition of competence in Creole is an expression of racial identity and solidarity as well as a demonstration of determination to acquire status and power (Wong, 1986). The secrecy and hostility inherent in the existence of different language codes present obvious but nevertheless strong barriers to effective interethnic communication.

In a comparative study of two generations of African Caribbeans and Asians, Modood et al. (1994) explored the attitudes of first generation African Caribbeans toward the use and transmission of Creole and Patois languages. Half of the first generation of African Caribbeans in the sample felt that it was not important for them or their children to maintain an oral Creole or Patois tradition. The group felt that the use of such language was limited as a mode of communication to other Caribbean peoples only, and would not therefore offer employment opportunities to their children. However, the other half of the African Caribbean group sampled felt that it was important for their language to be transmitted to their children as part of a cultural identity. Hewitt (1986) found that many black parents equate Creole use with economic failure and discouraged children from using Creole. These parents did not want it taught at schools.

The second generation of African Caribbeans in Modood et al.'s (1994) study felt that it was important to maintain their oral tradition as part of their cultural identity. Thus, one respondent said: 'It gives me a sense of identity, it gives me something I can relate to'. Another respondent stated that 'It is an expression of blackness' (p. 38). Where Creole use is equated with African Caribbean group identity, youngsters often feel the need to display some facility with socially marked Creole forms (Hewitt, 1986). Hewitt suggests that for this reason self-reports of language may over-report use of this language form. One 16 year old reported to Hewitt (p. 107): 'I feel black and I'm proud of it, to speak like that'.

Most of the second generation respondents in Modood et al.'s (1994) study felt that it was essential for African Caribbeans to be able to communicate in Creole and Patois. Those African

Caribbeans who were unwilling or unable to use Creole or Patois were viewed negatively by some of the respondents. They were considered to be out of touch with 'where they were coming from' (p. 38). These respondents also felt that Caribbean languages should be offered in schools.

Summary

Bilingualism is the ability to understand and make oneself understood in two or more languages. It is clear that Asians would like to preserve their mother tongues as they see this as an integral part of their ethnic and cultural identity. While many Asian children are able to speak their mother tongue or community languages, they are not in the same way proficient in reading and writing these languages. The use of standard English to communicate with one another may unfairly discriminate against those from a bilingual background.

One major function of language is the expression of identity. Language is vital to any group's identity and is particularly salient for ethnic groups. Giles et al. (1977) developed ethnolinguistic identity theory to explain how members of language communities maintain their linguistic distinctiveness, and how and when language strategies are used. In Modood et al.'s (1994) study, second generation African Caribbeans maintain that it was important their oral tradition as part of their cultural identity.

Culture-bound values and intercultural communication

This section will focus on some culture-bound values that are especially relevant for intercultural communication with minority ethnic children, young people and their families. These include individualism-collectivism; power-distance; uncertainty avoidance; direct versus indirect communication; low and high context communication; emotional and behavioural expressiveness; and self-disclosure. An understanding of minority ethnic children and adolescents' cultural values will enable social workers to communicate effectively with them. However, we need to recognize individual differences within cultures, as there is the ever-present danger of overgeneralizing and stereotyping. Within any culture, people differ according to how strongly they adhere to or comply with the values of that culture. Thus, information about Asian and African Caribbean cultural values should act as guidelines rather than absolutes.

Individualism-collectivism

Individualism-collectivism provides a powerful explanatory framework for understanding cultural similarities and differences in intercultural communication (Triandis, 2001). According to Hecht et al. (1989, p. 170), the 'extreme individualism in the US makes it difficult for its citizens to interact with those from less individualistic cultures'. For instance, in individualistic countries, 'affiliativeness, small talk, and initial acquaintance are more important than in collectivist countries, where the social network is more fixed and less reliant on individual initiative' (p. 171). In a more recent study, Bond and Smith (1996) found that conformity was significantly higher in collectivistic than individualistic communities.

Collectivism has important influences on the ways people raise children. In collectivistic families, particularly in Asian cultures, a keynote of family existence is harmony and the maintenance of social order (Chen, 1998). In many Asian cultures, one of the most important values taught to children is the principle of 'filial piety': honouring, respecting, and obeying one's parents. Asians value conformity and obedience as child rearing values (Dosanjh and Ghuman, 1996; Stopes-Roe and Cochrane, 1990). Children must not bring shame or loss of face to their parents. In order to maintain order and harmony, the roles and ranks of individual family members are ascribed and delineated. Typically the father is the ultimate authority. The principle of respect for rank and authority of family members can influence parent–child communication patterns. In Euro-American families, verbal assertiveness is valued. Children have the right to challenge the directives and decisions of adults. In cultures where individualism is highly valued, people are expected to take the initiative in advancing their personal interests and well-being and to be direct and assertive in interacting with others.

Harmony plays a critical role in influencing Asian behaviour in various human interactions. Self-limits, shame, cooperation with the group and embarrassment are natural products under this value system. Ho (1976) warns that the conflict or confrontation approach, rather than helping Asian clients may violate their cultural rules. Harmony is what Asians consciously or unconsciously seek and is evidenced by their behaviour. Harmony is a cultural pattern that touches all aspects of Asian life, including child rearing practices. For example, 'the concern of adults to create a secure and an attentive environment for a small child is part of this emphasis in Japanese society on harmony in social relationships' (Hendry, 1993, p. 43). Parkes et al. (1997, p. 9) point out that 'in [Japanese] society values and norms forcefully promote self-control and the avoidance of direct personal confrontation'. Communication problems can therefore arise when cultures that value assertiveness come in contact with cultures that value accord and harmony.

Triandis (1995, p. 48) estimated that 'about 70 per cent of the population of the world lives in collective cultures'. As noted earlier, in Britain, Asians and African Caribbeans tend to be more collectivist than white people. Individualism has been central to the life of Western industrialized societies such as the US and Britain (Hofstede, 1984; Matsumoto and Juang, 2004; Triandis, 2001). It is therefore important for members from individualistic cultures to understand the perceptions and communication behaviours of these collective cultures. Knowledge of these differences in communication styles should facilitate successful intercultural communication for social workers interviewing clients from different cultural backgrounds.

Power distance

People within each culture develop ways of interacting with different people according to the status differential that exists between the individual and the person with whom he or she is interacting. Power-distance (PD) refers to the degree to which different cultures encourage or maintain power and status differences between interactants. Cultures high on PD develop rules, mechanisms and rituals that serve to maintain and strengthen the status relationships among their members (Hofstede, 1980, 1984). Cultures low on PD, however, minimize those rules and customs, eliminating if not ignoring the status differences that exist between people (Hofstede, 1980, 1984). Hofstede (1980) found that the Philippines, Mexico, Venezuela and India had the highest score on the power-distance dimension and New Zealand, Denmark and Austria had the lowest marks on the dimension. Britain had a relatively low score, reflecting some degree of minimizing of power differences.

Uncertainty avoidance

Hofstede (1980, 1984) also proposed the dimension of uncertainty avoidance (UA) – the degree to which cultures develop institutions and rituals to deal with the anxiety created by uncertainty and ambiguity. Different degrees of uncertainty avoidance exist in every culture, but one tends to predominate. Pakistan had a higher score on uncertainty avoidance than Britain and India (Hofstede, 1980).

Cultures with a strong uncertainty avoidance are typified as active, aggressive, emotional, compulsive, security-seeking and intolerant; while cultures with a weak uncertainty avoidance are likely to be contemplative, less aggressive, unemotional, relaxed, accepting personal risks, and relatively tolerant. Differences in the level of uncertainty avoidance can result in unexpected problems in intercultural communication. For instance, when white British social workers communicate with a client from Pakistan, they are likely to be perceived as too nonconfirming and unconventional by the client, and the social workers may view their client as rigid and overly controlled. Social workers need to have an understanding of the consequences of uncertainty avoidance for intercultural communication.

Direct versus indirect communication

Direct versus indirect communication refers to the degree to which culture influences whether people prefer to engage in direct or indirect communication. Most cultures have both direct and indirect modes of communication. Members of individualistic cultures tend to communicate in a direct fashion, while members of collectivistic cultures tend to communicate in an indirect fashion. Levin (1985) describes communication in the US (a low context culture) in this way: 'The [North] American way of life, by contrast, afford little room for the cultivation of ambiguity . . . It expresses itself in such common injunctions as "Say what you mean", "Don't beat around the bush" and "Get to the point" ' (p. 28). Samovar and Porter (2002) note that 'the communication style of Americans tends to be frank and blunt . . . this level of openness is often shunned by Asian Americans, particularly first generation immigrants' (p. 228). Okabe (1983) points out that 'the cultural assumptions of interdependence and harmony require that Japanese speakers limit themselves to implicit and even ambiguous use of words' (p. 36). In African American communication, value is placed on circumlocution and paraphrase, instead of on direct statements and definitions (Hale, 1982). A direct and succinct language style is considered crude and inelegant. Thus, individuals from individualistic cultures tend to be direct whereas collectivists tend to be indirect in order to maintain harmony (Gudykunst, 1998).

Low and high context communication

Hall's (1976) low and high context scheme focuses upon cultural differences in communication processes. A high context communication or message is one in which 'most of the information is either in the physical context or internalized in the person, while very little is in the coded, explicit, transmitted part of the message' (p. 79). In high context cultures, much of the information is conveyed through the physical context, shared knowledge, and past experiences instead of by specific verbal messages. Communication is nonverbal and indirect. Many black people require fewer words than their white counterparts to communicate the same content (Jenkins, 1982).

A low context communication or message, in contrast, is one in which 'the mass of information is vested in the explicit code' (Hall, 1976, p. 70). Low context cultures therefore place a greater reliance on the verbal part of the message.

Manrai and Manrai (1996) classified individuals from cultures of Western Europe as low context and individuals from Asia, Japan, the Middle East and South America as high context. People from low context cultures are often perceived as excessively talkative by those from high context cultures, while people from high context cultures may be perceived as nondisclosing, sneaky and mysterious by those from low context cultures (Andersen, 1990). The level of context influences all other aspects of communication:

> High-context cultures make greater distinction between insiders and outsiders than low-context cultures do. People raised in high-context systems expect more of others than do the participants in low-context systems. When talking about something that they have on their minds, a high-context individual will expect his [or her] interlocutor to know what's bothering him [or her], so that he [or she] doesn't have to be specific. The result is that he [or she] will talk

around and around the point, in effect putting all the pieces in place except the crucial one. Placing it properly – this keystone – is the role of his [or her] interlocutor.

(Hall, 1976, p. 98)

As with individualism-collectivism, low and high context communication exists in all cultures, but one tends to predominate (Hall, 2000). Understanding that a client is from a high or low context culture, and the form of communication that predominates in these cultures, will make the client's behaviour less confusing and more interpretable to the practitioner (Lum, 2003).

Emotional and behavioural expressiveness

Emotional expressiveness refers to the communication of feelings and thoughts. It 'can refer to both one's own and one's partner's expression, with lack of expressiveness on either one's part seen as dissatisfying' (Hecht et al., 1989, p. 329). Cultures vary in what is considered 'appropriate channelling' of emotions. Hecht et al. (1989) report that African Americans perceive emotional expressiveness as important to their communication satisfaction with whites (European Americans). Africans and African Caribbeans tend to be emotionally expressive while whites have a more emotionally self-restrained style and often attempt to understate, avoid, ignore, or diffuse intense or unpleasant situations. One of the dominant stereotypes of African Caribbeans in British society is that of the hostile, angry, prone-to-violence black male. It is not unusual for white social workers to describe their black clients as being 'hostile and angry' (for example see Littlewood and Lipsedge, 1997; Fernando, 2001). In contexts where Eurocentric norms prevail, young black people will find their more intense expressive behaviour and the more animated communication style criticized and pathologized.

There are many cultural groups in which restraint of strong feelings is highly valued. For example, traditional Asian cultures emphasize that maturity and wisdom are associated with one's ability to control emotions and feelings. Social workers interviewing/assessing Asian children and adolescents need to consider cultural factors that dictate against public disclosures and feelings because these may have serious consequences for the assessment process.

Self-disclosure

Self-disclosure refers to the client's willingness to tell the practitioner what she/he feels, believes or thinks. Intercultural comparisons of self-disclosure patterns show that European Americans are more disclosive than African Americans (Diamond and Hellcamp, 1969) and Asians (Segal, 1991). Indeed, Segal (1991, p. 239) describes Indians as being 'reserved and reluctant to discuss their problems outside the family'. According to Segal, for most Indians 'family integrity is sacred, and any threat to it is viewed as a failure on the part of the parents' (p. 239). An individual's emotional problems bring shame and guilt to the Asian family, preventing any family member from reporting such problems to others outside the family. Segal indicates that 'even when counseling is sought voluntarily, [Indians] often feel they have been "reduced" to a level beneath their dignity' (p. 239). Thus, the family may exert strong pressures on the Asian client not to reveal personal matters to 'strangers' or 'outsiders'. Similar conflicts have been reported for Hispanic clients (Laval et al., 1983).

Social workers unfamiliar with these cultural ramifications may perceive their clients in a very negative light. They may erroneously conclude that the client is repressed, inhibited, shy or passive. On the other hand, Asian clients may perceive the 'direct and confrontative techniques [of white practitioners] in communication as "lacking in respect for the client", and a reflection of insensitivity' (Sue and Sue, 1999, p. 51).

Black people may also be reluctant to disclose to white practitioners because of hardships they have experienced via racism (Sue and Sue, 1999; Vontress, 1981). The reality of racism in British society needs to be acknowledged in any social work relationship involving a black client (Phung, 1995).

Some young black clients, because of their previous experiences and current expectations, may sense that whites cannot be trusted, that they will ultimately harm or cheat them. White social workers who experience distrust from young black clients need to have an understanding of the historical and cultural reasons for young black clients' distrust of whites and should recognize the adaptive and survival role that distrust often serves for young blacks. According to Davis and Proctor (1989, p. 27), 'the underlying "healthy paranoia" should be recognized and respected'.

Summary

Culture-bound values that are especially relevant for intercultural communication with black children, young people and their families include: individualism-collectivism; power-distance; uncertainty-avoidance; direct versus indirect communication; low and high context communication; emotional and behavioural expressiveness; and self-disclosure. Individualism has been central to the life of Western industrialized societies such as the US and Britain. Collectivism is particularly high among Asian and African societies. However, diversity within each country is very possible. Power-distance refers to the degree to which different cultures encourage or maintain power and status differences between interactants. Uncertainty avoidance refers to the degree to which cultures develop institutions and rituals to deal with the anxiety created by uncertainty and ambiguity. Differences in the level of uncertainty avoidance can result in unexpected problems in intercultural communication. Direct versus indirect communication refers to the degree to which culture influences whether people prefer to engage in direct or indirect communication. Members of individualistic cultures tend to communicate in a direct fashion, while members of collectivistic cultures tend to communicate in an indirect fashion.

In high context cultures, much of the information is conveyed through the physical context, shared knowledge, and past experiences instead of by specific verbal messages. Communication is nonverbal and indirect. On the other hand, low context cultures place a greater reliance on the verbal part of the message.

Emotional expressiveness refers to the communication of feelings and thoughts. Cultures vary in what is considered 'appropriate channelling' of emotions. Self-disclosure refers to the client's willingness to tell the practitioner what she/he feels, believes or thinks. Intercultural comparisons of self-disclosure patterns show that European Americans are more disclosive than Asians and African Caribbeans.

Nonverbal behaviour

In the broadest sense, nonverbal behaviours are all the behaviours that occur during communication other than words. Many studies have reported that only a small fraction of the meaning people get in an interaction derives from the words that are spoken; most of the messages conveyed and perceived in interactions are nonverbal (for example, Mehrabian, 1981).

Nonverbal cues are often the best indicators of an individual's true attitudes or intentions, irrespective of what has been said. Unlike spoken language, which is used as often to conceal thought as it is to express thought, and which people largely control for their own purposes, much nonverbal behaviour seems impossible to control. Individuals are not aware of most of their nonverbal behaviour, which is enacted mindlessly, spontaneously and unconsciously (Samovar and Porter, 2002). We can get conflicting messages from nonverbal behaviours. The words coming out of someone's mouth may tell you one thing, but their nonverbal behaviours (for example, tone of voice, gaze) may tell you something else. Social workers must accept that at least some of the time their nonverbal behaviour and their spoken words may not seem to match.

The following section explores how culture may influence the following areas of nonverbal behaviour: kinesics, touching behaviour, perception of time, proxemics, silence, and gesture. It is important to remember that not all nonverbal behaviours described below are exhibited by all black people; and behaviours or patterns may be modified by class, age or gender.

Kinesics

This is the study of body language. It refers to 'gestures, facial expressions, eye contact, body positions, body movement, and forms of greeting and their relation to communcation' (Dodd, 1987, p. 173). Considerable intercultural differences have been reported in people's kinesic behaviour (Burgoon et al., 1989; Gudykunst and Kim, 1984; Hall, 1976). In this section I will examine visual behaviour, which is one of the most studied aspects of nonverbal behaviour.

A number of studies have shown that African Americans tend to gaze less directly than do European Americans when interacting with someone (e.g., LaFrance and Mayo, 1978). LaFrance and Mayo (1978) suggest that white authority figures (e.g. teachers, educators, social workers etc.) often misread African American eye behaviour (e.g., inferring that black people are uninterested, less honest, withhold information, and have poor concentration). In Euro-American culture, direct eye contact is expected, especially when speaking to someone (Jandt, 2000). In Euro-American culture, members expect direct eye contact as a sign of listening and showing respect for authority. Black people, on the other hand, may associate eye contact and gaze with negative overtones and a lack of respect.

Hanna's (1984) data showed some African Americans were reluctant to look directly in the eye of persons who occupied an authority position. Many black children are taught not to look another person (particularly older persons) in the eye when the older person is talking to them. To do so is to communicate disrespect. Avoiding eye contact is a non-verbal way of communicating recognition of the authority-subordinate relationship of the participants in a social situation. Also among Asian families, eye contact with authority figures is generally considered disrespectful (Chen, 1998; Chiu, 1987). In contrast, white children are socialized to do just the opposite; looking away from a speaker is seen as disrespectful.

Valsiner (2000) notes that 'in Columbian *mestizo* community, respectful conduct of children towards adults is expected to occur in early childhood. At two years of age, the child is expected to show respect to adults by sitting quietly, not passing in front of the adult, or looking into the adult's face while speaking to him or her' (p. 233). The author notes that if this behaviour is 'viewed within the framework of European or North American type of social interaction rules, such conduct (absence of eye-contact) would be immediately viewed as impolite or abnormal (for example autistic)' (p. 233).

Differences in white and black visual behaviour have clear applications in the social work interview. Instead of assuming that the client's averted eyes indicate lack of understanding, a social worker more familiar with patterns of black nonverbal behaviour might well attribute it to a culturally learned behaviour pattern.

Touching

Touch, or the study of haptics, provides a rich area of intercultural communication insight. There are substantial intercultural differences in interpersonal patterns of tactile communication (Malandro and Barker, 1983; Samovar, Porter and Jain, 1981). Many white people feel uncomfortable when a person from a culture whose members touch a lot greets the white person 'by touching the shoulders and arms for what seems like a long time' (Dodd, 1987, p. 11).

Conversely, many members of a 'haptically active' host culture feel equally uncomfortable when the white person maintains a lack of touch and distance, since this behaviour is perceived as unfriendly and cold. There are also gender differences in how individuals use and react to touch (Jandt, 2002).

People in collectivistic cultures (such as Asian, African and African Caribbean) tend to engage in more tactile interaction than people in individualistic cultures. Social workers need to be aware of these differences.

Perception of time

Our perception of time is culturally determined and differs greatly among different groups. Hall (1994) proposed that cultures organize time in one of two ways: either monochromic (M-time) or polychronic (P-time). Although he did not intend these as either/or categories, they do represent two distinct approaches to time. As the word monochromic implies, this approach sees time as lineal, segmented, and manageable. Time is something you must not waste; you must be doing something or feel guilty. Appointments and schedules are very important to members of monochromic cultures. Most Western cultures think of time in lineal-spatial terms.

People from cultures on P-time live their lives quite differently. P-time cultures deal with time holistically. They can interact with more than one person or do more than one thing at a time. According to Dresser (1998, p. 109), this multidimensional approach to the moment 'explains why there is more interrupting in conversations carried on by people from Arabic, Asian, and Latin American cultures'.

In the 'US [and Britain] promptness is highly prized . . . People make attributions regarding the person depending on how prompt or late that person is' (Brislin and Yoshida, 1994, p. 47). A large share of white people's relationships are governed by the clock. If black people arrive late for an appointment, they are labelled as being 'irresponsible', 'lazy', 'never on time'. Deviation from the set of rules people have learned in their culture regarding time 'tends to provoke strong emotional reactions' (Brislin and Yoshida, 1994, p. 47). This can result in intercultural misunderstandings.

In Asian, African and African American culture, orientations to time are driven less by a need to 'get things done' and conform to external demands than by a sense of participation in events that create their own rhythm. Thus, African Americans 'often use what is referred to as BPT (Black People's Time) or hang loose time, maintaining that priority belongs to what is happening at that instant' (Samovar and Porter, 2002, p. 190). However, black people are capable of code switching with time just as with language.

Proxemics

Another nonverbal difference in intercultural communication is the communication of interpersonal space and distance. Hall (1964) was the first researcher to study personal space, systematically referring to the study of spatial usage as proxemics. Various studies have indicated that cultures differ greatly in their use of personal space, the distances they maintain, and their regard for territory, as well as the meanings they assign to proxemic behaviour (Hall, 1976; Samovar et al., 1981; Gudykunst and Kim, 1984).

The degree to which a culture is individualistic or collectivist has an impact on the nonverbal behaviour of that culture in a variety of ways. People from individualistic cultures are comparatively remote and distant proximically. Collectivistic cultures are interdependent and, as a result they work, play, live and sleep in close proximity to one another (Samovar and Porter, 2002).

Silence

The intercultural implications of silent behaviours are diverse because the value and use of silence as communication vary markedly from one culture to another. The Western tradition is relatively negative in its attitude toward silence and ambiguity, especially in social and public relations. In a Western context, silences can convey all the various kinds and degrees of messages that may be described as cold, oppressive, defiant, disapproving or condemning, calming, approving, humble, excusing and consenting (Samovar and Porter, 2002).

Traditionally, Eastern societies such as India have valued silence more than Western societies. Oliver (1971, p. 264) observed that 'silence in Asia has commonly been entirely acceptable, whereas in the West silence has generally been considered socially disagreeable'. In India silence is used to promote harmony, cooperation and other collectivistic values. Silence is a sign of interpersonal sensitivity, mutual respect, personal dignity, affirmation and wisdom (Jain and Matukumalli, 1993).

Social workers should, therefore, pay more attention to the cultural views of silence and the interpretations given to silence in communication interactions. Intercultural misunderstanding can occur if practitioners do not know when, where and how to remain silent.

Gesture

In a large study involving forty different cultures, Morris (1995) isolated twenty common hand gestures that had a different meaning in each culture. Gestures are movements of the body, usually the hands, that are generally reflective of thought or feeling. One example of how gestures can communicate different meanings from culture to culture is the act of pointing. In the US and Britain, people point at objects and people with the index finger. However, in much of Asia, pointing with the index finger is considered rude (Samovar and Porter, 2002).

When social workers use gestures in intercultural contexts, they need to be aware that their gestures may have a different meaning for the client. Being unaware of these differences can cause problems. According to Barna (1994, p. 32), 'the lack of understanding of nonverbal signs and symbols, such as gestures . . . is a definite communication barrier'.

Summary

Broadly speaking, nonverbal behaviours are all the behaviours that occur during communication other than words. Culture may influence the following areas of nonverbal behaviour: visual behaviour, touching behaviour, perception of time, proxemics, silence and gesture. In Euro-American culture, direct eye contact is expected, especially when speaking to someone. In Asian and African cultures, avoiding eye contact is a nonverbal way of communicating recognition of the authority-subordinate relationship of the participants in a social situation. Also, eye contact with authority figures is generally considered disrespectful. Touch provides a rich area of intercultural communication insight. People in collectivistic cultures tend to engage in more tactile interaction than people in individualistic cultures. Collectivistic cultures are interdependent and, as a result they work, play, live and sleep in close proximity to one another. Our perception of time is also culturally determined and differs greatly among different groups. The value and use of silence as communication also vary markedly from one culture to another.

Implications for social work practice

Practitioners need to respect the right and need of black people to establish and maintain their own languages. It is important to develop the self-concept and self-worth of black children and young people by allowing them to preserve and perpetuate their own languages. The problem introduced into the intercultural communication situation by the existence of codes, e.g., black English, needs to be acknowledged by social workers. According to d'Ardenne and Mahatani (1990, p. 64), 'Black clients who speak another form of English are even less likely to be understood by their counselors [and other service providers] than those who speak another language and require interpreters.' Social workers need to be aware that the dominant white society's rejection of black English as a legitimate linguistic style may influence their perceptions of clients speaking black English. The devaluation of black English in British and American society is consistent with the devaluation of African and African Caribbean people in general, and must be addressed. Practitioners who view black English as a legitimate code spoken by many African Caribbean people, notwithstanding the importance of learning English, are likely to attain greater satisfaction from communication with speakers of black English than are those who see the language as negative.

Social workers in interethnic communication should have an understanding of different language habits – different denotations, connotations, grammar, accents and concepts of the function of language. A sensitivity to such differences and a willingness to make the adjustments necessary for common understanding is a big step toward resolving the difficulties resulting from linguistic diversity. Social workers should resist judging and evaluating a black child and young person's language, since ethnocentric judgements will interfere with effective communication.

Wilson (1978, p. 157) outlines the following implications and recommendations of using black English:

Black English is a language like any other. Therefore, it is not 'bad' English and does not represent mental inferiority. Do not permit a child to be made to feel bad because he [she] does not speak standard English and do not allow him [her] to be degraded because of his dialect. However, we need to recognize that in order for the black child to fully function in a white middle class dominated world he [she] must learn to handle standard English as competently as any white middle class child. Consequently, we need to teach the black child to become truly bilingual – teach him [her] to speak fluently standard English while at the same time not denying him the use of his [her] black English under the appropriate circumstances; tell the child that in order to attain his [her] career goals which more than likely lies within the realm of white middle class functioning he [she] must learn to speak standard English, build his [her] vocabulary, read and write well, but that there is nothing 'wrong' with the language spoken by his [her] people.

(p. 157)

Social workers need to have an understanding of the relationship between racial identities and use of black English. A black person with high pre-encounter attitudes may choose not to use black English and may feel embarrassed by those who do. Instead, he or she may use standard English exclusively. On the other hand, an individual at the immersion-emersion level of racial identity development embraces black culture and history and may choose to use black English in order to gain self-esteem and racial pride.

The use of interpreters

The term 'interpretation' emphasizes the exchange of connotative meaning between languages so that both affect and meaning are conveyed; whereas 'translation' refers to the exchange of the denotative meaning of a word, phrase or sentence in one language for the same meaning in another language. The 'translator should be someone with cultural knowledge and appropriate professional background' (Lago and Thompson, 1996, p. 61). Most of the literature and studies intercultural communication refer to 'interpreting' services.

One stereotyped image which exists about Asian people is that 'they do not speak English'. However, a large proportion of the Asian community speak English as a second language and many people, as noted earlier, speak two or three languages as well as English. Asian women who do not work outside the home, and older Asians who migrated to Britain in their later years, are more likely not to speak English. Those Asians who do not speak English tend to take their children to social services to interpret. For example, social services tend to use children to translate for their elders (Dominelli, 1997). In sensitive situations this can result in distress and humiliation and/or vital information not being elicited. Dominelli (1997) cites an example in which a child is used for interpreting. A Sikh woman who spoke Punjabi but virtually no English was referred by a health visitor to social services because the woman was suffering from post-natal depression. However, 'as there were no Punjabi-speaking social workers, a white social worker visited the woman and used the woman's 9 year old daughter as a translator' (Dominelli, 1997, p. 102). Dominelli (1997) argues that 'Such exploitation of black children is racist because it facilitates the continuation of inadequate services for black people. . . . the black child becomes an integral part of the interaction between black people and powerful white agencies and bureaucracies which hold direct power over them' (p. 106). Furthermore, 'the black child's knowledge of English also becomes a tool through which parental authority can be under-mined' (p. 106). Keats (1997) also discusses the problems of using children as interpreters. She points out that 'the substance of the discussion may be beyond the child's real understanding, in which case there is a loss of precision as well as a loss of face, or it may involve knowledge which the parent may consider inappropriate for the child to have and so the response will not reflect the true situa-tion' (p. 68).

Dominelli (1997) has noted that the inappropriate use of inter-preters and translators has continued for several decades in order to cut costs because they are cheaper to employ than qualified black social workers. The lack of 'either sufficient bilingual social workers or appropriate translation services has led to bad practice on a wide scale regardless of setting' (Dominelli, 1997, p. 159). Humphreys et al. (1999, cited in O'Hagan, 2001, p. 163) found 'that Asian fami-lies experience discrimination in child protection work due to the inadequacy of the interpretative service' (cited in O'Hagan, 2001,

p. 163). In an article on 'The over-representation of Black children in the child protection system' Chand (2000) argues that as 'the concepts associated with child abuse and neglect are very different from those concerning, for example, welfare rights, . . . an interpreter who specializes in the latter may not be able to communicate the sensitivity and seriousness of the abusive situation' (p. 71). Also, 'In some Asian languages the words necessary for the description of sexual abuse do not exist, or are so rarely used that people would be shocked by their usage (Farmer and Owen, 1995, p. 114). This means that it is important that special training is made available to interpreters working in the area of child protection. Social workers 'need to understand [that] the interpreter [will] require time to explain unfamiliar terms and procedures like child protection, abuse and neglect, assessments . . . without causing the service user unnecessary anxiety' (Chand, 2000, p. 71). Thus, a comprehensive translation service is necessary in establishing anti-racist social work (Dominelli, 1997).

Racist language

Racism is 'a major hindrance to successful intercultural communication . . . one reason racism is so pervasive is that it is often learned early in life, . . . and becomes part of our world view without our realization' (Samovar and Porter, 2001, p. 271).

Dominelli (1997, p. 6) argues that 'the very language we use is riddled with racism'. When social workers speak of Britain, they usually mean white, 'English' Britain. Howitt and Owusu-Bempah (1994) found 55 negative connotations of the word 'black' as compared to only 21 for the word 'white' in the dictionary. Conversely, the authors found 9 and 19 positive connotations of black and white respectively. Practitioners need to be aware of the 'implicit racism in the word [black]' (Domnelli, 1997, p. 6). The social worker's choice of language sends messages continuously to the child and young person about his or her values. The language used will betray the practitioner if he or she does not genuinely respect his or her client's culture. For example, is negative language being used, such as in blatant derogatives ('nigger', 'Paki'), colour symbolism (white as good, black as bad), political evaluations ('underdeveloped', 'cultural 'deprivation') and in ethnocentric descriptions ('huts' in Africa). Or conversely, are positive terms being used when they would not be used for whites in the same context (blacks being called 'quite intelligent'). Are the religions of other cultures treated with respect? Is black people's culture trivialized or ridiculed? Finally, is a distinction made between 'us' and 'them', in such a way that black people are not part of 'us' or Britain. The racism in language such as that expressed in words like 'nigger', 'Paki' is so obvious that they are seldom heard in interethnic/racial encounters in social service settings. More common today is the subtle racism in language. A refusal on the part of white people to say 'black' or 'African Caribbean' instead of 'coloured', and a constant reference to black groups as 'you people' are all interpreted by black adolescents in intercultural settings as indications of racist attitudes on the part of the white language user. The language of racism, be it overt or subtle, is a deterrent to effective intercultural communication.

Racist attitudes (when expressed even in the most subtle or unconscious fashion in the interethnic setting) disrupt the communication process. According to Ridley (1995, p. 39), 'counsellors [and social workers], in many ways, are socialized and trained to behave as racists without even knowing it'. There is no reason to believe that counsellors, therapists and social workers are any less vulnerable to manifesting various types of intentional and unintentional racism than other members of society (Locke, 1992). According to Sue and Sue (1999) 'it is the unintentional and covert forms of [racial] bias that may be the greater enemy [than overt acts] because they are unseen and more pervasive' (p. 30). Indeed, Ridely (1995) argues that 'unintentional behaviour is perhaps the most insidious form of racism . . . the major challenge facing counselors [and social workers] is to overcome unintentional racism and provide more equitable service delivery (Ridley, 1995, p. 38).

Social workers who want to communicate with black children and adolescents in a productive fashion must become as sensitive to their offensive racist expressions as black people have become. The major challenge facing social workers is to become sensitized to the racism inherent in language usage and to make a conscious effort to discard the overt and covert language of racism. The use of overt or subtle racism in language in interethnic interviews will result in anger and hostility toward the practitioner and disrupt or often terminate the possibility for interethnic communication. Social workers need to modify their personal linguistic habits in order to ensure effective interethnic communication.

If effective interethnic communication is to take place, the establishment of trust is imperative. Overcoming the black client's mistrust is the greatest contribution practitioners can make to the 'working alliance' (Gelso and Fretz, 1992). But trusting a white social worker is often difficult for young black clients. Towards this end, practitioners must demonstrate their goodwill; that is, they must convey that they are well meaning individuals who have elected to work with people whom they value. In particular they must be as free as possible of racism. Trust is also enhanced by the worker's demonstration of the skills necessary to address the black client's problems (Davis and Proctor, 1989).

In general, black people tend to disclose more when they are interviewed by someone from their own ethnic group (Davis and Proctor, 1989). However, some Asians may reject practitioners who belong to the same ethnic group, due to concerns about breach of confidentiality. Thomas (1998, p. 190) suggests that

> The children of African and Asian heritage [in Britain] communicate with white [therapists] by putting forward a 'proxy self'. This communication by proxy served the function of protecting the black child in a society where adults or people with power over them might be harmful to their psychological and emotional development. If we were living in a racism-free society, there would be no 'race' obstacle for black children to overcome on the route towards therapy [and communication] with White professionals.

A black child or adolescent will tend to reveal the 'real self' only 'when some safety [in the relationship] is established' (Thomas, 1998, p. 188). Social workers need to be aware of the effects of racism on black children and adolescents' self-disclosure patterns.

Speech and communication style

Social workers may interpret culturally appropriate behaviour patterns as indicative of passivity, submissiveness, excessive dependency, or even resistance. By failing to acknowledge certain behaviour patterns as manifestations of deference to authority, social workers may directly contribute to intercultural communication problems. For example, when interacting with professionals, Asian clients may convey respect for authority by engaging in prescribed behaviours such as repeated head nodding, avoidance of direct eye contact and refraining from asking questions, interrupting for clarification, or making their needs/desires explicit, and withholding critical comments. This can result in a persistent reluctance from Asian clients to seek explanations of services and policies or to clarify specific verbal communications. Furthermore, limited or non-English speaking Asian clients who are unfamiliar with the system are most likely to demonstrate such reluctance while remaining in a great need of relevant information. Social workers are viewed as authority figures who are directive; who employ structured, practical problem-solving approaches; and who provide specific advice and recommendations. Social workers who are relatively nondirective and who fail to offer practical assistance promptly may be perceived as indifferent or uncaring.

The following case study illustrates the failure of service providers 'to understand the complexity of bilingualism' (Canino and Spurlock, 2000, p. 11).

> Carmen, an 8 year old Latina, was referred to an outpatient clinic for evaluation because of her poor academic performance. Family problems were suspected to be a root cause. Carmen's parents came from the Dominican Republic and spoke Spanish at home. A monolingual English-speaking clinician performed the assessment and found Carmen to be inhibited, shy, and unduly concrete in her responses. She had difficulty answering questions about her feelings and family background. The clinician suspected family problems, as well as a possible learning disability in Carmen, but recommended an evaluation of the child by a bilingual clinician. The bilingual consultant found Carmen to be quite expressive when describing her family and feelings in Spanish . . . there was no evidence of family or cognitive dysfunction. It was clear that the child needed extra help with English grammar and vocabulary. . . . At a 6-month follow-up Carmen was reported to be doing well.
>
> (Canino and Spurlock, 2000, p. 15)

Canino and Spurlock note that the above case 'exemplifies the multiple variables that must be considered for a child in the process of acquiring a second language' (Canino and Spurlock, 2000, p. 15).

Thus, in Carmen's case, 'the introduction of a second language had temporarily affected her native language, and as she was in the process of becoming bilingual she was using both English and Spanish, but her academic and school-peer language was English. . . . The need for a competent bilingual evaluator was crucial . . .' (Canino and Spurlock, 2000, p. 15). Social workers need to respond patiently to clients who have a limited knowledge of English. They need to be aware of the jargon in their speech and provide a clear definition of technical terms. They must withhold judgements and negative evaluations; instead, they must show respect for the difficulties associated with learning a new language. Social workers tend to assume that black people are familiar with the dominant ways of conducting interviews. If a black client gives what is felt to be an irrelevant answer to a question, this is likely to be put down to the client's uncooperativeness, and so forth, and not to the possibility of miscommunication. Thus, black clients may be denied valuable services 'through misconceptions based upon cultural insensitivity and dominance' (Fairclough, 1989, p. 64). Social workers may attribute the difficulty they experience in dealing with black clients to the clients' 'incompetence or unco-operativity or some other stereotyped trait, rather than to different dialect or discourse norms, perhaps low proficiency in a second language or stress in an unfamiliar environment' (Giles and Coupland, 1991, p. 123). According to Sue et al. (1992, p. 79), 'promoting bilingualism rather than monolingualism should be a major goal to the provision of mental health [and social] services: it is an expression of personal freedom and pluralism'.

Mares et al. (1985), working in the field of health care, have suggested some practical ways in which practitioners can communicate more effectively with people who speak little or no English or who speak as a second language. These are: a) to reduce stress-for example, practitioners should allow more time for interviewing the client than they would for an English-speaking client, and practitioners should also give plenty of nonverbal reassurance; b) to simplify English – for example, practitioners should speak clearly but must not raise their voice and must not use slang or idioms; c) to check back properly – for example, practitioners need to develop a regular pattern of checking that what they have said has been understood.

Ting-Toomey (1996) suggests that effective intercultural communication requires knowledge of and respect for cultural differences in worldviews and behaviours, as well as sensitivity to differences between high- and low-context communication patterns and differences in cultural perceptions of time. For example, when social workers (from low context cultures) interview black children and youngsters from high context cultures, they are liable to have difficulty in communicating because the high context messages do not contain sufficient information for practitioners to gain true or complete meaning. Social workers may interpret a high context culture's message according to their low context disposition and reach entirely the wrong meaning. Children and young people from high context cultures are more likely to be adept at reading nonverbal behaviour. They have an expectation that social workers are also able to understand the unarticulated communication; hence they do not speak as much as people from low context cultures. As discussed earlier, nonverbal behaviours comprise the bulk of communication messages in any culture. Misunderstandings in relation to the interpretation of nonverbal behaviours can easily lead to conflicts or confrontations that break down the communication process.

In a high context culture, much more is taken for granted and assumed to be shared, and consequently nearly all messages are coded in such a way that they do not need to be explicitly and verbally transmitted. Instead, the demands of the situation and the shared meanings among the interactants mean that the preferred interpretation of the messages is already known.

Asians may assess the feelings of the social worker and tend to give their opinions in an indirect manner (Lum, 2003; Servaes, 1988) in order to avoid offending the social worker. Unlike the Western ideal of self-expression, the Eastern cultures aim to express feelings in such a way that it is not harmful either to oneself or to others. This, therefore, influences the style of communication, placing more value on indirect and metaphorical communication rather than direct and clear communication as emphasized in the Western culture. According to Lau (1988, p. 194) 'The Western trained therapist's expectation of clear, direct verbal communication is often at variance with cultural rules where direct communication and confrontation are avoided because this may lead to loss of face within the family group'.

Finally, in a study of the inspection of services for minority ethnic children and families, O'Neale (2000) put forward the following standard for social service departments in communicating with ethnic minority families:

> Communication needs of ethnic minority children and their families are met when they have contact with the SSD. The SSD provides information about available services in ways which they can understand . . . The front line and reception staff respond appropriately to people who do not speak English, whose first language is not English or who have communication difficulties . . . Ethnic minority families know what communication support is available from the SSD and how to access it.
>
> (p. 50).

6

Socialization: Cultural/Racial Influences

Introduction

What is socialization? Like many concepts in developmental psychology, socialization can be variously defined. According to Kao et al. (1997) socialization refers to 'an explicit transmission of appropriate values through deliberate attempts to shape, coax, and mould children's behaviour' (Segall et al., 1990) (p. 154). Chambers and Patterson (1995) state that 'socialization is something that emerges from thousands of exchanges between the child and family members spread out over a period of many years. During these exchanges, the child is altering the behaviour of the parent at the same time that the parent is presumably 'socializing' the child. It is this mutuality of effects that makes it very difficult to analyze cause and effect relations' (1995, pp. 211–12). According to Maccoby (1992), contemporary theories of socialization place greater stress on the interactive exchanges between parent and child as contributors to behaviour. In addition, explanations have become more complex and multidimensional than those offered by earlier approaches. Closely related to the process of socialization is the process called enculturation. This is the process by which youngsters learn and adopt the ways and manners of their culture. Another term closely related to enculturation is the concept of acculturation (see Chapter 3).

Edwards (1996) has noted that socialization theories have also undergone substantial revision as theorists and researchers have recognized the cultural limitations of these theories. According to Edwards (1996) socialization theories and their proponents were ethnocentric (e.g., proposing that explanations of behaviour in one society applied equally well in others) for far too long. Such theories relied heavily on research and assumptions based in Western societies, with the result that the theories were neither nongeneralizable to other cultures or failed to take into account the richness of human diversity.

As the number of black and minority children continue to increase in US and Britain, the socialization of black/ethnic minority children and adolescents has become a topic of growing interest and concern (e.g., Boykin and Toms, 1985; Harrison et al., 1990; Knight et al., 1993; Phinney and Rotherham, 1987; Thornton et al., 1990). According to Harrison et al. (1990) 'Socialization refers to the processes by which individuals become distinctive and actively functioning members of the society in which they live' (Harrison et al., 1990, p. 354). The authors state that although 'the mechanisms for transmittal of the culture are the same for both ethnic minority and majority children (e.g., reinforcement, modelling, identification, etc). . . . ethnicity is potent in the socialization process of families since it includes group patterns of values, social customs, perceptions, behavioural roles, language usage, and rules of social interactions that group members share in both obvious and subtle ways' (Phinney and Rotheram, 1987, p. 354).

Much of the literature on socialization has been based on white, middle class samples (Harrison et al., 1990). Because black/minority children and adolescents face different developmental issues, conclusions from research that does not include black/minorities cannot be generalized to include them. Socialization patterns differ among ethnic groups with regard to issues such as child rearing (Dosanjh and Ghuman, 1996; Ellis and Petersen, 1992; Gardiner and Kosmitzki, 2005; Lin & Fu, 1990), e.g., Kao and Sinha (1997) note that 'socialization practices that promote individualism help to foster a conception of self that is discrete, autonomous, and abstract. Socialization practices that inculcate collectivism promote a conception of self that is embedded, ensembled, and situated (p. 156).

These differences can be explained by the concept of the developmental niche put forward by Super and Harkness (1986). The developmental niche stresses the role of the cultural context in which the socialization of the child takes place. According to Harkness and Super (1995), there are three major components of the developmental niche, each of which is directly related to parents. First, there are the physical and social settings in which a child lives (e.g., nuclear family living typically found in many Western cultures versus extended family arrangements found in many Asian or African countries). Aspects of this component include a) the kind of company a child keeps (e.g., large families where children serve as playmates and caretakers); b) the size and shape of one's living space; and c) eating and sleeping schedules. The second component of the developmental niche focuses on culturally regulated customs and childrearing practices (e.g., informal versus formal schooling and independence versus dependence training). Finally, there is the third component relating to the psychological characteristics of a child's parents (e.g., developmental expectations or parental cultural belief systems). According to Super and Harkness (1994) this component 'is an important channel for communicating general cultural belief systems to children, through very specific context-based customs and settings' (p. 98).

This chapter will examine cultural/racial influences on socialization. It will examine Baumrind's (1971) classic conceptualization of three parenting styles – authoritative, authoritarian, and permissive, and cross-cultural differences. It will also explore racial socialization; socialization differences in individualistic and collectivistic societies; cultural differences in discipline and implications for social work practice.

Parenting styles

Baumrind (1971) has identified three major patterns of parenting: authoritative, authoritarian, and permissive. Authoritative parents are those who set and enforce clear standards of conduct but also value and encourage adolescents' independence and autonomy. Authoritarian parents value and enforce obedience and respect for authority; independence, individuality, and verbal give and take are not encouraged. Permissive parents tend to make few demands and permit their children ample opportunity for self-regulation.

Other researchers (Maccoby and Martin, 1983) have identified a fourth type of parenting style called 'uninvolved'. Uninvolved parents are often too absorbed in their own lives to respond appropriately to their children and often seem indifferent to them.

Research has assessed the association of parenting styles with various indexes of adolescent adjustment (Dornbusch et al., 1987; Steinberg et al. 1991) and has shown that authoritative parenting generally is positively associated with adjustment assessed by a variety of indicators. However, Dornbusch et al. (1987) found little association between any of the parenting styles and the school achievement of African American youngsters. The styles of parenting identified and measured are based on investigations of middle class European-American parents. The question of whether the parenting styles assessed measure parenting practices typical of non-Euro-American parents has not been addressed. Chao (1994) showed that parenting styles and their meaning vary as a function of the cultural background of the families assessed. Thus, for example, authoritarian parenting, when understood in the context of Asian cultural values and traditions, does not have the negative connotations apparent for middle class European-American families. Chao argues that 'to explain Chinese school success using Baumrind's (1971) parenting styles would not be adequate because Baumrind's conceptualizations are specific only to European-American culture, or European-American individuals. Other indigenous concepts capturing parenting style must be offered and also tested for their relevancy to Chinese [and other] culture[s] or Chinese individuals' (p. 1113).

Significant differences in discipline strategies are frequent sources of misunderstanding between minority/black and dominant/European cultures. The use of corporal punishment and authoritarian parenting styles are described in the literature as characteristic of African American and Asian families (Chao, 1994). It is common for African Caribbeans and Indians to include physical punishment as part of their disciplinary repertoire (Gopaul-McNicol, 1999; Segal, 1999).

A study by Deater-Deckard et al. (1996) compared European American and black elementary school age children. They found that although children who were black, male, poor, and living with single mothers were more likely to have received physical discipline, they were not more likely to display externalizing or aggressive behaviours at school. These researchers suggest that the sociocultural meaning of physical punishment may vary based on ethnicity.

In one study Gopaul-McNicol (1993) found that 84% of West Indians from the West Indies and 56% of West Indians from the UK, the US and Canada agreed with using spanking as a form of child discipline. However, Hylton (1997) found that there was a 'generational change among minorities [in Britain] in child rearing practices . . . with growing emphasis on co-operation rather than the discipline of physical control' (p. 33). In Hylton's (1997) study [the first generation] black minorities believed that school teachers and social workers had more control over their children and that 'physical discipline, or the threat of such discipline from parents to their children, can result in children being removed from their parents' (p. 33). Consequently, Hylton (1997) found that attitudes to child rearing were changing among African and African Caribbean families, with less use of physical discipline.

In a study of child rearing practices among Punjabi families in Britain, Dosanj and Ghuman (1996) found that Punjabi mothers of both first and second generation did not approve of physical punishment – smacking – as a way of disciplining their children, although a minority used 'it as a last resort' (p. 172). One mother stated; 'I don't mind a little smack, but I don't like it' and 'Nearly two-thirds of the second generation mothers thought parents should manage without smacking' (p. 172).

Individualism-collectivism

Lau (2003) writes that in non-western European minority families

> The importance given to interdependence and the need to preserve harmonious family relationships has given rise to structures that do not conform to western European norms, such as extended family groups within the same household. Life-cycle transitions are managed in the context of different rules with regard to authority, continuity and interdependence. In the traditional Asian family, relationships are hierarchical between the sexes as well as between the generations. Authority is invested in grandparents or the most senior male members. . . . Where kinship systems are highly structured, kinship terms delineate the individual's place in the family, including duties and expected obligations, within a system of mutual dependence.
>
> (p. 95)

The values of the society in which children are raised provide a framework that shapes parental behaviours and interactions with children and the resulting developmental outcomes (Kagitcibasi, 1996; Super and Harkness, 1997).Within all cultures, parents engage in practices aimed at socializing the child to become a responsible adult member of the society (Whiting and Whiting, 1975). Yet the patterning of values varies widely across cultural groups (Kluckhohn and Strodtbeck, 1961).

Two fundamental values (mentioned in Chapter 5) that have been shown to differentiate European American culture from most non-Western cultures are individualism and collectivism (Hofstede, 1980; Kagitcibasi, 1996; Kim et al. 1994). Many writers in the social science disciplines have used this dimension to understand differences in social behaviours across the cultures they have studied (e.g., Hofstede, 1980; Kluckhohn and Strodtbeck, 1961). Some writers believe that the individualism-collectivism dimension is the most important attribute that distinguishes one culture from another. The definitions of the two cultural types are extreme in that they only broadly describe cultural patterns. However, it is useful to examine the dimension of individualism-collectivism in terms of the different behaviour patterns their members present. These underlying values shape the processes of development through the ways in which parents socialize their children (Greenfield and Cocking, 1994).

Individualism refers to 'the subordination of the goals of the collectivities to individual goals, and a sense of independence and lack of concern for others', and collectivism refers to 'the subordination of individual goals to the goals of a collective and a sense of harmony, interdependence, and concern for others' (Hui and Triandis, 1986, pp. 244–5). These constructs reflect individual societal values regarding self, others, family and community, and thus are related to attitudes and social behaviour. Individualistic societies value autonomy, independence, achievement, identity, self-reliance, solitude and creativity. Collectivistic societies value loyalty to the group, dependence, tradition, harmony, respect for authority, and cooperation (Triandis, 1990; 2001). In individualistic cultures, 'people are supposed to look after themselves and their immediate family only', and in collectivistic cultures, 'people belong to ingroups or collectivities which are supposed to look after them in exchange for loyalty' (Hofstede, 1984, p. 419). In individualistic cultures, the development of the individual is foremost, even when this is at the expense of the group, whereas in collectivistic cultures the needs of the group are more important, with individuals expected to conform to the group (Gudykunst, 2003). Conformity is valued in collectivistic cultures, but diversity and dissent are more esteemed in individualistic cultures. The 'I' identity has precedence in individualistic cultures over the 'we' identity which takes precedence in collectivistic cultures. The emphasis in individualistic societies is on individuals' initiative and achievement, while emphasis is placed on belonging to groups in collectivistic societies. Collectivistic cultures stress the needs of a group; individuals are identified more through their group affiliation than by individual position or attributes. Hierarchical differences and vertical relationships are emphasized, and role, status, and appropriate behaviours are more clearly defined by position. Collectivistic cultures require a greater degree of harmony, cohesion, and cooperation within their ingroups and place greater burdens on individuals to identify with the group and conform to group norms. Sanctions usually exist for nonconformity. Individualistic cultures, however, depend less on groups and more on the uniqueness of their individuals. The pursuit of personal goals rather than collective ones is of primary importance. As a result, individualistic cultures require less harmony and cohesion within groups and place less importance on conformity of individuals to group norms.

Greenfield and Cocking (1994, p. 7) 'hypothesized that a value orientation stressing interdependence would characterize the cultural and cross-cultural roots of socialization practices and developmental goals for minority groups . . . [and] would . . . contrast with the independence scripts that characterize the cultural roots of Euro-American socialization and developmental goals'. Greenfield (1994) notes that 'value judgments concerning the superiority of the independent individual became reified . . . [hence] respect for elders and the socialization practices that support it have been given a negative evaluation in developmental psychology as lack of initiative and authoritarian childrearing (cf. Baumrind, 1980). They have not been considered as simply derivatives of a contrasting value system-an interdependence developmental script' (Greenfield, 1994, p. 30). However, the authors argue that, 'a value that is adaptive for socialization under one set of societal conditions becomes maladaptive under another' (Greenfield, 1994, p. 28). In a comparative study of Korean parental strictness in Korea and US and Canada, Kim et al. (1994) found that a 'collectivistic childrearing practice such as strictness can become maladaptive under new societal conditions' (p. 28). Because people from collectivistic cultures view 'interdepence as important [they] foster it through children's socialization processes' (Brislin and Yoshida, 1994, p. 93). While cultures tend to be predominantly either individualistic or collectivistic, both exist in all cultures. Individualism has been central to the life of Western industrialized societies such as the USA and the UK (Hofstede, 1984). Collectivism is particularly high among Asian and African societies. However, diversity within each country is very possible. In the USA, for instance, Hispanics and Asians tend to be more collectivistic than other ethnic groups (Triandis, 1990; 2001), and in the UK, Asians and African Caribbeans tend to be more collectivist than white people. Dwivedi (2002) notes that 'in western culture, "independence" is viewed as the cherished ideal and "dependence" is seen as a despicable state . . . professionals working with their clients consider that fostering independence is the most important aspect of their work' (p. 47).

Western psychology and its associated views of human nature, maturity and mental health are based on individualistic values and are thus one-sided. Indeed, 'modern views of child development are steeped in individualism' (Woodhead, 1999, p. 11). Social workers need to understand the importance of family responsibility and respect for elders within this framework. Extended families are important in collectivistic cultures and respect for elders is an important element in the collectivistic or interdependence socialization complex (Triandis, 1989).

Asians are allocentric, not idiocentric, and the individual is expected to make sacrifices for the good of the group – more specifically, the family (Hofstede, 1980; Segal, 1991). Asians typically place great emphasis upon the individual-family relationship (Sue and Sue, 1999) and upon the extended family. South Asians attach great importance to the traditions and values of their family and kinship groups (Ghuman, 2003). Thus, South Asian families' 'orientation towards "collectivity" leads to such customs and traditions as extended families, helping and supporting close family relatives, and arranged marriages' (Ghuman, 2003, p. 33).

Dwivedi (2002) notes that in India the pure form of the extended family (in which the brothers, wives and children live together with their parents) is not so common but variations such as the 'joint family' and the 'intergenerational family' are still very common. The joint family refers to 'where some of the brothers (with their wives and children) live together without their parents' (p. 49). The 'intergenerational family' refers to 'where the parents live together with

one of their grown-up children and their spouse and children'
(p. 49). Dwivedi (2002) argues that the disruption of the extended
family is a 'source of stress for ethnic minorities . . . in a culture
where the emotional support from one's extended family, especially
in times of stress, is the essential ingredient of any coping strategy'
(p. 22).

First generation Asian parents, in general, brought up their children and trained their young people as they themselves were brought
up in their country of origin (Ghuman, 1999). Thus, children are
brought up to be obedient and respectful of their elders in the family
and the community. Children are taught to be interdependent and
not 'individualistic' and independent and young people are expected
to be loyal to the family, to be obedient to their parents and respect
their elders (Ghuman, 2003). However, second generation Asians
have changed their socializing practices and parents were more likely
to give freedom to their children to pursue their interests and
hobbies (Ghuman, 2003).

In a study of Gujerati Hindu families from India who settled in
the US, Patel et al. (1996) found that the Indian dedication to the
collectivity (family, clan, Hindu religious community) motivated
them to maintain such traditions, emphasizing the importance of
the extended family, obedience to elders, established sex roles,
arranged marriages, and the discouragement of autonomy in the
young. Segal (1991, p. 239) points out that 'traditionally, Indians
have retained their own culture and religious values, regardless of
the country to which they have migrated'. However, in the USA,
Segal notes that these traditional Asian values are 'eroded to a large
degree as a result of living in the US . . . [which] is especially apparent in the individualistic behaviour of the children and grandchildren of Indian immigrants' (1991, p. 235). It is possible that similar
findings can be found among second generation Asians living in the
UK. Modood et al. (1994) found that among second generation
Asians there was a strong commitment to the immediate family,
which was not translated into a strong commitment to the extended
family, whereas for first generation Asians 'it was extremely important to be in contact with the [immediate and extended] family'
(Modood et al., 1994, p. 24). Thus, 'variants of extended
family, where the parents live together with one of their grown-up
children and their spouse and children, are still very common today'
(p. 49). In another study Shaw (2000) found a 'non-residential

extended family' situation, where newly married sons/daughters live in close proximity to their parents, to be common amongst the second generation of Muslims in Oxford. Most second generation Muslims maintain close links with relatives and friends, and take part in family and community events. They also accept the obligation to support and take care of their parents. In a study of African, African Caribbean, Bangladeshi, Indian and Pakistani families living in Britain, Hylton (1997) found that many South Asian young people 'wish to live within a nuclear family organizational form, although they are keen to maintain or perform extended family obligations' (p. 23). Among most African and African-Caribbean families 'few grandparents live as part of an extended family . . . [though] many African Caribbeans . . . may live close to their children and grandchildren' (Hylton, 1997, p. 23). All respondents regarded family relations as absolutely central to their lives in Britain. According to Owusu-Bempah (2002) Hylton's study 'demonstrated the importance of collectivist values to the well-being of ethnic minority families' (p. 31).

Harrison et al. (1990) argue that African Americans, like other ethnic groups of colour in the US, have stressed collective values and group solidarity as response to exploitation and blocked opportunties. Parents emphasize interdependence and sharing as socialization goals for children. This observation is consistent with the finding that African American children are more willing to share within a group, and that African American college students score higher on collectivism than do European Americans (Gaines, 1997). Close ties with the extended family are important (White and Parham, 1990).

The African view of the world encompasses the concept of 'groupness' (Holdstock, 2000; Nobles, 1986). In the theoretical model of black psychology presented by Nobles (1986), interrelatedness, connectedness and interdependence are viewed as the unifying philosophic concepts in the African American experience base. The African philosophical tradition recognizes that 'only in terms of other people does the individual become conscious of his [or her] own being' (Mbiti, 1970, p. 5). Only through others does one learn his or her duties and responsibilities towards himself or herself and others. An essential point in understanding the traditional African's view of oneself is that one believes 'I am because we are; and because we are, therefore, I am' (Mbiti, 1970, p. 10).

Summary

Child rearing approaches to discipline are closely related to the values and goals of socialization. In general, higher levels of control are common wherever child rearing does not stress the development of individualistic independence in the child. Baumrind's (1971) parenting styles (authoritative, authoritarian, and permissive) are based on investigations of middle class European American parents. Parenting styles and their meaning vary as a function of the cultural background of the families assessed. Differences in discipline strategies are frequent sources of misunderstanding between minority/black and dominant/European cultures.

Two fundamental values that have been shown to differentiate European American culture from most non-Western cultures are individualism and collectivism. These underlying values shape the processes of development through the ways in which parents socialize their children. Extended families and respect for elders are important in collectivistic cultures. Parents emphasize interdependence and sharing as socialization goals for children.

Racial socialization

This section will focus on parental communications to children about race, a process researchers commonly refer to as 'racial socialization'. An important issue for black/minority parents is that of protecting their children from the adverse effects of racism, prejudice, and discrimination. Johnson et al. (2003) point out that

> components of parenting not assessed in traditional studies of child care become relevant in future studies of families of color. An example is racial socialization, preparation for the experience of ethnic or racial bias.
>
> (2003, p. 19)

McAdoo (1983) argued that being a member of a minority group in the US means being treated differently, and this societal stressor places huge demands on family life. Among the stressors identified by McAdoo are unemployment, inadequate health care, she argues that, although these stressors are experienced by other families, ethnic minority families experience these stressors within a racist environment, 'which changes and intensifies the meaning and impact of these sources of stress' (1983, p. 202). These stressors are also experienced by black/minority families in Britain. There is considerable evidence that there is discrimination against Asians and African Caribbeans in education, employment, the health care system, and law, including the criminal justice system (Brown, 1984; 1990; Parekh, 2000). Indeed, racial violence and racial abuse appear to be on the increase in Britain (Macpherson, 1999; Skellington and Morris, 1992). Thus, an important part of ethnic minority parenting is to teach children to cope with racism, prejudice, and discrimination. This is an area that has not received much attention in the consideration of parenting in black/minority families in Britain. Although most of the literature concentrates on African American parents, we can posit that the processes may be similar in other ethnic and racial groups that are considered minority groups in the US and Britain.

Parents have an important role to play in children's racial knowledge. As key socializing agents, their values, attitudes and behaviours convey important information to children about their own and other racial and ethnic groups. Parents of children as young as 3 years undertake racial socialization (Peters, 1985). Both the content and method of communicating race-related information vary widely across families (Hill, 1999). Some parents intentionally discuss racial issues with their children; other parents avoid the topic. Some black parents do not make their children aware of issues of racism or the potential for discrimination for various reasons. Some believe that the problem is too great for children to understand and that they will need to experience racism before they can truly learn. Fewer still believe racism is not as much a problem now as it was when they were growing up (Spencer, 1984). Some parents emphasize group differences and disadvantage; others emphasize similarities among all people (McAdoo, 2002). According to Johnson et al. (2003) 'Social position variables (parent and child experiences with discrimination) and residential and social segregation influence parental socialization messages to younger children about race' (p. 19).

Early studies showed that children's racial attitudes were unrelated to those of their parents (see Aboud, 1988). However, more recent research among black families suggests that parents' race-related messages may have important consequences for children's identity formation and development (Marshall, 1995; Peters, 1985; Sanders-Thompson, 1994; Spencer, 1984). Thus, children's orientations toward race are derived, in part, from parental practices and world views.

The process whereby children procure a sense of their unique ethnic and racial identity has been identified with several terms. Those terms include racial socialization, cultural transmission, socialization environment, race related messages, parental values transmission, cultural parenting, ethnic socialization and others (Bowman and Howard, 1985; Peters, 1985; Phinney and Rotheram, 1987). African American scholars have begun to acknowledge the importance of child rearing in a racially hostile world (Boykin and Toms, 1985; McAdoo, 2002; Peters, 1985; Thornton et al., 1990). The concept of racial socialization originated in scholars' efforts to identify strategies that black/minority ethnic parents use to rear competent and effective children in a society that is largely stratified by 'race'. The majority of research and theoretical writing on racial socialization has focused on African Americans.

Ethnic socialization has been defined by Phinney and Rotheram (1987) as 'developmental processes by which children acquire the behaviors, perceptions, values, and attitudes of an ethnic group, and come to see themselves and others as members of such groups' (p. 11). Racial socialization is defined by Peters (1985) as the 'tasks black parents share with all parents – providing for and raising children – but include the responsibility of raising physically and emotionally healthy children who are black in a society in which being black has negative connotations' (p. 161).

Thornton et al. (1990) defined racial socialization as including 'specific messages and practices that are relevant to and provide information concerning the nature of race status' (p. 401). They further specified three realms of relevant information that parents may communicate: a) information related to personal and group identity, b) information related to intergroup and interindividual relationships, and c) information on group position in the social hierarchy. Other conceptualizations have incorporated aspects of these definitions, focusing on the transmission of cultural practices, racial knowledge, and awareness of racism through verbal, nonverbal, deliberate, and inadvertent mechanisms (Bowman and Howard, 1985; Marshall, 1995; Sanders-Thompson, 1994; Stevenson, 1994, 1995). Thus, the term refers to parental practices that communicate messages about race or ethnicity to children. It is applicable across multiple racial/ethnic groups.

While the definitions are varied, the concept that black families have a special role in buffering the impact of racism and promoting a sense of cultural pride for their children has received significant attention over the last decade. Many studies have attempted to define, measure, and promote racial or ethnic socialization for black children and adolescents. Demo and Hughes (1990) found that adults who had received racism preparation messages from parents while growing up were more likely to have stronger feelings or closeness to other blacks and to hold stronger support for black separatism. Other researchers found a clear sense of and communication about one's racial identity from family members contributed to academic, and career success (Bowman and Howard, 1985; Edwards and Polite, 1992).

Boykin and Toms (1985) developed a conceptual framework for understanding the socialization environment that African American families find themselves raising children in. The authors described African Americans as facing a 'triple quandary'. They argue that black American children 'must simultaneously negotiate through three distinctively different realms of experience . . . the mainstream, minority, and Black culture experience' (pp. 38–9). The mainstream culture is the dominant culture in America, often based on white, middle class norms and values. Black people are widely exposed to the dominant culture and vary in their interest and ability to embrace its value system. The minority culture arises directly as a result of adaptations to racism and oppression. These areas are very important and seem to capture the variety of parenting strategies that are implemented. The acknowledgement of the bicultural nature of raising black children to survive in American society is implicit within this conceptual framework. One implication of this framework is the identification of African American families which fit into either a mainstream, minority, or black cultural socialization styles in their child rearing practices. These three themes recur in various forms throughout the literature on African American socialization.

The socialization process involves dynamic exchanges of information and interaction between parents and their children. Although scholars studying racial socialization have focused primarily on goals initiated by parents for their children, racial socialization is a bi-directional process shaped by parents and children.

Parents' race-related messages to their children take a variety of forms: verbal, nonverbal, explicit, and implicit. Most empirical studies of racial socialization focus on parents' deliberate (and explicit) race-related messages to children. Studies that have examined African American parents' reports about their current racial socialization practices (Marshall, 1995; Peters, 1985; Thornton et al., 1990) have found that the majority of them teach their children about racial/ethnic background, history, and heritage, and prepare them for racial bias.

Studies have also found that the majority of African American adults recall receiving messages about race from their parents (Sanders-Thompson, 1994; Demo and Hughes, 1990). Child rearing among Latino and Asian parents also emphasizes the importance of preserving the cultural traditions and values of their countries of origin and of teaching children about prejudice and discrimination in the US (Garcia Coll et al., 1995; Garcia Coll and Magnuson, 1997; Kibria, 1997).

Proactive and reactive

Stevenson (1998) suggests that racial socialization messages may be proactive or protective. That is, they may originate from parents' preconceived values, goals, and agendas (proactive) or they may occur in reaction to discrete events in parents' or children's lives (reactive). Proactive racial socialization is linked to parents' views of the strengths and competencies their children will need in order to function effectively in their adult social roles. Proactive racial socialization among black parents is guided by parents' expectations that their children will inevitably encounter racism and discrimination (e.g., Essed, 1990). However, other racial socialization agendas also may be proactive. For example, parents who value diversity and pluralism may choose racially-ethnically diverse versus homogeneous settings for their children. An important feature of proactive racial socialization messages is that they are closely linked to parents' worldviews.

Reactive racial socialization occurs inadvertently in response to race-related incidents that parents or children have experienced, or in response to children's general queries about racial issues. Children can disagree with parents' socialization messages, choosing instead to stick to their own worldviews. Uba (1994) cites a case of conflict between a 17-year-old Korean American boy and his immigrant parents, which illustrates the ways in which children may choose to incorporate or ignore parents' racial socialization efforts. Uba states: 'Although his parents tried to teach him to be proud to be Korean and to learn about Korean culture, Jack did not identify with Koreans as much as his parents wanted. Jack's father had threatened to disown him for being so disrespectful and attributed Jack's behaviours to being too Americanized' (Uba, 1994, p. 113).

The different dimensions of racial socialization include: a) emphasizing racial and ethnic pride, traditions, and history (termed cultural socialization); b) promoting an awareness of racial prejudice and discrimination (termed preparation for bias); c) issuing cautions and warnings about other racial and ethnic groups, or about inter-group relations (termed promotion of mistrust); and d) emphasizing the need to appreciate all racial and ethnic groups (termed egalitarianism) (Boykin and Toms, 1985; Thornton et al., 1990; Demo and Hughes, 1990; Sanders-Thompson, 1994). Although dimensions of racial socialization are described separately, particular racial socialization messages as they occur in everyday conversation are less readily distinguishable. For example, messages emphasizing cultural pride and history (cultural socialization) also may contain messages about historical discrimination and prejudice (preparation for bias), at least among minority populations in the US and Britain.

Cultural socialization

The term cultural socialization has been used normally to refer to parental practices that teach children about cultural heritage, ancestry, and history; that maintain and promote cultural customs and traditions; and that instil cultural, racial and ethnic pride (Boykin and Toms, 1985; Thornton et al., 1990). Cultural socialization may be evidenced in the following behaviours: talking to children, or reading books to them, about prominent people in the history of their ethnic or racial group; celebrating cultural holidays; exposing children to positive role models (Bowman and Howard, 1985; Knight et al., 1993; Peters, 1985; Sanders-Thompson, 1994; Stevenson, 1994; Thornton et al., 1990).

Most minority parents engage in cultural socialization practices with their children. For example, in Phinney and Chavira's (1995) study of parents with adolescent children, 88% of Mexican American, 83% of African American, and 67% of Japanese American parents described behaviours associated with cultural socialization.

Empirical studies have suggested that cultural socialization is associated with more favourable child outcomes among minority youth, particularly in terms of children's ethnic identity and their knowledge and attitudes regarding their ethnic group. For example, Demo and Hughes (1990) found that black adults who recalled that their parents had emphasized racial pride, cultural heritage, and racial tolerance reported greater feelings of closeness to other blacks and more Afrocentric racial attitudes than did those who reported no racial socialization. In their study of Chinese American families, Ou and McAdoo (1993) found that parents' pride in Chinese culture was related to their children's racial-ethnic preferences. In particular, more parental cultural socialization was associated with greater preferences for same-race/ethnic peers among first- and second-grade girls. Several studies have also reported significant relationships between overall racial socialization and favourable identity outcomes among youth (Marshall, 1995; Sanders-Thompson, 1994).

Preparation for bias

The term 'preparation for bias' is used to refer to parents' efforts to promote their children's awareness of racial bias, and to prepare them to cope with prejudice and discrimination. Several scholars have suggested that enabling children to navigate around racial barriers and to negotiate potentially hostile social interactions are important parenting tasks within ethnic minority families (Thornton et al., 1990; Garcia Coll et al., 1995; Harrison et al., 1990).

Parents' discussion of racial bias with their children appears to vary as a function of racial-ethnic group membership. Studies among Asian American and Latino parents have found comparatively low levels of racial socialization in this regard (Phinney and Chavira, 1995). Phinney and Chavira (1995) found that 93.8% of African American parents reported discussing racial bias and discrimination with their children, but only 73% of Mexican American parents and 44.5% of Japanese American parents reported such discussions.

Socialization of mistrust

The term 'promotion of mistrust' has been used to refer to parental practices that discourage children from interacting with people of other racial/ethnic out-groups or that fosters a sense of distrust across racial/ethnic boundaries. Where preparing children for racial bias may have helpful influences on children's developmental outcomes, socialization practices that foster intergroup mistrust and alienation from mainstream values may promote maladaptive behaviours. For example, in Ogbu's (1974) research among high school students in California, parents' over-emphasis on racial barriers and discrimination seemed to undermine children's sense of efficacy and promote distrust of and anger toward mainstream institutions. Children who showed these attitudes were more likely to perform badly in school.

Egalitarianism and silence about race

There are few studies on the influences of egalitarian socialization or silence about race in terms of their consequences for children's development. However, scholars have emphasized that black children socialized from an egalitarian perspective may have unrealistic expectations concerning intergroup relations. They may also be unable to understand and cope with experiences involving racial bias (Spencer, 1984; Stevenson, 1995).

Although most of the theory and research on racial and cultural socialization is US based, I believe that many of the issues raised are applicable to black and minority ethnic groups in Britain.

Summary

An important part of ethnic minority parenting is to teach children to cope with racism, prejudice, and discrimination. The concept of racial socialization originated in scholars' efforts to identify strategies that black/minority ethnic parents use to rear competent children in a society that is largely stratified by 'race'. However, this is an area that has not received much attention in Britain. Although most of the research and theoretical writing on racial socialization has focused on African American parents, we can posit that the processes may be similar in other ethnic and racial groups that are considered minority groups in the US and Britain.

Boykin and Toms (1985) described black families as facing a 'triple quandry'. These are: mainstream culture, minority culture, and black culture. These three themes recur in various forms throughout the literature on African American socialization. Parents race-related messages to their children take a variety of forms: verbal, nonverbal, explicit, and implicit. Most empirical studies of racial socialization focus on parents' deliberate (and explicit) race-related messages to children. Racial socialization messages may be proactive or protective. Proactive racial socialization is tied to parents' views of the strengths and competencies their children will need in order to function effectively in their adult social roles. Reactive racial socialization occurs inadvertently in response to race-related incidents that parents or children have experienced, or in response to children's general queries about racial issues.

The different dimensions of racial socialization include: cultural socialization; preparation for bias; promotion of mistrust; and egalitarianism. Cultural socialization has been used commonly to refer to parental practices that teach children about cultural heritage, ancestry, and history; that maintain and promote cultural customs and traditions; and that instil cultural, racial and ethnic pride. A number of studies have indicated that most parents of colour engage in cultural socialization practices with their children. Empirical studies have suggested that cultural socialization is associated with more favourable child outcomes among minority youth, particularly in terms of children's ethnic identity and their knowledge and attitudes regarding their ethnic group.

The term 'preparation for bias' is used to refer to parents' efforts to promote their children's awareness of racial bias, and to prepare them to cope with prejudice and discrimination. The extent to which parents discuss racial bias with their children appears to vary as a function of racial-ethnic group membership. Empirical studies regarding the influences of preparation for bias on youth have produced inconsistent results.

The term 'socialization of mistrust' has been used to refer to parental practices that discourage children from interacting with people of other racial-ethnic out-groups or that fosters a sense of distrust across racial-ethnic boundaries.

Racial socialization and racial identity

Parham and Williams (1993) examined the impact of race-specific messages on racial identity attitudes. Participants were classified into one of six groups based on self-reported messages they received from parents regarding race. In that study, none of the four subscales of the Racial Identity Attitude Scale (see Chapter 3) was found to be uniquely related to the parental messages received while growing up. There was no significant relationship between the set of four racial identity attitudes and six racial message categories. Parham and Williams (1993) stated that it was likely that their question on racial messages was not sensitive enough to detect a relationship between parental racial socialization and racial identity attitudes. It should also be noted that Demo and Hughes (1990) found a relationship between the impact of parental racial socialization on dimensions of racial identification rather than attitudes associated with the racial identity stage. This may account for the difference in their findings. Thompson et al. (2000) also found a positive relationship between aspects of racial socialization and positive racial identity attitudes.

Demo and Hughes (1990), using data from the National Black Survey (US) reported a relationship between parental socialization messages and racial identity. They assessed black identity in three ways: feelings of closeness to other blacks, commitment to African culture and the extent to which blacks should confine their social relationships to other blacks, and the evaluation of blacks as a group. Parental socialization messages assessed what individuals had been taught about what it is to be black and about getting along with whites. When 'feelings of closeness to other blacks' and commitment to black separatism were examined, parental racial socialization was one of the strongest correlates. Blacks who were told to view 'all races as equal' identified more closely with black people, their history, and their culture than did blacks who were told to 'work hard' or to view 'whites as superior'. The individualistic 'work hard' approach was weakly but positively related to black group evaluation. Demo and Hughes (1990) noted that their findings also supported a multidimensional approach to the study of racial identity.

Spencer (1983) found that children with some knowledge of black history as reported by parents were more likely to report black/Afrocentric racial attitudes, while children who were limited in knowledge about civil rights, who had parents who did not discuss race discrimination issues or teach about civil rights were more likely to report Eurocentric racial attitudes. She also found that young children (3–6 years) in general tended to hold Eurocentric racial attitudes but as they got older (7–9 years), an orientation toward Afrocentric racial attitudes increased. This finding was true irrespective of geographic region. In her study, she asked parents rather than youth about their cultural values transmission.

In uncovering the various culture child rearing strategies and messages identified by the parents in her different geographic samples, Spencer (1983) noted several themes. Those themes include parental teaching of the importance of civil rights, that integration leads to greater experiences, that the current racial climate is better than that of the 1950s or 1960s, and that racial discrimination exists. Parent and children's knowledge of black history was found to be correlated with children's pro-black racial awareness, racial attitudes, and racial preferences. Direct and active teaching from parents about cultural values is most crucial in instilling Afrocentric or pro-black thought processes in children. That is, without direct intervention, black children's pro-black identities may be subject to confusion and instability.

British studies

Very little is known in Britain about how racial/cultural socialization is carried out in different ethnic and minority groups. In Britain, Fatimilehin (2002) found that racial socialization influenced the racial and ethnic identity development of African Caribbean adolescents. She notes that 'racial socialisation messages relating to black culture and history, racism, pride, and the family [influenced racial and ethnic] development' (p. 355). There was also a strong relationship between 'receiving messages about racism [and] being more immersed in a black racial identity' and concludes that 'racial socialization has a major impact on racial and ethnic identity development' (p. 355).

Rodriguez et al. (2003) argue that 'By avoiding any conversations about race or ethnicity or ignoring situations that arise, adults may unintentionally send a subtle message that race or ethnicity is unimportant or not to be discussed openly' (p. 3012).

Reynolds (1998) notes that an important mothering function of African Caribbean mothers living in Britain is to provide children with strategies to cope with racism. Reynolds (2001) notes that 'As a result of particular concerns facing African Caribbean young males . . . in educational underachievement, schools exclusion, police harassment and incarceration, racial violence . . . [it is important for parents to provide] them with the necessary guidance and advice to resist systems of racism and inequalities' (p. 144).

In a study of Punjabi families in Britain, Dosanjh and Ghuman (1996) found that over 50% of the Punjabi mothers in their sample 'said that they talk to their child about racism in general, and how to cope with the racism which they are likely to meet in their daily lives' (p. 132). For example, one mother described her son's first encounter with racism: 'He had a few people say to him Paki. And he said to me: "mum, am I a Paki". I said: "No, you are not a Paki". I went to his school and saw his teacher and told him: "He is not a Paki; he is a Sikh" ' (pp. 132–3). In a study of permanent family placement for children of minority ethnic origin in Britain, Thoburn et al. (2000) found that young people's comments 'about growing up as a member of a minority ethnic group in Britain were often linked with comments about racism' (p. 133). Most of the young people in the study 'felt that their adoptive or foster parents, whether of the same or a different ethnic background had been helpful [in helping them cope with racism]' (p. 133). For the young minority ethnic people in their sample, good parenting 'must include help to deal with racism and with issues of identity and racial pride' (Thoburn et al., 2000, p. 208).

To conclude:

> Children and adolescents who are socialized about race and ethnicity are further along in identity than children who are not (Knight et al., 1993; Marshall, 1995) and they demonstrate more positive mental health outcomes and competencies (Parham and Helms, 1985; Phinney and Chavira, 1995; Pyant and Yanico, 1991; Taub and McEwen, 1992).
>
> (Rodriguez et al., 2003, p. 302)

Implications for social work practice

In general social work has operated within a 'problem oriented' framework, which is characterized by deficit and dysfunctional theories of black families. Dominelli argues that: 'Black children and families are over-represented in the controlling aspects of social work and underrepresented in the welfare aspects of social work . . . We need a shift from a deficit model of social work control to a strength model of social work empowerment' (Dominelli 1992, p. 166).

Many social work texts paint crude cultural stereotypes of black families. The 'norm' against which black families are, implicitly or explicitly, judged is white. The norm presents a myth of the normal family as nuclear, middle class, and heterosexual. Black families are seen as strange, different, and inferior. The pathological approach to black family life is evident in the British research on black people. It is also evident in social workers' perception of black families. Social workers tend to rely on Eurocentric theory and practice, that devalues the strength of black families (Ahmad, 1990; Robinson, 1995). The traditional method of studying black families in the social science literature has often focused on the pathological rather than on the strengths of the black family (Robinson, 1995). Barn (2002) writes that: 'Negative thinking feeds into policy and practice, leading to discriminatory behaviour and poor outcomes for black families' (Barn, 2002, p. 9).

Dominelli (1997) argues that 'White social workers are anxious about the appropriateness of black families' child rearing practices, relationships between black parents and their children, and women's roles within black families. These anxieties are central in the social work equation of pathologising black families' (p. 99). Social work models have tended to pathologize black families and encourage practitioners to perceive the families as being the 'problem'. Consequently, social work interventions focus almost exclusively on clients' weaknesses, inabilities, and inadequacies. Dominelli (1997) cites some examples of stereotypes held by social workers about black families – 'West Indian families are deemed unstable because they are run by domineering women who are morally loose. The strength and unity of the Asian family is problematised. Asian women are too docile and sexually repressed . . . Asian men are too powerful . . . in other words, a "deficit" model of human relations is the outcome of these (racist) evaluations' (Dominelli, 1997, p. 97).

The negative perceptions and assumptions about black families, and lack of understanding, awareness, and knowledge of black experience, become pervasive forces within social work that can endanger the welfare of black families. Traditional social work is not effective in meeting the needs of black families. Social workers must have an understanding of African Caribbean and Asian kinship ties and family patterns. For instance, as was emphasized earlier, kinship bonds are more extensive in these families than in a white nuclear family. Social workers need to be aware that extended family values are an important element in the family assessment.

In Britain, immigration controls have made it difficult for 'black family units to be reconstructed in their traditional totality' (Dominelli, 1997, p. 97). In addition 'poor employment prospects and bad housing also deny black people choices in establishing their preferred family forms. White social workers continue to divide black families by taking disproportionate numbers of black children into care by "inappropriately intervening in the family process" . . . [this] has led black people to perceive white social workers as child snatchers' (Dominelli, 1997, pp. 98–9). Social workers need to assess black families in the context of a racist society. They need to be aware that: 'ethnic minority families face many issues . . . [which] include personal and institutional racism and the impact of immigration, nationality laws and separated families' (O'Neale, 2000, p. 1).

In a study of local authority provision for black and ethnic minority families, Richards and Richards and Ince (2000) found that the 'overall picture remains extremely bleak' (p. 7). For example, services 'had very few of the most basic structures, for example comprehensive equal opportunities policies and ethnic record keeping and monitoring systems. Very few had placement policies for Black children and effective programmes for Black foster carers' (p. 79). However, there were a few examples of good practice. For example, in one local authority 'Anti-racist practice and culturally sensitive service provision was kept consistently on the agenda, with rolling programmes of training . . . and responsibility on team managers to ensure that culturally sensitive services were not seen as an "add on" ' (Richards and Ince, 2000, p. 80).

In another study, 'Inspection of services for ethnic minority children and families', O'Neale (2000) found that 'many of the case files [that were] examined failed to indicate that issues of race and culture had been taken into account by [social] workers when they undertook assessments' (p. 33). O'Neale (2000) points out that social workers need to also take into account 'The experience of racism [that] is likely to affect the responses of the child and family to the assessment process' (p. 33).

A lack of knowledge of black families has contributed 'to unnecessary intervention of social workers in black families which often
results in devastating consequences for the family' (ABSWAP, 1983,
p. 14). More recently Barn (2002) argues that 'the extent to which
education and training equip students in the helping professions to
develop their skill and competence in engaging black families is
questionable (Penketh, 2000)' (p. 12). It is important that all social
workers 'develop their skill and competence in working with minority ethnic birth and substitute families' (Barn, 2002, p. 12)

Child abuse and use of physical punishment

Boushel (2000) writes that: 'Childrearing approaches to control and
discipline are closely related to the values and goals of socialization'
(p. 74). Kagitcibasi (1996) notes that 'In general, higher levels of
control are common wherever childrearing does not stress the development of individualistic independence in the child' (p. 21).

In a study of six local authorities in Britain, Gibbons et al. (1995)
found that black families were often referred for using physical methods of punishment, such as a stick, than were white families. Also,
compared to white children, black children were over-represented
among referrals for physical abuse. Gibbons et al. (1995) argue that
'the consequences of the injuries inflicted on black and Asian children
were no more likely to be long-lasting' and that it was 'the form the
punishment took that was unacceptable to community agents who
referred these children' (p. 40). In another study, Barn et al. (1997)
also found that black children were over-represented among referrals
for physical abuse compared to white children. According to Gopaul-
McNicol (1999) 'when a culture views corporal punishment as an
acceptable form of discipline, as Caribbean cultures tend to, then
"physical abuse" is more likely to occur' (p. 82).

As noted earlier in the chapter, cultures vary in their styles of
discipline. It is common for some cultures, for example, to include
physical punishment as part of their disciplinary repertoire (Fontes,
2005). In an article on the over-representation of black children in
the child protection system, Chand (2000) points out that 'the issue
of punishment is one of the most controversial areas relating to black
families, child abuse and social work intervention' (p. 72) He argues
that social workers may be confused about 'the reasons why punishment is employed in certain situations' (p. 72). Social workers,

therefore, need 'to have some knowledge and understanding about acceptable and unacceptable behaviours within the service user's culture, since it seems that the severity of the punishment needs to somehow match the severity of the "crime" in order for it to be more acceptable' (p. 73)

A leading authority on the cultural aspects of child abuse, Korbin (1981, 1987, 1997) 'exposed the weaknesses of the child abuse knowledge basis in working with cultural minorities since it was based almost entirely on research and clinical experience in Western nations' (O'Hagan, 2001, p. 111). Korbin (1987) pointed out that a particular behaviour may be viewed by one cultural group as abusive but may be perceived as a mode of discipline by another cultural group.

The child abuse inquiry reports of Jasmine Beckford (Blom-Cooper, 1985) and Tyra Henry (Lambeth, 1987) noted that 'abusive behaviours were interpreted as aspects of culture and that the workers . . . had no right to criticize the supposedly cultural (child abusing) practices of others. This gave rise to the concepts of cultural relativism and the rule of optimism' (O'Hagan, 2001, p. 114). Cultural relativism 'provides one explanation for incompetence . . . Instead of an exposure of the behaviours which have been wrongfully interpreted as culture, and the ineffectual response to such behaviours, cultural relativism speaks of those interpretations as if they are fact' (O'Hagan, 1999, p. 278). I agree with Segal's (1999) statement that: 'Ethnocentrism must be avoided, but extreme cultural relativism may justify acceptance of physically, socially and emotionally damaging practices' (Segal, 1999, p. 41).

Chand argues that black children and their families may 'be more or less likely to be subjected to child abuse investigations by social work agencies' (Chand, 2000, p. 67). This may be due to either the pathologization of black families or cultural relativism. Thus, 'the potential consequences of either approach for black families will be either [unnecessary investigation] or there will not be appropriate intervention for black children at risk' (p. 67). Practitioners must be able to assess when the cultural norm of physical punishment becomes abusive and dangerous (Brophy et al., 2003). Culturally sensitive social work practice 'does not mean accepting inhumane acts as "normal" in any culture . . . Social workers will have to exercise their judgement over contentious issues and not use "culture" as an excuse for not doing so. Not spotting child abuse in black families because they are perceived as disciplinarian is one example' (Dominelli, 1997, p. 33). In his article, Chand (2000) concludes that 'overall cultural differences in the way families rear their children should be acknowledged and respected, but where child abuse does occur it should be understood that this particular family has gone beyond what is acceptable not only in the British culture, but also in their own . . . Hence, causing significant harm to a child physically, emotionally, sexually or through neglect is not acceptable in any culture' (p. 75).

An important distinction between corporal punishment and abuse, according to Straus and Donnelly (2001), is whether the child is psychologically damaged. Abuse is not condoned by any ethnic group. Children need to be protected. Thoburn et al. (2005) discuss Brophy et al.'s (2003) research which stresses 'the importance of differentiating between 'normal' child care practices and deviant . . . behaviours that are [unacceptable] in any community (p. 84).

To work effectively and assess whether abuse is taking place we need to understand the context. Gopaul-McNicol (1999, p. 79) writes that 'Researchers in the Caribbean [and Britain] should focus on elucidating the differences in disciplinary practices in various subcultures, so that advocates for children do not erroneously diagnose a parent as abusive when he or she is, in the eyes of that culture, merely disciplining the child'.

Acculturation

Social workers need to be aware that acculturation levels vary not only within cultural groups but also within families (i.e., intergenerational). Different levels of acculturation within families can result in 'disagreement and conflict about family values and parenting behaviours' (Zuniga, 1992), (Bornstein, 1995, p. 199). Culturally competent social work practice with minority groups should include an assessment of the individual client's acculturation level as well as an assessment of the family's cultural values, including those of siblings and parents.

Garcia Coll et al. (1995) note that 'parents determine, to some extent, familiar ethnic minority aspects of parenting (e.g., disciplinary practices, educational expectations) they uphold and those they relinquish in favor of the dominant culture parental values, attitudes, and practices' (p. 201).

Racial socialization

In addition to understanding the cultural dimension, social workers need to recognize the racism which affects the lives of black people. Social workers need to understand that racial socialization – particularly how to cope with discrimination, racism, and prejudice – is relevant to understanding the socialization practices of black families. Social workers need to be aware that the socialization of children in black families occurs within the environment of real or potential racial discrimination and prejudice. Thus, according to McAdoo (2002):

> The tasks Black parents share with all parents – providing for and raising children – not only are performed within the mundane extreme environmental stress of racism but include the responsibility of raising physically and emotionally healthy children who are Black in a society in which being Black has negative connotations. This is racial socialization.
>
> (p. 59)

In African American families, parents often see their primary teaching role as enabling their children to cope with racism (Peters, 1985; Hill, 1999). Peters (1985) found that the black parents 'recognized that being Black brought a different dimension to the way they were raising their children' (Peters, 1985, p. 171).

Social workers need to be aware of the three primary goals of ethnic and racial socialization identified by Boykin and Toms (1985). As noted earlier, these include promoting a group's cultural traditions, preparing children and young people to deal with racism and discrimination, and preparing children and young people to operate in the mainstream. These 'goals have implications for the socialization process for many racial and ethnic groups in US [and British] society' (Rodriguez et al., 2003, p. 302). The authors point out that 'children and adolescents who are socialized about race and ethnicity are further along in identity development than children who are not . . . and they demonstrate more positive mental health outcomes and competencies' (p. 302).

Collectivism-individualism

Greenfield and Cocking (1994) writes that:

> when interdependently oriented people are minority members of a dominant society oriented toward independence, an unequal meeting of values occurs. There is a tendency for members of the dominant individualistic society to evaluate negatively members of a minority whose behaviour, goals, and attitudes reflect an emphasis on interdependence.
>
>   (p. 20)

White Euro-American cultures are seen as not only desirable, but normative as well. As noted earlier, individualism-collectivism is a dimension that has been used to understand differences in socialization practices between different cultures. Social workers need to understand that collectivistic cultures – for example Asian – foster interdependence within the family. Individuals are expected to sacrifice their own personal needs and goals for the sake of a common good. Social workers need to take into account the 'collective' nature of the South Asian family. However, social workers professional training in general stresses an 'individualistic' approach to working with families. As a result social workers may find it difficult to empathise with the concerns of the South Asian parents about community connectedness and obligations.

Dwivedi and Varma (2002) write: 'In western culture, relationships of the individual to society are viewed from an "ego-centric" perspective focusing on the reproduction of individuals rather than on the reproduction of relationships, with an emphasis on separateness, clear boundaries, individuality and autonomy within the relationships, while in eastern cultures there is a "socio-centric" conception of these relationships' (p. 22). Collectivism has important influences on the ways people raise children. In a study of child rearing practices of Punjabi families, Dosanjh and Ghuman (1996) write that 'there is no conscious attempt made to train the children to be independent as is understood in Britain and America . . . children from the age of four or five years onwards are encouraged to be obedient and to honour the elders . . . the popular notion of a good child is . . . firmly tied to the notion of [doing] as you are told' (p. 51). It is important for social workers to note that for some black children, there is a conflict among the black cultural emphasis on survival of the group, interdependence, and cooperation and the dominant culture's emphasis on competition and individualism.

Conclusions

Knowledge about child rearing values, attitudes, and behaviours among Asian and African Caribbean parents in Britain is limited. The consequences of migration, biculturalism, and bilingualism and their impact on both children and parents have also been relatively neglected in research in Britain. Also, most minority groups in Britain have lower socio-economic status than the population at large, with some few exceptions. Unemployment, lower educational attainment are more prevalent among such minority populations. Ogbu (1988) emphasized socio-economic circumstances as a major explanatory variable for understanding the development of child rearing techniques within minority groups in the US. There is a need to understand child rearing and socialization practices among minority ethnic parents in Britain.

In cross-cultural studies of child rearing it is necessary to take into account the traditional cultural values and attitudes particular to each of the minority groups as well as the values, attitudes, and conventions of the cultural environments in which they currently reside. It is also necessary to recognize the interactions among various social institutions and their impact on parental child rearing practices. In doing so, we may better understand the consequences of cultural differences and similarities in child rearing.

Social workers in Britain need more training in working with black families and children. They need to be aware, for example, that individualism-collectivism differences between countries and cultures are associated with differences in socialization practices. Indeed, all the issues addressed in this chapter need to be addressed by social work educators and practitioners.

7

Conclusion

> Children growing up in multicultural environments are not a new phenomenon but they are a feature of a world in which the international movement of large numbers of people is ever increasing.
>
> (Keats, 1997, p. 23)

There are now a considerable proportion of children living in Britain who belong to ethnic minority groups and who differ ethnically and culturally from the majority population. However, there is a dearth of research/literature on the development of ethnic minority children in social work textbooks and professional journals. Social work texts on childcare make little reference to culture. For example, the only reference to culture in Hill and Aldgate's (1996) text is a warning that 'a stance of cultural pluralism may oversimplify complex issues' (p. 115).

The body of literature representing the deficit view of black children and families has most strongly influenced the professional and personal perceptions of social workers in Britain (see Robinson, 1995; 2000).

In this book, I have argued that the failure to include black children in our conceptual thinking about service delivery has occurred in spite of strong empirical evidence supporting the need to integrate culturally sensitive perspectives in social work research and practice (Davis and Proctor, 1989; Lum, 2003; Pinderhughes, 1989). As a result, black children and families are seen by white, middle class workers whose standards of behaviour, often perceived as being the norm, have little or nothing to do with designing ways to ensure effective outcomes for black children (Fontes, 1995; Pinderhughes, 1989).

I have attempted to articulate from a cross-cultural and black perspective a framework for understanding the development of minority ethnic children. This book has offered an introduction to cross-cultural perspectives in child development that both challenges the Eurocentric assumptions implicit in much traditional psychology and relates theory and research to social work practice. It has examined cultural similarities and differences across groups of white and black people in relation to a range of key topics: attachment theory; racial/ethnic identity; cognitive development; communication; and cultural/racial influences on socialization practices. As Asante (1992) suggests 'there is space for Eurocentrism in a multicultural enterprise as long as it does not parade as universal' (1992, p. 267).

I have argued that one of the major ways of conceptualizing principles in cross-cultural psychology is through the use of the terms etics and emics. An etic refers to a universal truth or principle, whereas an emic refers to truths that are culture specific. Etic versus emic goals provides social workers with a theoretical framework for working with culturally diverse children and young people and adults. When a social worker assumes that his or her own emic-etic distinction is true for all cultures, he/she is operating from an ethnocentric point of view and cultural misunderstanding will result. I have argued that it is critical for social workers to acknowledge the extent of individual differences within a given cultural or ethnic group. Thus, recognizing intragroup differences is critical and helps avoid stereotyping.

I have examined the concept of attachment and its relevance in cross-cultural settings. I have argued that cultures differ in their notions of 'ideal' attachment. The cross-cultural validity of the methods of assessing attachment and the meaning of the attachment classifications themselves have been questioned. The meaning of the Strange Situation, a widely used measure of attachment, has also been challenged. Some cross-cultural studies have also challenged the notion that closeness to the mother is necessary for secure and healthy attachment. Social workers need to be aware that notions about the quality of attachment and the processes by which it occurs are qualitative judgements made from the perspective of each culture. What is considered an optimal style of attachment may not necessarily be optimal across all cultures. It should be clear from the descriptions of the attachment categories that the diagnostic system is built up on the European-kind middle social class system of meanings (see LeVine and Miller, 1990; Gardiner and Kosmitzki, 2005). The mother (or her substitute caregiver) – rather than a social group (for example, mother, aunt and grandmother together) – is assumed to be in control over the child. I have argued that multiple caregiving is common in Asian and African families. Thus, the experiences of a child growing up in these situations can be quite different from those of a child in a Euro-American household. Rashid (1996) argues that 'the challenge to British social work practitioners is to recognise the need for cultural relativism and cultural humility in thinking about attachment and parenting' (p. 75).

I have examined Cross's racial and Phinney's ethnic identity development models and Berry's acculturation model. I have argued that maintenance of a strong ethnic identity is generally related to psychological well-being among members of acculturating groups.

Berry's acculturation framework is useful for social workers to examine acculturation strategies of minority adolescents and to make comparisons between generations within families. As Phinney et al. (2000) point out 'because the rates of adaptation following immigration may vary between parents and adolescents (Portes, 1997), intergenerational discrepancies in cultural values may increase' (Phinney et al., 2000, p. 528). I have argued that the construct of levels of acculturation provides an important way to begin to think about intracultural differences in black child development. It is important for social workers to determine the potential impact of different levels of acculturation upon black child development.

Social workers need to take an active approach in helping black children build positive self-images of themselves. Banks (2003) argues that 'all children have an identity development need', but for black children 'additional help, in the form of overt intervention is necessary to counter the negative images that they may encounter' (p. 157). He cites the following messages (implicit and explicit): 'you will not succeed', 'you are inferior'; 'your features are unattractive'. Social workers need to 'support and develop a child's knowledge, understanding, acceptance and positive regard of self in the context of his or her "racial" group' (Banks, 2001, p. 163). Goldstein and Spencer (2000) outline practice guidelines in promoting the development of positive identity and self-esteem of black children. These include: 'carers who . . . give positive images to the child about all aspects of their identity, including ethnicity/'race', culture, religion and language; [and] placements where there is a continuity of experiences with the child's and birth family's previous background in terms of ethnicity, culture, language and religion (p. 11).

I have explored cognitive development as studied by Piaget and the testing approach to intelligence. I have discussed cross-cultural research in these areas and implications for social work practice. I have examined the continuous recycling of ideologies arguing that black people are innately intellectually inferior – ideologies that adversely affect the confidence of students and the willingness of teachers to invest in them. These notions have more recently been reignited by Hernstein and Murray's (1994) book *The Bell Curve: Intelligence and Class Structure in American Life*. One result of these theories is that black children have often been ignored and stigmatized by educators who have labelled them as unintelligent and, according to Holliday (1985), as children who generally are 'unable to talk right, think right, act right, or feel right' (p. 53). Similarly, black parents have been described as uninterested or investing too little in their children's education. However, black parents are more involved in some school-related activities than are white parents, often in an effort to supplement or compensate for the inadequate education their children receive in schools.

In US, African American scholars have challenged the negative assessments of black children's intellectual ability by delineating the structural-cultural barriers that they face, studying the unique learning styles of black children and creating alternative schools to meet their needs. In Britain, the increase in the number of exclusions from school affects a disproportionately large number of black pupils, in particular African Caribbean boys. Supplementary schools have [also] been set up for African Caribbean children in Britain. These schools 'attended not only to the basic skills but also to other aspects of the curriculum that children and parents felt were being neglected in the mainstream schools . . . however, it is still only a small number of children who attend these schools' (German, 2002, p. 204). Supplementary schools also exist for African, Chinese and Asian children.

I have examined from a psychological point of view issues relating to intercultural communication with black children and adolescents and their families. Intercultural communication includes both verbal and nonverbal interaction. In this book I have identified some of the characteristics of nonverbal communication which are of special importance in intercultural communication. White social

workers need to have an understanding of the nonverbal communication styles of minority children and adolescents. Nonverbal
communication styles – for example, patterns of eye contact, expression of feeling, physical distance and directiveness are likely to vary
for minority clients. I have argued that white social workers' attributions about the nonverbal communication of black people can
sometimes be wrong. However, understanding that a client is from
a collectivistic or individualistic culture or a high or low context
culture will make his or her behaviour less confusing or interpretable.

I have argued that social workers must be alert to the impact of
culture on speech and style of communication. For example, is code
switching present (e.g., when an African Caribbean child slips into
use of non-Standard English after using Standard English during
most of the interview)? I have explored the use of black English
among African Caribbean youngsters and the implications of interacting with Asian clients who may have English as a second
language, or may not speak English at all. I have stressed that white
social workers should avoid judging and evaluating a black person's
language and communication style, since ethnocentric judgements
will interfere with effective communication.

In assessment and intervention, the questions to pursue and the
interventions to offer must be informed by substantial understanding of the client's cultural reality. Interviewing, assessment, and
intervention skills grow out of the knowledge base described in this
book. Culturally appropriate interviewing techniques consider the
manner in which questions are asked, level of intrusiveness, direct-
ness, formality, forms of address. For example, as noted in this book,
studies have shown that 'Indians often defer to figures of authority
and persons in positions of power, seeking precise guidance and
direction when in need (Roland, 1988). This would therefore
suggest that a non-directive form of counselling [communication] is
unlikely to lead to positive outcomes (Laungani, 1997)' (Palmer and
Laungani, 1999, p. 65).

Within all cultures, parents engage in practices aimed at socializing the child to become a responsible adult member of the society.
I have argued that the parenting concepts of 'authoritarian' and
'restrictive' are not very relevant for Asians, although they may be
important for understanding European-American parenting. Indeed,
these concepts are more pertinent to American parenting values in

which 'strictness' is sometimes equated with manifestations of parental hostility, aggression, mistrust and dominance (Rohner and Pettengill, 1985). For Asians, parental obedience and some aspects of strictness may be equated with parental concern, caring, or involvement (Chao, 1994, p. 1112).

I have argued that he individualism-collectivism dimension allows for similarities and differences in socialization practices to be identified and explained across cultures. According to Dosanjh and Ghuman (1996, p. 190) 'Asian families still tend to emphasise inter-dependence rather than the independence that is valued in western European countries'. Social workers in Britain need more training in working with black families and children. They need to be aware, for example, that individualism-collectivism differences between countries and cultures are associated with differences in socialization practices.

I have explored racial socialization practices among black families. I have argued that it is important for black parents to teach children to cope with racism, prejudice and discrimination. Garcia Coll (1995) argues that 'the effects of racism and discrimination and how to prepare children to cope with these particular demands are not part of the core formulations of mainstream models, even though these issues are of concern to parents (Burgess, 1980) and are central to the processes of parenting in ethnic and minority families (McAdoo, 1983)' (p. 192). Several authors have suggested that cultural socialization promotes children's positive racial identity development and self-esteem by preparing children to interpret and cope with prejudice, discrimination, and negative group images from the outside world (e.g., Demo and Hughes, 1990).

In this book, I have drawn on case examples to illustrate important practice issues. Throughout the book I have argued that social work practice needs to be anti-discriminatory and anti-racist. Anti-discriminatory practice 'is an attempt to eradicate discrimination and oppression from our own [social work] practice and challenge them in the practice of others and the institutional structures in which we [social workers] operate. In this respect, it is a form of emancipatory practice' (Thompson, 2001, p. 34).

I have argued that racial prejudice is extensive, and not even well-intentioned social workers escape its impact on their thoughts, attitudes and values. As Ridley (1995, p. 39) notes, 'racism exists in numerous counseling [and social work] behaviours, bringing harm to [black] clients . . . counselors [social workers], in many ways, are socialized and trained to behave as racists without even knowing it'. White social workers need to avoid racist behaviour (overt and covert) and language in their interactions with black clients. Many white professionals who wish to work 'interculturally' live in social isolation from the minority ethnic groups; their only experience of these groups is when individuals are under stress. Negative stereotypical images about the client's family organization, child rearing practices, derived from moments of dysfunction, become the basis for everyday knowledge (Boyd-Franklin, 2003). Cultural racism is 'evident in defining black families' child rearing practices as inferior to white ones' (Dominelli, 1997, p. 95). I would agree with Parham et al. (1999) that society must confront the fact 'that racism is not a people of colour problem; it is a white people's problem. Until whites decide to clean up their house, little progress will continue to be made' (p. 133).

Social workers' own cultural beliefs may affect the manner in which they interact with black clients. It is therefore important for social workers to examine their own beliefs about black families and children and how they play out in relation to the beliefs and practices of their culturally diverse clients. This means examining one's own cultural lens and cultural filters through which one views others, especially those who are different. Exploring one's own culture and examining how culture has shaped one's values, beliefs, behaviours, conceptions of 'family', and notions of others who are different help reduce personal biases and stereotyping of others.

There is increasing recognition both of the dearth of research dealing with ethnic minorities (Graham, 1992) and of the need for greater attention to culture and ethnicity in psychological research (Betancourt and Lopez, 1993). However, in spite of the awareness of its importance, there is very little guidance available to researchers on how to carry out such research. Research methods textbooks do not generally address the topic, and researchers are often unclear about how to incorporate the study of ethnicity into their own work. Appropriate paradigms and models are very much needed to study ethnic minority children and families. Future research in child development needs to fully articulate how variables such as racism, prejudice and discrimination, and other sources of oppression operate and influence developmental outcomes in black children. Thus, social work theory and practice with black children needs to be more reflexive, inclusive and cultural.

Various authors (Gardiner, 1994; 2001; Gardiner and Kosmitzki, 2005; Greenfield and Cocking, 1994) predict that there will be an increasing interest in viewing human development within a cross-cultural developmental perspective in the 21st century. Throughout the book, I have argued that cross-cultural findings on child development can be used to develop intervention strategies relevant to children and families within different cultural contexts. Rogoff and Morelli (1989) state that:

> The inclusion of cultural issues in the field of developmental psychology, be it in theory building or in its application to field situations, can serve as a mutually enriching experience for expanding the theoretical horizons as well as the extension of knowledge to promote the well-being of children in cultural contexts where the need for intervention is pressing.
>
> (p. 347).

The main aim of this book has been to sensitize students, educators and practitioners to cross-cultural and black perspectives in child development. The literature that addresses these issues in Britain is limited at best. If we are to understand minority child development in Britain from these perspectives and its implications for social work practice, much more must be written, researched and published. I would like to conclude with this quote from Gardiner (2004):

> Cross-cultural study of development frequently resembles a confused mosaic of often contradictory findings. Yet therein lies the promise and excitement of future endeavors ... Much more needs to be done, and as the cross-cultural perspective reveals, discovery of similarities and dissimilarities in human behaviour will make our understanding both easier and more difficult.
>
> (p. 72)

Bibliography

Aboud, F. (1988) *Children and Prejudice.* Cambridge, MA: Basil Blackwell.

ABSWAP (1983) *Black Children in Care – Evidence to the House of Commons Social Services Committee.* London: Association of Black Social Workers and Allied Professionals.

Ahmad, B. (1990) *Black Perspectives in Social Work.* Birmingham: Venture Press.

Ahmed, S. (1996) Anti-racist social work: a black perspective. In C. Hanvey and T. Philpot (eds) *Practising Social Work.* London: Routledge.

Ahmed, S., Cheetham, J., Small, J. (1986) *Social Work with Black Children and their Families.* London: Batsford.

Ainsworth, M. D. S. (1978) *Patterns of Attachment: a Psychological Study of the Strange Situation.* NJ: Lawrence Erlbaum Associates.

Ainsworth, M. D. S. (1982) Attachment: Retrospect and prospect. In C. M. Parks and J. Stevenson-Hinde (eds) *The Place of Attachment in Human Behavior.* New York: Basic Books.

Ainsworth, M. D. S. and Wittig, B. A. (1969) Attachment and exploratory behavior of one-year-olds in a strange situation. In B. M. Foss (ed) *Determinants of Infant Behavior IV.* London: Methuen.

Alexander, C. (1996) *The Art of Being Black: The Creation of Black British Identities.* Oxford: Clarendon Press.

Andersen, P. A. (1990) Explaining intercultural differences in nonverbal communication. In L. A. Smovar and R. E. Porter (eds) *Intercultural Communication: A Reader.* Belmont, CA: Wadsworth.

Anwar, M. (1978) *Between Two Cultures: A Study of Relationships between Generations in the Asian community in Britain.* London: Commission for Racial Equality.

Anwar, M. (1998) *Between Two Cultures: A Study of Relationships between Generations in the Asian Community in Britain,* 2nd edn. London: Commission for Racial Equality.

Arce, C. A. (1981) A reconsideration of Chicano culture and identity. *Daedalus,* 110: 177–92.

Aries, E. and Moorehead, K. (1989) The importance of ethnicity in the development of identity of black adolescents. *Psychological Reports,* 65: 83–93.

Arnold, R. (1997) Raising levels of achievement in boys. London: National Foundation for Research.

Asante, M. K. (1992) *Afrocentricity*. Trenton, NJ: Africa World Press.

Atkinson D. R., Morten, G. Sue and Derald, W. (1979) *Counseling American Minorities: A Cross-cultural Perspective*. Dubuque, Iowa: W. C. Brown Co.

Atkinson D. R., Morten, G. Sue and Derald, W. (1983) *Counseling American Minorities: A Cross-cultural Perspective*. Dubuque, Iowa: McGraw Hill.

Atkinson D. R., Morten, G. Sue and Derald, W. (1989) *Counseling American Minorities: A Cross-cultural Perspective*. Dubuque, Iowa: McGraw Hill.

Atkinson D. R., Morten, G. Sue and Derald, W. (1993) *Counseling American Minorities: A Cross-cultural Perspective*. Madison, Wis.: Brown & Benchmark.

Atkinson, D. R., Ponterotto, J. G. and Sanchez, A. R. (1984) Attitudes of Vietnamese and Anglo-American Students toward Counseling. *Journal of College Student Development*, 25: 448–452.

Bagley, C. (1993) *International and Transracial Adoptions: A Mental Health Perspective*. Aldershot: Avebury.

Baker, C. (1995) *Foundations of Bilingual Education and Bilingualism*. Clevedon: Multilingual Matters.

Baldwin, J. A. (1984) African Self-Consciousness and the Mental-Health of African-Americans. *Journal of Black Studies*, 15: 177–194.

Banks, N. (1992) Techniques for direct identity work with Black children. *Adoption and Fostering*, 16(3): 19–25.

Banks, N. (2001) Assessing the children and families who belong to minority ethnic groups. In J. Horwath (ed) *The Child's World*. London: Jessica Kingsley Publishers.

Banks, N. (2003) What is a black identity? In Dwivedi, K. N. (ed) *Meeting the Needs of Ethnic Minority Children: Including Refugee, Black, and Mixed Parentage Children: A Handbook for Professionals*. London: Jessica Kingsley Publishers.

Banks, W. (1976) White preference in blacks: a paradigm in search of a phenomenon. *Psychological Bulletin*, 83: 1179–1186.

Barn, R. (1990) Black children in local authority care: admission patterns. *New Community*, 16(2): 229–46.

Barn, R. (1993) *Black Children in the Public Care System*. London: Batsford.

Barn, R., Ferdinand, D. and Sinclair, R. (1997) *Acting on Principle: An Examination of Race and Ethnicity in Social Services Provision for*

Children and Families. London: British Agencies for Adoption & Fostering.

Barn, R. (2002) 'Race', ethnicity and child welfare. In B. Mason and A, Sawyer (eds) *Exploring the Unsaid.* London: Karnac.

Barna, L. (1994) Stumbling blocks in intercultural communication. In L. A.Samovar and R. E. Porter (eds) *Intercultural Communication: A reader.* 2nd edn. Belmont, CA: Wadsworth.

Baumrind, D. (1971) *Current Patterns of Parental Authority.* Washington, DC: American Psychological Association.

Baumrind, D. (1995) *Child Maltreatment and Optimal Caregiving in Social Contexts.* New York: Garland.

Bebbington, A. and Miles, J. (1989) The background of children who enter local authority care. *British Journal of Social Work,* 19: 349–68.

Beck, A. T., Ward, C. H., Mendelson, M., Mock, J. and Erbaugh, J. (1961) An inventory for measuring depression. *Arch Gen Psychiatry,* 4: 561–571.

Beishon, S., Modood, T. and Virdee, S. (1998) *Ethnic Minority Families.* London: Policy Studies Institute.

Berk Laura, E. (1998) *Development through the Lifespan.* Boston: Allyn and Bacon.

Berk Laura, E. (2001) *Development through the Lifespan.* Boston: Allyn and Bacon.

Berrington, B. (1995) Marriage patterns and inter-ethnic unions. In D. Coleman and J. Salt (eds) *Ethnicity in the 1991 Census.* London: OPCS.

Berry, J. (1980) Acculturation as adaptation. In A. M. Padilla (ed) *Acculturation: Theory, Models and Some New Findings.* Boulder, CO: Westview.

Berry, J. W. (1969) On Cross-Cultural Comparability. *International Journal of Psychology,* 4: 119–28.

Berry, J. W. (1974) Psychological aspects of cultural pluralism. *Culture Learning,* 2: 17–22.

Berry, J. W. (1980) Acculturation as varieties of adaptation. In A. M. Padilla (ed) *Acculturation: Theory, Model, and Some New Findings.* Boulder, CO: Westview.

Berry, J. W. (1990) Psychology of acculturation. In J. Berman (ed) *Cross-cultural Perspectives.* Nebraska Symposium on motivation, Vol. 37, (pp. 201–234). Lincoln: University of Nebraska Press.

Berry, J. W. (1997) Immigration, acculturation and adaptation. *Applied Psychology: An International Review,* 46: 5–68.

Berry, J. W. and Sam, D. (1997) Acculturation and adaptation. In J. W.

Berry, M. H. Segall, and Ç. Kagitçibasi (eds) *Handbook of Cross-cultural Psychology (Vol. 3): Social Behavior and Applications.* 2nd edn. Boston: Allyn & Bacon.

Berry, J. W., Kim, U., Minde, T. and Mok, D. (1987) Comparative studies of acculturative stress. *International Migration Review,* 21: 491–511.

Berry, J. W., Kim, U., Power, S., Young, M. and Bujaki, M. (1989) Acculturation attitudes in plural societies. *Applied Psychology: An International Review,* 38: 185–206.

Berry, J. W., Poortinga, Y. H., Segall, H. and Dasen, P. R. (1992) *Cross-cultural Psychology: Research and Applications.* Cambridge: Cambridge University Press.

Berry J. W., Poortinga Ype, H. and Pandey, J. (eds) (1997) *Handbook of Cross-cultural Psychology.* Boston: Allyn and Bacon.

Berry, J. W., Poortinga, Y. H. and Pandey, J. (eds) (2002) *Handbook of Cross-Cultural Psychology.* (2nd edn). Boston: Allyn & Bacon.

Berry, J. W. and Dasen, P. R. (1974) *Culture and Cognition: Readings in Cross-cultural Psychology.* London: Methuen.

Betancourt, H. and Lopez, S. R. (1993) The Study of Culture, Ethnicity, and Race in American Psychology. *American Psychologist,* 48: 629–637.

Binet, A. and Simon, T. (1905) *Upon the Necessity of Establishing a Scientific Diagnosis of Inferior States of Intelligence.*

Binet, A. and Simon, T. (1916) *The Development of Intelligence in Children: (the Binet-Simon scale).* Baltimore: Williams & Wilkins.

Black and In Care (1984) *Black and In Care: Conference Report.* London: Children's Legal Centre.

Black and In Care Steering Group (1985) *Black and in Care: Conference Report (Report of a Conference Organized by the Black and In Care Steering Group held in October 1984).* London: Black and In Care Steering Group.

Blom-Cooper, L. (1985) *A Child in Trust: The Report of the Panel of Inquiry into the Circumstances Surrounding the Death of Jasmine Beckford.* London: Brent.

Bond, M. H. and Smith, P. B. (1996) Cross-cultural social and organizational psychology. *Annual Review of Psychology,* 47: 205–235.

Bornstein M. H. (ed) (1995) *Handbook of Parenting.* Vol 2. New Jersey: Lawrence Erlbaum Associates.

Boulton, M. J. and Smith, P. K. (1992) The social nature of play fighting and play chasing: Mechanisms and strategies underlying cooperation and compromise. In J. H. Barkow, L. Cosmides and J. Tooby (eds) *The Adapted Mind.* New York: Oxford University Press.

Boushel, M. (2000) What kind of people are we? 'Race', anti-racism and social welfare research. *British Journal of Social Work*, 30: 71–89.

Bowlby, J. (1969) *Attachment and Loss*. London: Hogarth Press.

Bowlby, J. (1982) *Attachment and Loss*. London: Hogarth Press.

Bowman, P. J. and Howard, C. (1985) Race-related socialization, motivation, and academic achievement: A study of black youths in three-generation families. *Journal of the American Academy of Child Psychiatry*, 24: 134–141.

Boyd-Franklin, N. (2003) *Black Families in Therapy*. New York: The Guilford Press.

Boykin, A. W. (1994) Afrocultural Expression and its Implications for Schooling. In E. Hollins, J. King and W. Hayman (eds) *Teaching Diverse Populations: Formulating a Knowledge Base*. Albany: SUNY Press.

Boykin, A. W. (1997) *Culture Matters in the Psychosocial Experiences of African Americans: Some Conceptual, Process and Practical Considerations*, unpublished manuscript.

Boykin, A. W. and Toms, F. D. (1985) Black child socialization: A conceptual framework. In H. P. McAdoo and J. L. McAdoo (eds) *Black Children: Social, Educational, and Parental Environments*. Beverly Hills, CA: Sage.

Braham, P., Rattansi, A., Skellington, R. and Open, U. (1992) *Racism and Antiracism: Inequalities, Opportunities and Policies*. London: Sage Publications in association with the Open University.

Brainerd, C. J. (1978) *Piaget's Theory of Intelligence*. Englewood Cliffs, NJ: Prentice-Hall.

Branch, C. W. and Newcombe, N. (1986) Racial Attitude Development among Young Black-Children as a Function of Parental Attitudes – A Longitudinal and Cross-Sectional Study. *Child Development*, 57: 712–721.

Bretherton, I. (1992) The Origins of Attachment Theory – Bowlby, John and Ainsworth, Mary. *Developmental Psychology*, 28: 759–775.

Bretherton, I. and Waters, E. (1985) *Growing Points of Attachment Theory and Research*. Chicago: University of Chicago Press.

Brislin Richard, W. and Yoshida, T. (1994) *Improving Intercultural Interactions: Modules for Cross-cultural Training Programs*. Thousand Oaks, CA: Sage Publications.

Brislin Richard, W. and Yoshida, T. (1994) *Intercultural Communication Training: An Introduction*. Thousand Oaks, CA: Sage Publications.

Bronfenbrenner, U. (1977) Toward an experimental ecology of human development. *Proceedings of the American Philosophical Society*, 119: 439–469.

Bronfenbrenner, U. (1979) *The Ecology of Human Development: Experiments by Nature and Design.* Cambridge, Mass: Harvard University Press.

Bronfenbrenner, U. (1993) The ecology of cognitive development: Research models and fugitive findings. In R. H. Wozniak and K. W. Fischer (eds*) Development in Context: Acting and Thinking in Specific Contexts.* Hillsdale, NJ: Erlbaum.

Brophy, J., Jhutti-Johal, J. and Owen, C. (2003) Assessing and documenting child ill-treatment in ethnic minority households. *Family Law*, 33: 756–764.

Brown, C. (1984) *Black and White in Britain: The Third PSI Survey.* Aldershot: Gower.

Brown, C. (1990) Racial inequality in the British Labour Market. *Employment Institute Economic Report*, 5.4 (June).

Bruner, J. S. and Gil, A. (1971) *The Relevance of Education.* London: Allen & Unwin.

Burg, B. and Belmont, I. (1990) Mental Abilities of Children from Different Cultural Backgrounds in Israel. *Journal of Cross-Cultural Psychology*, 21: 90–108.

Burgoon, J. K., Buller, D. B. and Woodall, W. G. (1996) *Nonverbal Communication: The Unspoken Dialogue.* New York: McGraw-Hill.

Burgoon Judee, K., Buller, David, B. and Woodall, W. G. (1989) *Nonverbal Communication: The Unspoken Dialogue.* New York: Harper & Row.

Burkard, A. W., Ponterotto, J. G., Reynolds, A. L. and Alfonso, V. C. (1999) White counselor trainees' racial identity and working alliance perceptions. *Journal of Counseling and Development*, 77: 324–329.

Butler, I. and Roberts, G. (2004) *Social Work with Children and Families.* London: Jessica Kingsley Publishers.

Byers, P. and Byers, H. (1972) Nonverbal communication and the education of children. In C.B. Cazden, V. John and D. H. Hymes (eds), *Functions of Language in the Classroom* (pp. lx, 394). New York: Teachers College Press.

Byrnes, J. P. (1988) Formal operations: A systematic reformulation. *Developmental Review*, 8: 66–87.

Callanan, A. and O'Hagan, G. (2001) *Inspection of Social Care Services for Older People, West Sussex County Council, May 2001.* London: Dept. of Health.

Canino, I. A. and Spurlock, J. (2000) *Culturally Diverse Children and Adolescents: Assessment, Diagnosis, and Treatment.* 2nd edn. New York: Guilford Press.

Carter, R. T. (1991) Racial identity attitudes and psychological functioning. *Journal of Multicultural Counseling and Development*, 19: 105–115.

Carter, R. T. (1995) *The Influence of Race and Racial Identity in Psychotherapy*. New York: John Wiley & Sons.

Census (2001) www.statistics.gov.uk

Central Council for Education and Training in Social Work (1983) *Teaching Social Work for a Multi-racial Society: Report of a Working Group*. London: Central Council for Education and Training in Social Work.

Central Council for Education and Training in Social Work (1991) *One Small Step towards Racial Justice: The Teaching of Antiracism in Diploma in Social Work Programmes*. London: Central Council for Education and Training in Social Work.

Chambers, P. and Patterson, G. R. (1995) Discipline and child compliance in parenting. In M. Bornstein (ed) *Handbook of Parenting (Vo 14)*. Hillsdale, NJ: Erlbaum.

Chand, A. (2000) The over-representation of Black children in the child protection system: possible causes, consequences and solutions. *Child and Family Social Work*, 5: 67–77.

Chao, R. K. (1994) Beyond parental control and authoritarian parenting style: Understanding Chinese parenting through the cultural notion of training. *Child Development*, 65: 1111–1119.

Chaplin, J. P. (1975) *Dictionary of Psychology*. New York: Dell.

Charles, M., Rashid, S. and Thoburn, J. (1992) The placement of Black children with permanent new families. *Adoption and Fostering*, 16(3): 13–19.

Chavajay, P. and Rogoff, B. (2002) Schooling and traditional collaborative social organization of problem solving by Mayan mothers and children. *Developmental Psychology*, 38: 55–66.

Chen, L. A. (1998) *A contextual examination of parental ethnic socialization and children's ethnic attitudes and knowledge among immigrant Chinese families*. Unpublished doctoral dissertation: New York University.

Chiu, L. H. (1987) Child rearing attitudes of Chinese, Chinese-American, and Anglo-American mothers. *International Journal of Psychology*, 22: 409–419.

Clark, K. and Clark, M. (1940) Skin color as a factor in racial identification of Negro preschool children. *Journal of Social Psychology*, 11: 159–169.

Clark, K. and Clark, M. (1947) Racial identification and preference in

Negro children. In *Readings in Social Psychology*. Theodor, M. Newcomb and Eugene L. Hartley (eds). New York: Holt.

Coard, B., The Caribbean and Community Workers (1971) *How the West Indian Child is made Educationally Subnormal in the British School System*. London: New Beacon Books.

Cole, M. (1984) The World Beyond our Borders: What Might Our Students Need to Know About It. *American Psychologist*, 39: 998–1005.

Cole, M. (1995a) From Cross Cultural to Cultural Psychology. *Swiss Journal of Psychology*, 54: 262–76.

Cole, M (1995b) Culture and cognitive development: From cross-cultural research to creating systems of cultural mediation. *Culture and Psychology*, 1: 25–52.

Cole, M. (1998) Culture in development. In M. Woodhead, D. Faulkner and K. Littleton (eds) *Cultural Worlds of Early Childhood*. London: Routledge.

Cole, M. and Cole, S. R. (1996) *The Development of Children*. New York: Freeman.

Coleman, J. C. and Hendry, L. B. (1999) *The Nature of Adolescence*. London: Routledge.

Cole, M. and Scribner, S. (1974) *Culture and Thought: A Psychological Introduction*. New York: Wiley.

Cole, M. and Scribner, S. (1977) Cross-cultural studies of memory and cognition. In R.V. Kail, Jr and J. W. Hagen (eds) *Perspectives on the development of memory and cognition*. Hillsdale, NJ: Erlbaum.

Coleman, J. C. and Hendry, L. B. (1999) *The Nature of Adolescence*. 3rd edn. London: Routledge.

Coombe, V. (1994) Black children in residential care. In V. Coombe and A. Little (eds) *Race and Social Work in London*. London: Tavistock.

Corman, H. H. and Escalona, S. K. (1969)Stages in sensori-motor development: A replication study. *Merrill-Palmer Quarterly*, 15(4): 351–361.

Coupland, N., Coupland, J. and Giles, H. (1991) *Language, Society and the Elderly: Discourse, Identity and Ageing*. Oxford: Blackwell.

Coupland, N., Wiemann, J. M. and Giles, H. (1990) '*Miscommunication' and Problematic Talk*. Newbury Park, CA: Sage Publications.

Crawford, K. and Walker, J. (2003) *Social Work and Human Development*. Exeter: Learning Matters.

Crittenden, P. M. (2000) A dynamic-maturational exploration of the meaning of security and adaptation. In P. M. Crittenden and A. H. Claussen (eds) *The Organization of Attachment Relationships: Maturation, Culture and Context.* Cambridge: Cambridge University Press.

Crittenden, P. M. and Claussen, A. H. (2000) *The Organization of Attachment Relationships: Maturation, Culture and Context.* Cambridge: Cambridge University Press.

Cross, W. E. (1971) The Negro to black conversion experience: towards the psychology of black liberation. *Black World,* 20: 13–27.

Cross, W. E. (1978) The Thomas and Cross models of psychological nigrescence: a literature review. *The Journal of Black Psychology,* 5: 13–31.

Cross, W. E. (1980) Models of psychological negrescence: a literature review. In Reginald L. Jones (ed) *Black Psychology.* New York: Harper and Row.

Cross, W. E. (1985) Black identity: rediscovering the distinction between personal identity and reference group orientation. In Margaret B. Spencer, Geraldine K. Brookins and Walter R. Allen (eds) *Beginnings: The Social and Affective Development of Black Children.* Hillsdale, NJ: L. Erlbaum.

Cross, W. E. (1991) *Shades of Black: Diversity in African-American Identity.* Philadelphia: Temple University Press.

Cross, W. E. (1995)The psychology of nigrescence: revising the Cross model. In J. G. Ponterotto, J. M. Casas, L. A. Suzuki and C. M. Alexander (eds) *Handbook of Multicultural Counseling.* Thousand Oaks, CA: Sage.

Cross, W. E. (2001) Encountering nigrescence. In J. G. Ponterotto, J. M. Casas, L. A. Suzuki and C. M. Alexander (eds) *Handbook of Multicultural Counseling.* 2nd edn. Thousand Oaks, CA: Sage.

Cross, W. E., Parham, T. A. and Helms Janet, E. (1991) The stages of black identity development: nigrescence models. In Reginald L. Jones (ed) *Black Psychology.* Berkeley, Calif.: Cobb and Henry.

Cross, W. E., Parham, T. A. and Helms, Janet, E. (1995) The stages of black identity development: nigrescence models. In Reginald L. Jones (ed) *Black Psychology.* 2nd edn. Berkeley, Calif.: Cobb and Henry.

Cross, W. E. and Fhagen-Smith, O. (1996) Nigrescence and ego identity development. In P. Pedersen, J. Draguns, W. Lonner and J. Trimble (eds) *Counseling Across Cultures.* Thousand Oaks, CA: Sage.

Cross, W., Parham, T. and Helms, J. (1998) Nigrescence revisited: theory and research. In R. L. Jones (ed) *African American Identity Development.* Hampton, VA: Cobb & Henry.

Cross, W. E. and Vandiver, B. J. (2001) Nigrescence theory and measurement: Introducing the Cross Racial Identity Scale (CRIS). In J. G. Ponterotto, J. M. Casas, L. A. Suzuki and C. M. Alexander (eds) *Handbook of Multicultural Counseling.* 2nd edn. Thousand Oaks, CA: Sage.

Cummins, J. (1984) *Bilingualism and Special Education: Issues in Assessment and Pedagogy.* Clevedon: Multilingual Matters Ltd.

Daniel, B., Wassell, S. and Gilligan, R. (1999) *Child Development for Child Care and Protection Workers.* London: Jessica Kingsley Publishers.

d'Ardenne, P. and Mahtani, A. (1990) *Transcultural Counseling in Action.* London: Sage.

Darling-Hammond, L., Wise, A. E., Klein, S. P. (1995) *A License to Teach: Building a Profession for 21st-century Schools.* Boulder: Westview.

Dasen, P. R. (1977) *Piagetian Psychology: Cross-cultural Contributions.* New York: Gardner Press.

Dasen, P. R. (1982) Cross-cultural aspects of Piaget's theory: The competence-performance model. In L. L. Adler (ed) *Cross-cultural Research at Issue.* New York: Academic Press.

Dasen, P. R. (1984) The cross-cultural study of intelligence: Piaget and Baoule. *International Journal of Psychology* ,19: 407–424.

Dasen, P. R.(1994) Culture and cognitive development from a Piagetian perspective. In W. J. Lonner and R. Malpass (eds) *Psychology and Culture.* Boston: Allyn & Bacon.

Dasen, P. R. and Berry, J. W. (1974) *Culture and Cognition: Readings in Cross-cultural Psychology.* London: Methuen.

Dasen, P. R., Inhelder, B., Lavelle, M. and Retschitzki, J. (1978) *Naissance de l'intelligence chez l'enfant Boule de Cote d'Ivoire.* Berne: Hans Huber.

Dasen, P. R. and Heron, A. (1981) Cross-cultural tests of Piaget's theory. In H. C.Triandis and A. Heron (eds) *Handbook of Cross-cultural Psychology,* Vol. 4. Boston: Allyn &Bacon.

Davey, A. G. and Norburn, M. V. (1980) Ethnic awareness and ethic differentiations amongst primary school children. *New Community* ,8: 51–60.

Davis, Larry, E. and Proctor, Enola, K. (1989) *Race, Gender, and Class: Guidelines for Practice with Individuals, Families, and Groups.* Englewood Cliffs, N.J.: Prentice Hall.

Deater-Deckard, K., Bates, J. E., Dodge, K. A. and Pettit, G. S. (1996) Physical discipline among African American and European

American mothers: Links to children's externalizing behaviors. *Developmental Psychology*, 32: 1065–1072.

Demo, D. H. and Hughes, M. (1990) Socialization and racial identity among black Americans. *Social Psychology Quarterly*, 53(4): 364–374.

Department of Health (1991) *The Children Act 1989 Guidance and Regulations*. London: HMSO.

Department of Health (1999) *Adoption now: messages from research*. Chichester: Wiley & Sons.

Department of Health (2001) *The Children Act Now: Messages from Research*. London: HMSO.

Department of Health/OFSTED (1995) *The Education of Young Children who are Looked After by Local Authorities*. London: HMSO.

Diamond, R. and Hellcamp, D. (1969) Race, sex, ordinal position of birth, and self disclosure in high school. *Psychological Reports*, 35: 235–238.

Dodd, C. H. (1987) *Dynamics of Intercultural Communication*. 2nd edn. Dubuque, IA: William C. Brown.

Dominelli, L. (1992) An uncaring profession? An examination of racism in social work. In P. Baham, A. Rattansi and R. Skellington (eds) *Racism and Antiracism*. London: Sage.

Dominelli, L. (1997) *Anti-racist Social Work: A Challenge for White Practitioners and Educators*, 2nd edn. Basingstoke: Macmillan.

Dominelli, L. (2002) *Anti-Oppressive Social Work Theory and Practice*. London: Palgrave Macmillan.

Dornbusch, S. M., Ritter, P. L., Leiderman, P. H., Roberts, D. F. and Fraleigh, M. J. (1987) The Relation of Parenting Style to Adolescent School Performance. *Child Development*, 58: 1244–1257.

Dosanjh, J. S. and Ghuman, P. A. S. (1996) *Child-rearing in Ethnic Minorities*. Clevedon: Multilingual Matters.

Dovidio, J. F. and Gaertner, S. L. (1986) *Prejudice, Discrimination, and Racism*. Orlando, Fla.: Academic Press.

Dresser, C. (1998) *The Rainmaker's Dog: International Folktales to Build Communicative Skills*. Cambridge: Cambridge University Press.

Drury, B. (1991) Sikh girls and the maintenance of an ethnic culture. *New Community*, 17(3): 387–99.

Dwivedi, K. N. (2002) *Meeting the Needs of Ethnic Minority Children: Including Refugee, Black, and Mixed Parentage Children: A Handbook for Professionals*. 2nd edn. London: Jessica Kingsley Publishers.

Dwivedi, K. N. and Varma, V. P. (1996) *Meeting the Needs of Ethnic Minority Children: A Handbook for Professionals*. London: Jessica Kingsley Publishers.

Dykes, J., Ladly, P., Laungani, P. (1997) *The Physical Abuse of Children: A Study of Referral Records.* London: South Bank University School of Education Politics and Social Science.

Edwards, A. and Polite, C. (1992) *Children of the Dream: The Psychology of Black Success.* New York: Doubleday.

Edwards, C. P. (1996) Parenting toddlers. In M. H. Bornstein (ed) *Handbook of Parenting,* Vol 1. Hillsdale, NJ: Erlbaum.

Ellis, G. J. and Petersen, L. R. (1992) Socialization Values and Parental Control Techniques – a Cross-Cultural-Analysis of Child-Rearing. *Journal of Comparative Family Studies,* 23: 39–54.

Erikson, E. H. (1964) *Childhood and Society.* St. Albans: Triad/Paladin.

Erikson, E. H. (1968) *Identity, Youth, and Crisis.* London: Faber and Faber Ltd.

Erikson, Erik, H. (1993) *Childhood and Society.* New York: Norton.

Essed, P. (1990) *Everyday Racism: Reports from Women of Two Cultures.* Claremont, Calif.: Hunter House.

Fairchild, H. H. (1991) Scientific Racism – the Cloak of Objectivity. *Journal of Social Issues,* 47: 101–115.

Fairclough, N. (1989) *Language and Power.* Harlow: Longman.

Farmer, E. and Owen, M. (1995) *Child Protection Practice: Private Risks and Public Remedies: A Study of Decision-making, Intervention and Outcome in Child Protection Work.* London: HMSO.

Fatimilehin, I. (1999) Of jewel heritage: Racial socialization and racial identity attitudes among adolescents of mixed African Caribbean/White parentage. *Journal of Adolescence,* 22: 303–318.

Fatimilehin, I. (2002) *The Development of Racial and Ethnic Identity in Adolescence.* Unpublished PhD Thesis.

Fernandez, E. (1991) The cultural basis of child rearing. In B. Ferguson and E. Browne (eds) *Health Care and Immigrants: A Guide for the Helping Professions.* Artarmon NSW: Maclennan & Petty.

Fernando, S. (1991) *Mental Health, Race and Culture.* Basingstoke: Macmillan.

Fernando, S. (1995) *Mental Health in a Multi-ethnic Society: A Multi-disciplinary Handbook.* London: Routledge.

Fernando, S. (2001) *Mental Health, Race and Culture.* 2nd edn. London: Palgrave Macmillan

Fernando, S. (2002) *Mental Health, Race and Culture.* Basingstoke: Palgrave.

Firth, H. (1995) *Children First: A Framework for Action.* Hampshire County Council.

Fontes, L. A. (1995) *Sexual Abuse in Nine North American Cultures: Treatment and Prevention.* Thousand Oaks, Calif.: Sage Publications.

Fontes, L. A. (2005) *Child Abuse and Culture*. New York: The Guilford Press.

Fordham, S. and Ogbu, J. (1986) Black students' school success: Coping with the burden of acting white. *Urban Review*, 18, 176–206.

Franz, C. E. and White, K. M. (1985) Individualism and attachment in personality development: Extending Erickson's theory. *Journal of Personality*, 53(2): 224–256.

Fujino, D. C. and King, K. R. (1994) *Toward a Model of Womanist Identity Development*. Presentation at the Annual Convention of the American Psychological Association, Los Angeles, CA.

Gaertner, S. L. and Dovidio, J. F. (1986)The aversive form of racism. In J. F. Dovidion and S. L. Gaertner (eds) *Prejudice, Discrimination and Racism*. Orlando, FL: Academic Press.

Gaines, S. O. (1997) *Culture, Ethnicity, and Personal Relationship Processes*. New York: Routledge.

Garcia Coll, C. T. and Lourdes M. (1989) *The Psychosocial Development of Puerto Rican Women*. New York: Praeger.

Garcia Coll, C. T., Meyer, E. C. and Brillon, L. (1995) Ethnic and minority parenting. In M. H. Bornstein (ed) *Handbook of Parenting*. Vol 2. New Jersey: Lawrence Erlbaum Associates.

Garcia Coll, C. T. and Magnuson, K. (1997) The psychological experience of immigration: A developmental perspective. In A. Booth, A. C. Crouter, and N. Landale (eds) *Immigration and the Family; Research and Policy on US Immigrants*. Mahwah, NJ: Erlbaum.

Gardiner, H. W. (1994) Child Development. In L. L.Adler and U. P. Gielen (eds) *Cross-Cultural Topics in Psychology*. New York: Praeger.

Gardiner, H. W. (2001) Culture, context and development. In D. Matsumoto (ed) *The Handbook of Culture and Psychology*. Oxford: Oxford University Press.

Gardiner, H. W. (2004) Follow the yellow brick road: New approaches to the study of cross-cultural human development. In V. P. Gielen and J. L. Roopnarine (eds) *Childhood and Adolescence: Cross-cultural Applications*. Westport CT: Greenwood Press.

Gardiner, H. W. and Kosmitzki, C. (2005) *Lives Across Cultures*. Boston: Pearson.

Gelfand, M. J., Triandis, H. C. and Chan, D. K. S. (1996) Individualism versus collectivism or versus authoritarianism? *European Journal of Social Psychology*, 26: 397–410.

Gelso, C. J. and Fretz, B. R. (1992) *Counseling Psychology*. Fort Worth: Harcourt Brace Jovanovich College Publishers.

German, G. (2002) Anti-racist strategies for educational performance facilitating successful learning for all children. In K. N. Dwivedi (ed) *Meeting the needs of ethnic minority children including refugee, Black, and mixed parentage children: a handbook for professionals.* London: Jessica Kingsley Publishers.

Ghuman, P. A. S. (1994) *Coping with Two Cultures: British Asian and Indo-Canadian Adolescents.* Clevedon: Multilingual Matters.

Ghuman, P. A. S. (1997) Assimilation or integration? A study of Asian adolescents. *Educational Research,* 39: 23–35.

Ghuman, P. A. S. (1999) *Asian Adolescents in the West.* Leicester: British Psychological Society.

Ghuman, P. A. S. (2003) *Double Loyalties: South Asian Adolescents in the West.* Cardiff: University of Wales Press.

Ghuman Paul, A. S. and Dosanjh, J. S. (1996) *Child-rearing in Ethnic Minorities.* Clevedon: Multilingual Matters.

Gibbs, J. T. and Huang, L. N. (2003) *Children of Color: Psychological Interventions with Culturally Diverse Youth.* San Francisco: Jossey-Bass.

Gibbons, J., Conroy, S. and Bell, C. (1995) *Operating the Child Protection System.* London: HMSO.

Giles, H., Coupland, J. and Coupland, N. (1991) *Contexts of Accommodation: Developments in Applied Sociolinguistics.* Cambridge: Cambridge University Press.

Giles, H. and Coupland, N. (1991) *Accommodating Language.* Milton Keynes: Open University Press.

Giles, H. and Coupland, N. (1991) *Language: Contexts and Consequences.* Milton Keynes: Open University Press.

Giles, H. and Johnson, P. (1981) The role of language in ethnic group relations. In Turner J. C. (ed) *Intergroup Behaviour.* Oxford: Blackwell.

Giles, H., Bourhis, R. Y. and Taylor, D. M. (1977) Towards a theory of language in ethnic group relations. In H. Giles (ed*) Language, Ethnicity and Intergroup Relations.* London: Academic Press.

Gillborn, D. and Gipps, C. (1996) *Recent Research on the Achievements of Ethnic Minority Pupils.* London: HMSO.

Gilroy, P. (1987) *There Ain't No Black in the Union Jack: The Cultural Politics of Race and Nation.* London: Routledge.

Goldberg, S. (1972) Infant care and growth in urban Zambia. *Human Development* 15: 77–89.

Goldstein, B. P. and Spencer, M. (2000) *'Race' and Ethnicity: A Consideration of Issues for Black, Minority Ethnic and White Children in Family Placement.* London: British Agencies for Adoption & Fostering.

Goodnow, J. J. (1990) The socialization of cognition. In J. W. Stigler, R. A. Shweder and G. Herdt (eds) *Cultural Psychology: Essays on Comparative Human Development.* Cambridge: Cambridge University Press.

Goodnow, J. J. and Bethon, G. (1966) Piaget's tasks: The effects of schooling on intelligence. *Child Development,* 37: 573–582.

Gopaul-McNicol, S. A. (1988) Racial identification and racial preference of black preschool children in New York and Trinidad. *The Journal of Black Psychology,* 14(2): 65–68.

Gopaul-McNicol, S. A. (1993) *Working with West Indian families.* New York: Guilford Press.

Gopaul-McNicol, S.-A. (1999) Ethnocultural perspectives on childrearing practices in the Caribbean. *International Social Work,* 42(1): 79–86.

Gopaul-McNicol, S.-A. and Thomas-Presswood, T. (1998) *Working with Linguistically and Culturally Different Children: Innovative Clinical and Educational Approaches.* Boston: Allyn and Bacon.

Gormly, A. V. and Brodzinsky, D. (1997) *Lifespan Human Development.* Fort Worth: Harcourt Brace College Publishers.

Graham, S. (1992) Most of the subjects were white and middle class: Trends in published research on African Americans in selected APA journals, 1970–1989. *American Psychologist,* 47: 629–639.

Graves, T. (1967) Psychological acculturation in a tri-ethnic community. South-Eastern *Journal of Anthropology,* 23: 337–350.

Greenfield, P. M. (1966) *Culture, Concepts and Conservation: A Comparative Study of Cognitive Development in Senegal.* Unpublished PhD dissertation, Harvard University, Cambridge, MA.

Greenfield, P. M. and Cocking, R. R. (1994) *Cross-cultural Roots of Minority Child Development.* Hillsdale, NJ: Hove, L. Erlbaum Associates.

Grossman, K. E. and Grossman, K. (1990) The wider concept of attachment in cross-cultural research. *Human Development,* 33(1): 31–47.

Grossmann, K. E., Grossmann, K., Huber, F. and Wartner, U. (1981) German Children's Behavior Towards Their Mothers at 12 Months and Their Fathers at 18 Months in Ainsworth Strange Situation. *International Journal of Behavioral Development,* 4: 157–181.

Grugeon, E. and Woods, P. (1990) *Educating All: Multicultural Perspectives in the Primary School.* London: Routledge.

Gudykunst, W. B. (2003) *Bridging Differences: Effective Intergroup Communication.* London: Sage.

Gudykunst William, B. (1998) *Bridging Differences: Effective Intergroup Communication.* Thousand Oaks, Calif.: Sage Publications.

Gudykunst, W. B. and Kim, Y. Y. (1984) Communicating with strangers: An approach to intercultural communication. New York: McGraw-Hill.

Gudykunst, W. B. and Ting-Toomey, S. (1988) Culture and affective communication. *American Behavioral Scientist,* 31: 384–400.

Guernina, Z. (1995) Ethnic minority adolescents' identity in the new Europe: A transcultural approach. *International Journal of Psychotherapy,* 13(1): 52–9.

Guilford, J. P. (1985) The structure of intellect model. In B. B. Wolman and R. J. Sternberg (eds) *Beyond IQ.* Cambridge: Cambridge University Press.

Gushue, G. V. (1993) Cultural-Identity Development and Family Assessment – an Interaction-Model. *Counseling Psychologist,* 21: 487–513.

Guthrie, R. (1998) *Even the Rat was White,* 2nd edn. Needham Heights, MA: Allyn & Bacon.

Hackett, L. and Hackett, R. (1994) Child-Rearing Practices and Psychiatric-Disorder in Gujarati and British Children. *British Journal of Social Work,* 24: 191–202.

Hale, J. (1982) *Black children: their roots, culture and learning styles.* Provo, UT: Brigham Young University Press.

Hall, E. T. (1964) Adumbration as a feature of intercultural communication. *American Anthropologist,* 66: 154–63.

Hall, E. T. (1976) *Beyond Culture.* New York: Anchor Press/Doubleday.

Hall, E. T. (1994) Monochronic and polychronic time. In L. A. Smovar and R. E. porter (eds) *Intercultural Communication: A Reader.* Belmont, CA: Wadsworth.

Hall, E. T. (2000) Context and Meaning. In L. A. Samovar and R. E. Porter (eds) *Intercultural Communication: A Reader.* 9th edn. Belmont, CA: Wadsworth Publishing Company.

Hall, W. S., Cross, William, E. and Freedle, R. (1972) *Stages in the Development of a Black Identity.* Research and Development Division. Iowa City: American Testing Program.

Hanna, J. L. (1984) Black/white nonverbal differences, dance and dissonance: implications for desegregation. In A.Wolfgang (ed) *Nonverbal Behavior: Perspectives, Applications, Intercultural Insights.* Lewinson, NY: C. J. Hogrefe.

Hannerz, U. (1996) *Transnational Connections: Culture, People, Places.* New York: Routledge.

Harkness, S. and Super, C. M. (1995) Culture and Parenting. In M. Bornstein (ed) *Handbook of Parenting.* Vol 2. Hillsdale, NJ: Erlbaum.

Harkness, S. and Super, C. M. (1996) *Parents' Cultural Belief Systems: Their Origins, Expressions, and Consequences.* New York: Guilford Press.

Harlow, H. F. and Harlow, M. K. (1962) Social deprivation in monkeys. *Scientific American* 207: 136–146.

Harrison, A. O., Wilson, M. N., Pine, C. J., Chan, S. Q. and Buriel, R. (1990) Family Ecologies of Ethnic-Minority Children. *Child Development,* 61: 347–362.

Harwood, R. L., Miller, J. G. and Irizarry, N. L. (1995) *Culture and Attachment: Perceptions of the Child in Context.* New York: Guilford Press.

Hecht, M. L., Ribeau, S. and Alberts, J. K. (1989) An Afro-American Perspective on Interethnic Communication. *Communication Monographs,* 56: 385–410.

Helms, J. E. (1986) Expanding racial identity theory to cover counseling process. *Journal of Counseling Psychology,* 33(1): 62–64.

Helms J. E. (1990) *Black and White Racial Identity: Theory, Research, and Practice.* New York: Greenwood Press.

Helms, J. E. (1995) An update of Helms 's white and people of color racial identity models. In A. J. Ponterotto, J. M. Casas, L. S. Suzuki and C. M. Alexander (eds) *Handbook of Multicultural Counseling.* London: Sage.

Helms, J. E. and Piper, R. E. (1994) Implications of Racial Identity Theory for Vocational Psychology. *Journal of Vocational Behavior,* 44: 124–138.

Hendry, J. (1993) Becoming Japanese: The arenas and agents of socialization. In R. H. Wozniak (ed) *Worlds of Childhood Reader.* New York: Harper Collins.

Hernstein, R. J. and Murray, C. A. (1994) *The Bell Curve: Intelligence and Class Structure in American Life.* New York: Simon & Schuster.

Hewitt, R. (1986) *White Talk Black Talk: Inter-racial Friendship and Communication amongst Adolescents.* Cambridge: Cambridge University Press.

Hill, S. A. (1999) *African American Children: Socialization and Development in Families.* Thousand Oaks, CA: Sage Publications.

Hill, M. and Aldgate, J. (1996) *Child Welfare Services: Developments in Law, Policy, Practice and Research.* London: Jessica Kingsley Publishers.

Hilliard, A. G. (1981) IQ thinking as catechism: ethnic and cultural bias or invalid science. *Black Books Bulletin,* 17: 2–7.

Hilliard, A. G. (1987) The ideology of intelligence and IQ magic in education. *The Negro Educational Review,* 38: 136–145.

Ho, Man-Keung (1976) Social work with Asian Americans. *Social Casework*, 57(3): 195–201.

Hodes, M. (2000) Psychologically distressed refugee children in the United Kingdom. *Child Psychology and Psychiatry Review*, 5: 57–68.

Hofstede, G. (1980*) Culture's Consequences: International Differences in Work-related Values*. Beverly Hills, CA: Sage.

Hofstede, G. (1984) *Culture's Consequences: International Differences in Work-related Values*. Newbury Park: Sage.

Hofstede, G. H. (2001) *Culture's Consequences: Comparing Values, Behaviors, Institutions and Organizations across Nations*. Thousand Oaks, Calif.: Sage Publications.

Holdstock, T. L. (2000) *Re-examining Psychology: Critical Perspectives and African Insights*. London: Routledge.

Holliday, B. G. (1985) Developmental imperatives of social ecologies. In H. P. McAdoo and J. L. McAdoo (eds) *Black Children: Social Educational and Parental Environments*. Beverly Hills, CA: Sage.

Hopson, D. P. and Hopson, D. S. (1991) *Different and Wonderful: Raising Black Children in a Race-conscious Society*. New York: Prentice Hall Press.

Howe, D. (1995) *Attachment Theory for Social Work Practice*. Basingstoke: Macmillan.

Howe, D. (1996) *Attachment and Loss in Child and Family Social Work*. Aldershot: Avebury.

Howe, D. (1999) *Attachment Theory, Child Maltreatment and Family Support: A Practice and Assessment Model*. Basingstoke: Macmillan.

Howe, D. and Feast, J. (2000) *The Long Term Experience of Adopted Adults*. London: The Children's Society.

Howitt, D. and Owusu-Bempah, J. (1994) *The Racism of Psychology*. Hemel Hempstead: Harvester Wheatsheaf.

Hu, P. and Meng, Z. (1996) *An Examination of Infant-Mother Attachment in China*. Poster presented at the meeting of the International Society for the Study of Behavioral Development, Quebec City, Quebec, Canada.

Hui, C. H. and Triandis, H. C. (1986) Individualism-Collectivism – a Study of Cross-Cultural Researchers. *Journal of Cross-Cultural Psychology*, 17: 225–248.

Hutnik, N. (1991) *Ethnic Minority Identity: A Social Psychological Perspective*. Oxford: Oxford University Press.

Hylton, C. (1997) *Family Survival Strategies: Moyenda Black Families Talking*. London: Joseph Rowntree Foundation.

Ince, L. (1998) *Making it Alone: A Study of the Care Experiences of Young Black People.* London: BAAF.

Inhelder, B. and Piaget, J. (1958) *The Growth of Logical Thinking from Childhood to Adolescence.* New York: Harper & Row.

Ivey, A. E. (2002) *Intentional interviewing and counseling: Facilitating client development in a multicultural society.* 5th edn. Belmont, CA: Wadsworth.

Jackson, F. A. (1993) Multiple caregiving among African Americans and infant attachment: The need for an emic approach. *Human Development,* 36: 87–102.

Jacobs, J. H. (1992) Identity development in biracial children. In M. P. Root (ed) *Racially Mixed People in America.* Newbury Park, CA: Sage.

Jahoda, G. (1986) A Cross-Cultural-Perspective on Developmental-Psychology. *International Journal of Behavioral Development,* 9: 417–437.

Jain, N. C. and Matukumalli, A. (1993) *The Functions of Silence in India: Implications for Intercultural Communication.* Research paper presented at the Second International East meets West Conference in 'Cross-cultural communication, comparative philosophy, and comparative religion'. Long Beach, CA.

Jandt, Fred, E. (2000) *Intercultural Communication: An Introduction.* London: Sage.

Jandt, F. E. (2003) *Intercultural Communication: A Global Reader.* California: Sage Publications.

Jenkins, Adelbert, H. (1982) *Psychology of the Afro-American: A Humanistic Approach.* Pergamon Press.

Jensen, A. R. (1969) *Environment, Heredity, and Intelligence.* Cambridge, Mass.: Harvard Educational Review.

Jensen, A. R. (1969) *How Much Can We Boost IQ and Scholastic Achievement?* Cambridge, Mass: Harvard Educational Review.

Jensen, A. R. (1980) *Bias in Mental Testing.* London: Methuen.

Jensen, A. R. (1981) *Straight Talk about Mental Tests.* London: Methuen.

Johnson, D. J., Jaeger,, E., Randolph, S. M., Cauce, A. M. and Ward, J. (2003) Studying the effects of early child care experiences on the development of children of colour in the United States: Towards a more inclusive research agenda. *Child Development,* 74(5), 1227–1244.

Jones, A. (2001) Child asylum seekers and refugees. *Journal of Social Work,* 1(3): 253–271.

Jones Reginald, L. (1980) *Black Psychology.* New York: Harper and Row.

Jones Reginald, L. (1991) *Black Psychology*. 2nd edn. Berkeley, Calif.: Cobb and Henry.

Kagitcibasi, C. (1996) *Family and Human Development across Cultures: A View from the Other Side*. New Jersey: Lawrence Erlbaum Associates.

Kallgren, C. A. and Caudill, P. J. (1993) Current Transracial Adoption Practices – Racial Dissonance or Racial Awareness. *Psychological Reports*, 72: 551–558.

Kalu Ogbu, U. (1982) *African Cultural Development*. Enugu, Fourth Dimension.

Kao Henry, S. R. and Sinha, D. (1997) *Asian Perspectives on Psychology*. New Delhi: Sage.

Katz, J. (1985) The socio-political nature of counseling. *The Counseling Psychologist*, 13: 615–624.

Kaufman, Alan, S. (1990) *Assessing Adolescent and Adult Intelligence*. Boston: Allyn and Bacon.

Keats, D. M. (1981) The development of values. In J. L. M. Binnie-Dawson, G. H. Blowers and R. Hoosain (eds*) Perspectives in Asian Cross-cultural Psychology*. Lisse: Swets & Zeitlinger.

Keats, D. M. (1982) Cultural bases of concepts of intelligence: A Chinese versus Australian comparison. In P. Sukontasarp, N. Yongsiri, P. Intasuwan, N. Jotiban and C. Suvannathat (eds) *Proceedings of the Second Asian Workshop on Child and Adolescent Development*. Bangkok: Burapasilpa Press.

Keats, D. M. (1997) *Culture and the Child*. New York: John Wiley & Sons.

Keefe, Susan, E. and Padilla A. M. (1987) *Chicano Ethnicity*. Albuquerque: University of New Mexico Press.

Kelly, M. (1977) Papua New Guinea and Piaget – An eight-year study. In P. R. Dasen (ed) *Piagetian Psychology: Cross-cultural Contributions*. New York: Gardner Press.

Kermoian, R. and Leiderman, P. H. (1986) Infant attachment to mother and child caretaker in an East African community. *International Journal of Behavioral Development*, 9: 455–469.

Kerwin, C. and Ponterotto, J. G. (1995) Biracial identity development: Theory and research. In J. G. Ponterotto, J. M. Casas, L. A. Suzuki and C. M. Alexander (ed) *Handbook of Multicultural Counseling*. Thousand Oaks, CA: Sage.

Kerwin, C., Ponterotto, J. G., Jackson, B. L. and Harris, A. (1993) Racial Identity in Biracial-Children – a Qualitative Investigation. *Journal of Counseling Psychology*, 40: 221–231.

Kessler, C. and Quinn, M. E. (1987) Language Minority Childrens

Linguistic and Cognitive Creativity. *Journal of Multilingual and Multicultural Development*, 8: 173–186.

Kohli, R. and Mather, R. (2003) Promoting psychosocial well-being in unaccompanied asylum seeking young people in the United Kingdom. *Child and Family Social Work*, 8(3): 201–212.

Kibria, N. (1997) The construction of 'Asian American': Reflections on intermarriage and ethnic identity among second-generation Chinese and Korean Americans. *Ethnic and Racial Studies*, 20: 523–544.

Kim, U., Triandis, H. C., Kagitcibasi, C., Choi, S. and Yoon, G. (1994) Individualism and collectivism: Theory, method and application. Thousand Oaks, CA: Sage.

King, N. G. and James, M. J. (1983) *The Relevance of Black English to Intercultural Communication.* Paper presented at the Annual Conference of the Western Speech Communication Association, Albuquerque, NM.

Kirton, D. (2000) *'Race', Ethnicity and Adoption.* Buckingham: Open University Press.

Kirton, D. and Woodger, D. (1999) Experiences of transracial adoption: assessment, preparation and support: implications from research. In BAAF (ed) *Research Symposium Papers 1998.* London: BAAF.

Kluckhohn Florence, R. and Strodtbeck Fred, L. (1961) *Variations in Value Orientations.* Evanston, Ill., Elmsford, NY: Row Peterson & Co.

Knight, G. P., Bernal, M. E., Garza, C. A., Cota, M. K. and Ocampo, K. A. (1993) Family Socialization and the Ethnic-Identity of Mexican-American Children. *Journal of Cross-Cultural Psychology*, 24: 99–114.

Kohli, R. and Mather, R. (2003) Promoting psychosocial well-being in unaccompanied asylum seeking young people in the United Kingdom. *Child & Family Social Work*, 8(3), 201–212.

Korbin, J. E. (1981) *Child Abuse and Neglect: Cross-cultural Perspectives.* Berkeley: University of California Press.

Korbin, J. E. (1987) Child abuse and neglect: the cultural context. In R. Helfer and R. S. Kempe (eds) *The Battered Child.* 4th edn. Chicago: University of Chicago Press.

Korbin, J. E. (1997) Culture and child maltreatment. In M. E. Helfer, R. S. Kempe and R. D. Krugman (eds) *The Battered Child.* 5th edn. Chicago: University of Chicago Press.

Kroger, J. (1996) *Identity in Adolescence: The Balance between Self and Other.* 2nd edn. London: Routledge.

Labov, W. (1982) *The Social Stratification of English in New York City.* Washington, DC: Center for Applied Linguistics.

Ladner, J. A. (1977) *Mixed Families*. Garden City, NY: Anchor/Doubleday.

LaFrance, M. and Mayo, C. (1978) *Moving Bodies. Nonverbal Communication in Social Relationships.* Monterey: Brooks/Cole.

LaFromboise, T., Coleman, H. L. K. and Gerton, J. (1993) Psychological Impact of Biculturalism – Evidence and Theory. *Psychological Bulletin,* 114: 395–412.

Lago, C. and Thompson, J. (1994) Counselling and Race. In W. Dryden, D. Charles-Edwards and R. Woolfe (eds) *Handbook of Counselling in Britain.* London: Routledge.

Lago, C. and Thompson, J. (1996) *Race, Culture and Counselling.* Buckingham: Open University Press.

Lamb, M. E. (1992) *Child Care in Context: Cross-cultural Perspectives.* Hillsdale, NJ: L. Erlbaum.

Lamb, M. E., Hwang, C. P., Frodi, M., Frodi, M. (1982) Security of mother– and father–infant attachment and its relation to sociability with strangers in traditional and non-traditional Swedish families. *Infant Behavior and Development,* 5: 355–367.

Lambeth (1987) *Whose Child? The Report of the Public Enquiry into the Death of Tyra Henry.* London: London Borough of Lambeth.

Lancy David, F. (1983) *Cross-cultural Studies in Cognition and Mathematics.* New York: Academic Press.

Lau, A. (1988) Family therapy and ethnic minorities. In Street, E. and Dryden, W. (eds) *Family Therapy in Britain.* Buckingham: Open University Press.

Lau, A. (2003) Family therapy and ethnic minorities. In Dwivedi, K. N. *Meeting the Needs of Ethnic Minority Children: Including Refugee, Black, and Mixed Parentage Children: A Handbook for Professionals.* London: Jessica Kingsley Publishers.

Laungani, P. (1998) *India and England: A Psycho-cultural Analysis.* Amsterdam: Harwood Academic Publishers.

Laurendeau-Bendavid, M. (1977) Culture, schooling and cognitive development: A comparative study of children in French Canada and Rwanda. In P. R. Dasen (ed) *Piagetian Psychology: Cross-cultural Contributions.* New York: Gardner Press.

Laval, R. A., Gomez, E. A. and Ruiz, P. (1983) A language minority: hispanics and mental health care. *American Journal of Social Psychiatry,* 3: 42–49.

Levin, D. (1985) *The Flight from Ambiguity.* Chicago: University of Chicago Press.

LeVine, R. A. and Miller, P. M. (1990) Special Topic – Cross-Cultural

Validity of Attachment Theory – Commentary. *Human Development*, 33: 73–80.

LeVine, R. A., Miller, P. M. and West, M. M. (1988) *Parental Behavior in Diverse Societies*. San Francisco: Jossey-Bass.

Lewontin, R. C., Kamin, L. J. and Rose, S. (1984) *Not in our Genes: Biology, Ideology, and Human Nature*. New York: Pantheon Books.

Liebkind, K. and Jasinskaja-Lahti, I. (2000) Acculturation and psychological well-being among immigrant adolescents in Finland: A comparative study of adolescents from different cultural backgrounds. *Journal of Adolescent Research*, 15: 446–469.

Lin, C. Y. C. and Fu, V. R. (1990) A Comparison of Child-Rearing Practices among Chinese, Immigrant Chinese, and Caucasian-American Parents. *Child Development*, 61: 429–433.

Littlewood, R. and Lipsedge, M. (1989) *Aliens and Alienists: Ethnic Minorities and Psychiatry*. London: Routledge.

Littlewood, R. and Lipsedge, M. (1997) *Aliens and Alienists: Ethnic Minorities and Psychiatry*. London: Routledge.

Locke, D. C. (1992) *Increasing Multicultural Understanding: A Comprehensive Model*. Newbury Park, CA: Sage Publications.

Lonner, W. J. (1994) Culture and Human Diversity. In E. Trickett, R. Watts and D. Birman (eds) *Human Diversity*. San Francisco: Jossey-Bass.

Lum, D. (2003) *Culturally Competent Practice*. Pacific Group, CA: Brooks/Cole.

Lustig, M. and Koester, J. (1993) Intercultural competence. New York: Harper-Collins.

Maccoby, E. E. (1980) *Social Development: Psychological Growth and the Parent–Child Relationship*. New York: Harcourt Brace Jovanovich.

Maccoby, E. E. (1992) The role of parents in the socialization of children: An historical overview. *Developmental Psychology*, 28: 1006–1017.

Maccoby, E. E. and Martin, J. A. (1983) Socialization in the context of the family: Parent–child interaction. In E. M. Hetherington (ed) *Handbook of Child Psychology: Vol 4. Socialization, Personality, and Social Development*. 4th edn. New York: Wiley.

MacPherson (1999) *The Stephen Lawrence Inquiry*. London: Stationery Office.

Majors, R. (2001) *Educating our Black Children: New Directions and Radical Approaches*. London: Routledge.

Malandro, L. A. and Barker, L. (1983) *Nonverbal Communication*. Reading, MA: Addison-Wesley.

Mama, A. (1995) *Beyond the Masks: Race, Gender and Subjectivity*. London: Routledge.

Manrai, L. A. and Manrai, A. K. (1996) *Global Perspectives in Cross-cultural and Cross-national Consumer Research*. New York: London, International Business Press.

Marcia, J. (1966) Development and validation of ego-identity status. *Journal of Personality and Social Psychology*, 3: 551–558.

Marcia, J. (1980) Identity in adolescence. In J. Adelson (ed) *Handbook of Adolescent Psychology*. New York: Wiley.

Marcia, J. (1993) The relational roots of identity. In Kroger, J. (ed) *Discussions on Ego Identity*. Hillsdale, NJ: Lawrence Erlbaum.

Marcia, J., Waterman, A., Matteson, D., Archer, S. and Orlofsky, J. (1993) *Ego Identity: A Handbook of Psychosocial Research*. New York: Springer-Verlag.

Mares, P., Baxter, C., Henley, A. (1985) *Health Care in Multiracial Britain*. Cambridge: Health Education Council/National Extension College.

Marshall, S. (1995) Ethnic socialization of African American children: Implications for parenting, identity development, and academic performance. *Journal of Youth and Adolescence*, 24(4): 337–396.

Martinez, R. and Dukes, R. L. (1991) Ethnic and gender differences in self-esteem. *Youth and Society*, 32: 318–338.

Martinez, R. and Dukes, R. (1997) The effects of ethnic identity, ethnicity, and gender on adolescent well-being. *Journal of Youth and Adolescence*. 26(5): 503–516.

Matsumoto, D. and Juang, L. (2004) *Culture and Psychology*. Belmont, CA: Wadsworth/Thomson.

Maximé, J. (1986) Some psychological models of black self-concept. In S. Ahmed, J. Cheetham, and J. Small (eds) *Social work with Black Children and their Families*. London: Batsford.

Maximé Jocelyn, E. (1987) *Black Like Me: Workbook One*. Beckenham: Emani.

Maximé Jocelyn, E. (1991) *Black Like Me: Workbook Two: Black Pioneers*. Beckenham: Emani.

Maximé, J. (1993) The therapeutic importance of racial identity in working with Black children who hate. In V. Varma (ed) *How and Why Children Hate*. London: Jessica Kingsley Publishers.

Mbiti, J. (1970) *African Religions and Philosophies*. New York: Anchor Press.

McAdoo, H. P. (1981) *Black Families*. Beverly Hills, CA: Sage Publications.

McAdoo, H. P. (1983) Parenting styles. Mother–child interactions and self-esteem in young black children. In C. E. Obudo (ed) *Black Marriage and Family Therapy*. Westport, CT: Greenwood.

McAdoo, H. P. (ed) (2002) *Black Children*. 2nd edn. Thousand Oaks, CA: Sage Publications.

McAdoo, H. P. (1985) Racial attitude and self-concept of young black children over time. In H. P. McAdoo and J. L. McAdoo (eds) *Black Children: Social, Educational and Parental Environments*. Beverly Hills, CA: Sage Publications.

McAdoo, H. P. and McAdoo, John, L. (1985) *Black Children: Social, Educational, and Parental Environments*. Beverly Hills: Sage Publications.

McConahay, J. B. (1983) Modern Racism and Modern Discrimination – the Effects of Race, Racial-Attitudes, and Context on Simulated Hiring Decisions. *Personality and Social Psychology Bulletin*, 9: 551–558.

McLoyd, V. C. (1991) What is the study of African American children the study of? In R. L. Jones (ed) *Black Psychology*. Hampton, VA: Cobb & Henry.

Mehrabian, A. (1981) *Silent Messages: Implicit Communication of Emotions and Attitudes*. Belmont, Calif: Wadsworth Pub. Co.

Mehra, H. (2002) Residential care for ethnic minority children. In Dwivedi, K. N. (ed) *Meeting the Needs of Ethnic Minority Children: Including Refugee, Black, and Mixed Parentage Children: A Handbook for Professionals*. London: Jessica Kingsley Publishers.

Mendelberg, H. E. (1986) Identity Conflict in Mexican-American Adolescents. *Adolescence*, 21: 215–224.

Miles, R. (1989) *Racism*. London: Routledge.

Milne, R. and Clarke, P. (1993) *Bilingual Early Childhood Education in Child Care and Preschool Centres*. Richmond, Vic.: FKA Multicultural Resource Centre.

Milner, D. (1983) *Children & Race*. Beverly Hills: Sage Publications.

Mirza, H. S. (1992) *Young, Female, and Black*. London: Routledge.

Mishra, R. C. (2001) Cognition across cultures. In D. Matsumoto (ed) *The Handbook of Culture and Psychology*. Oxford: Oxford University Press.

Miyake, K., Chen, S. J. and Campos, J. J. (1985) Infant Temperament, Mothers Mode of Interaction, and Attachment in Japan – an Interim-Report. *Monographs of the Society for Research in Child Development*, 50: 276–297.

Modgil, S. and Modgil, C. (1976) *Piagetian Research: Compilation and Commentary*. Windsor: Nfer.

Modood, T., Beishon, S., Virdee, S. (1994) *Changing Ethnic Identities*. London: Policy Studies Institute.

Modood, T, Berthoud, R., Lakey, J., Nazroo, J., Smith, P., Virdee, S. and Beishon, S. (1997) *Ethnic Minorities in Britain: Diversity and Disadvantage.* London: Policy Studies Institute.

Montemayor, R., Adams, G. R., Gullotta, T. P. (eds) (2000) *Adolescent Diversity in Ethnic, Economic and Cultural Contexts.* Thousand Oaks: Sage.

Morelli, G. A., Oppenheim, D., Rogoff, B. and Goldsmith, D. (1992) Cultural Variation in Infants Sleeping Arrangements – Questions of Independence. *Developmental Psychology,* 28: 604–613.

Morelli, G. A., Rogoff, B. and Angelillo, C. (2003) Cultural variation in young children's access to work or involvement in specialised child-focused activities. *International Journal of Behavioral Development,* 27: 264–274.

Morris, D. (1995) *Bodytalk: The Meaning of Human Gestures.* New York: Crown Trade Paperbacks.

Mussen, P. H., Conger, J. J., Kagan, J. and Huston, A. C. (1984) *Child Development and Personality.* New York: Harper & Row.

Nesdale, D., Rooney, R. and Smith, L. (1997) Migrant ethnic identity and psychological distress. *Journal of Cross-Cultural Psychology,* 28: 569–588.

Nobles Wade, W. (1976) Black people in white insanity: an issue for black community mental health. *Journal of Afro-American Issues,* 4: 21–27.

Nobles Wade, W. (1986) *African Psychology: Towards its Reclamation, Reascension & Revitalization.* Oakland, CA: Black Family Institute.

Nsamenang, A. B. (1995) Theories of Developmental Psychology for a Cultural Perspective: A View from Africa. *Psychology and Developing Societies,* 7: 1–19.

Nyiti, R. M. (1982) The validity of 'cultural differences explanations' for cross cultural variation in the rate of Piagetian cognitive development. In D. A. Wagner and H. W. Stevenson (eds*) Cultural Perspectives on Child Development.* San Francisco: Freeman.

Ogbu John, U. (1974) *The Next Generation. An Ethnography of Education in an Urban Neighborhood.* New York: Academic Press.

Ogbu, J. U. (1988) Cultural diversity and human development. In H. P. McAdoo (ed) *Black Children and Poverty: A Developmental Perspective.* San Francisco, CA: Jossey-Bass.

Ogbu, J. U. (1994) From cultural differences to differences in cultural frame of reference. In Greenfield, P. M. and Cocking, R. R. (1994) *Cross-cultural Roots of Minority Child Development.* Hillsdale, NJ: Hove, L. Erlbaum Associates.

O'Hagan, K. (1999) Culture, cultural identity, and cultural sensitivity in child and family social work. *Child and Family Social Work*, 4: 269–281.

O'Hagan, K. (2001) *Cultural Competence in the Caring Professions.* London: Jessica Kingsley Publishers.

Okabe, R. (1983) Cultural assumptions of East and West: Japan and the United States. In W. Gudy Kunst (ed) *Intercultural Theory: Current Communication Perspectives.* Beverly Hills, CA: Sage.

Okitikpi, T. (1999) Educational needs of black children in care. In Barn, R. (ed) *Working with Black Children and Adolescents in Need.* London: British Agencies for Adoption and Fostering.

Oliver, R. T. (1971) *Communication and Culture in Ancient India and China.* Syracuse, NY: Syracuse University Press.

Olwig, K. F. and Hastrup, K. (1997) *Siting Culture: The Shifting Anthropological Object.* New York: Routledge.

O'Neale, V. (2000) *Excellence not Excuses: Inspection of Services for Ethnic Minority Children and Families.* London: Social Services Inspectorate.

O'Neale, V., Lloyd, J (2000) *Inspection of Child Protection and Planning and Decision Making for Looked after Children: London Borough of Barking and Dagenham.* London: London Inspection Group SSI.

Osler, A. H. (1998) Exclusion and Racial Equality: Implications for Policy Makers. In N. Donovan (ed) *Second Chances: Exclusion from School and Equality of Opportunity.* London: New Policy Institute.

Ou, Y. S. and McAdoo, H. P. (1993) Socialization of Chinese American children. In H. P. McAdoo (ed) *Ethnicity: Strength in Diversity.* Newbury Park, CA: Sage.

Owusu-Bempah, J., Howitt, D. (2000) *Psychology beyond Western Perspectives.* Leicester: BPS Books.

Owusu-Bempah, K. (2002) Culture, ethnicity and identity. In Davies, M. (ed) *The Blackwell Companion to Social Work.* 2nd edn. Oxford: Blackwell.

Palmer, S. and Laungani, P. (1999) *Counselling in a Multicultural Society.* London: Sage.

Paniagua, F. A. (1994) *Assessing and Treating Culturally Diverse Clients: A Practical Guide.* Thousand Oaks, Calif.: Sage Publications.

Parekh, B. (ed) (2000) *The Future of Multiethnic Britain.* London: Profile Books.

Parham, T. A. (1989) Cycles of psychological nigrescence. *The Counseling Psychologist,* 17(2): 187–226.

Parham, T. A. and Helms, J. E. (1981) The influence of black students' racial identity attitudes on preference for counselor's race. *Journal of Counseling Psychology.* 28: 250–257.

Parham, T. A. and Helms, J. E. (1985a) Attitudes of Racial Identity and Self-Esteem of Black-Students – an Exploratory Investigation. *Journal of College Student Development,* 26: 143–147.

Parham, T. A. and Helms, J. E. (1985b) Relation of Racial Identity Attitudes to Self-Actualization and Affective States of Black-Students. *Journal of Counseling Psychology,* 32: 431–440.

Parham, T. A. and Williams, P. T. (1993) The relationship of demographic and background factors to racial identity attitudes. *Journal of Black Psychology,* 19(1): 7–24.

Parham, T. A., White, J. L. and Ajamu, A. (1999) *The Psychology of Blacks: An African-Centered Perspective.* NJ: Prentice Hall.

Parkes, C. M. and Stevenson-Hinde, J. (1982) *The Place of Attachment in Human Behavior.* London: Tavistock Publications.

Parkes, L. P., Schneider, S. K. and Bochner, S. (1999) Individualism-Collectivism and self-concept. *Asian Journal of Social Psychology,* 2(3), 367–390.

Patel, K. (1996) *Cultural Heritage of Gujarat.* Vadodara: Good Companions.

Pedersen, P. B. (1988*) A Handbook for Developing Multicultural Awareness.* Alexandria, VA: American Counseling Association.

Penketh, L. (2000) *Tackling Institutional Racism: Anti-racist Policies and Social Work Education and Training.* Bristol: Policy Press.

Peters, M. F. (1985) Racial socialization of young black children. In Harriette, P. McAdoo and John McAdoo (eds) *Black Children: Social, Educational, and Parental Environments,* Beverly Hills: Sage Publications.

Phinney, J. (1989) Stages of ethnic identity development in minority group adolescents. *Journal of Early Adolescence,* 9: 34–49.

Phinney, J. (1990) Ethnic identity in adolescents and adults: Review of research. *Psychological Bulletin,* 108: 499–514.

Phinney, J. S. (1992) The multigroup ethnic identity measure: a new scale for use with diverse groups. *Journal of Adolescence,* 7(2): 156–76.

Phinney, J. S. (1993) Three stage model of ethnic identity development. In M. E. Bernal and G. Knight (eds) *Ethnic Identity: Formation and Transmission among Hispanics and other Minorities.* Albany: State University of New York Press.

Phinney J. S. and Rotheram M. J. (1987) *Children's Ethnic Socialization: Pluralism and Development.* Beverly Hills: Sage Publications.

Phinney, J. J. and Chavira, V. (1993) Ethnic-Identity and Self-Esteem – an Explanatory Longitudinal-Study. *Journal of Adolescence,* 16: 118–118.

Phinney, J., Cantu, C. and Kurtz, D. (1997) Ethnic and American identity as predictors of self-esteem among African American, Latino and White adolescents. *Journal of Youth and Adolescence*, 26: 165–185.

Phinney, J. S. (1996) When we talk about American ethnic groups, what do we mean? *American Psychologist*, 51: 918–927.

Phinney, L. 91999) An intercultural approach in psychology: cultural contact and identity. *Cross-Cultural Psychology Bulletin*, 33: 24–31.

Phinney, J. S. (2000) Identity formation across cultures: The interaction of personal, societal, and historical change. *Human Development*, 43: 27–31.

Phinney, J. S., Baumann, K. and Blanton, S. (2001) Life goals and attributions for expected outcomes among adolescents from five ethnic groups. *Hispanic Journal of Behavioral Sciences*, 23: 363–377.

Phinney, J. S. and Alipuria, L. L. (1990) Ethnic identity in college students from four ethnic groups. *Journal of Adolescence*, 13: 171–183.

Phinney, J. S. and Chavira, V. (1992) Ethnic-Identity and Self-Esteem – an Exploratory Longitudinal-Study. *Journal of Adolescence*, 15: 271–281.

Phinney, J. S. and Chavira, V. (1995) Parental Ethnic Socialization and Adolescent Coping with Problems Related to Ethnicity. *Journal of Research on Adolescence*, 5: 31–53.

Phinney, J. S. and Devich-Navarro, M. (1997) Variations in bicultural identification among African American and Mexican American adolescents. *Journal of Research on Adolescence*, 7: 3–32.

Phinney, J. S. and Flores, J. (2002) 'Unpackaging' acculturation – Aspects of acculturation as predictors of traditional sex role attitudes. *Journal of Cross-Cultural Psychology*, 33: 320–331.

Phinney, J. S., Horenczyk, G., Liebkind, K. and Vedder, P. (2001) Ethnic identity, immigration, and well-being: An interactional perspective. *Journal of Social Issues*, 57: 493–510.

Phinney, J. S., Madden, T. and Santos, L. J. (1998) Psychological variables as predictors of perceived ethnic discrimination among minority and immigrant adolescents. *Journal of Applied Social Psychology*, 28: 937–953.

Phinney, J. S., Ong, A. and Madden, T. (2000) Cultural values and intergenerational value discrepancies in immigrant and non-immigrant families. *Child Development*, 71: 528–539.

Phinney, J. S. and Kohatsu, E. L. (1997) Ethnic and racial identity development and mental health. In J. Schulenberg, Maggs and K.

Hurrelman (eds) *Health Risks and Developmental Transitions in Adolescence.* New York: Cambridge University Press.

Phinney, J. S. and Rotheram, M. J. (1987) *Children's Ethnic Socialization: Pluralism and Development.* Newbury Park: Sage.

Phoenix, A. (1999) Sensitive to 'race' and ethnicity. In D. Messer and F. Jones (eds) *Psychology and Social Care.* London: Jessica Kingsley Publishers.

Phung, T. (1995) An experience of inter-cultural counseling: views from a black client. *Counselling,* February: 61–2.

Piaget, J. (1952a) *The Origins of Intelligence in Children.* New York: International Universities Press.

Piaget, J. (1952b) *Play, Dreams and Imitation in Childhood.* New York: Norton.

Piaget, J. (1972) Intellectual evolution from adolescence to adulthood. *Human Development,* 15: 1–12.

Piaget, J. and Inhelder, B. (1969) *The Psychology of the Child.* New York: Basic Books.

Piaget, J., Inhelder, B. and Pomerans, A. J. (1974) *The Child's Construction of Quantities: Conservation and Atomism.* London: Routledge.

Pinderhughes, D. M. (1987) *Race and Ethnicity in Chicago Politics: A Reexamination of Pluralist Theory.* Urbana: University of Illinois Press.

Pinderhughes, E. (1989) *Understanding Race, Ethnicity and Power: The Key to Efficacy in Clinical Practice.* New York: Free Press.

Pinderhughes, E. (1995) Biracial identity: Asset or handicap? In H. Harris, H.Blue and E. Griffith (eds) *Racial and Ethnic Identity.* London: Routledge.

Polite, Craig, K. and Edwards, A. (1992) *Children of the Dream: The Psychology of Black Success.* New York: Doubleday.

Ponterotto, J. G. (1989) Expanding Directions for Racial Identity Research. *Counseling Psychologist,* 17: 264–272.

Ponterotto, J. G. (1991) The Nature of Prejudice Revisited – Implications for Counseling Intervention. *Journal of Counseling and Development,* 70: 216–224.

Ponterotto, J. G. (1993) White Racial Identity and the Counseling Professional. *Counseling Psychologist,* 21: 213–217.

Ponterotto, J. G. and Casas, J. M. (1991) *Handbook of Racial/Ethnic Minority Counseling Research.* Springfield, IL: Charles C. Thomas.

Poortinga, Y. (1997) Towards convergence? In J. W. Berry, Y. H. Poortinga, and J. Pandey (eds) *Handbook of Cross-Cultural Psychology.* Boston: Allyn & Bacon.

Porter, J. R. and Washington, R. E. (1993) Minority Identity and Self-Esteem. *Annual Review of Sociology*, 19: 139–161.

Porterfield, E. (1978) *Black and White Marriages: An Ethnographic Study of Black-White Families*. Chicago: Nelson-Hall.

Posada, G., Gao, Y., Wu, F., Posado, R., Tascon, M., Schoelmerich, A., Sagi, A., Kondo-Ikemura, K., Haaland, W. and Synnevaag, B. (1995) The secure-base phenomenon across cultures. Children's behavior, mothers' preferences and experts' concepts. In E. Waters, B. E. Vaughn, G. Posada and K. Kondo-Ikemura (eds) *Caregiving, Cultural, and Cognitive Perspectives on Secure-base Behavior and Working Models: New Growing Points of Attachment Theory and Research*. Monographs of the Society for Research in Child Development, 60 (2–3, Serial No. 244), 27–48.

Poston, W. S. C. (1990) The biracial identity development model: A needed addition. *Journal of Counseling and Development*, 69: 152–55.

Powell-Hopson (1985) *The Effects of Modeling, Reinforcement, and Color Meaning Word Associations on Doll Color Preferences of Black Preschool Children and White Preschool Children*. Unpublished doctoral dissertation, Hofstra University.

Prevatt-Goldstein, B. and Spencer, M. (2000) *'Race' and Ethnicity*. London: British Agencies for Adoption and Fostering.

Price-Williams, D. R., Gordon, W., and Ramirez, M. (1969) Skills and conservation: A study of pottery-making children. *Developmental Psychology*, 1: 769.

Pyant, C. T. and Yanico, B. J. (1991) Relationship of Racial Identity and Gender-Role Attitudes to Black Women's Psychological Well-Being. *Journal of Counseling Psychology*, 38: 315–322.

Rack, P. (1982) *Race, Culture, and Mental Disorder*. London: Tavistock Publications.

Rashid, S. (1996) Attachment reviewed through a cultural lens. In D. Howe (ed) *Attachment and Loss in Child and Family Social Work*. Avebury: Ashgate.

Redfield, R., Linton, R. and Herskovits, M. (1936) Memorandum on the study of acculturation. *American Anthropologist*, 38: 149–152.

Retschitzki, J. (1989) Evidence of formal thinking in Baule airele players. In D. M. Keats, D. Munro and L. Mann (eds) *Heterogeneity in Cross-cultural Psychology*. Amsterdam: Swets & Zeitlinger.

Reynolds, T. (1998) *Afro-Caribbean mothering: Reconstructing a new identity*. South Bank University, Unpublished PhD thesis.

Reynolds, T. (2001) *Parenting, motherhood and paid work: Rationalities and ambivalences*. London: ESRC Seminar Series.

Richards, A. and Ince, L. (2000) *Overcoming the Obstacles: Looked after Children: Quality Services for Black and Minority Ethnic Children and their Families.* London: The Family Rights Group.

Ridley, C. R. (1995) *Overcoming Unintentional Racism in Counseling and Therapy: A Practitioner's Guide to Intentional Intervention.* Thousand Oaks, Calif.; London, Sage Publications.

Robinson, L. (1995) *Psychology for Social Workers: Black Perspectives.* London: Routledge.

Robinson, L. (1998) *'Race', Communication, and the Caring Professions.* Buckingham: Open University Press.

Robinson, L. (2000) Racial identity attitudes and self-esteem of black adolescents in residential care: An exploratory study. *British Journal of Social Work,* 30: 3–24.

Robinson, L. (2001) A conceptual framework for social work practice with black children and adolescents in the United Kingdom. *Journal of Social Work,* 1(2): 165:185.

Robinson, L. (2003) The Adaptation of Asian and African Caribbean Second Generation Youth in Britain. Paper presented at the International Conference on Diversity in Organisations, Communities and Nations in Hawaii, 13–16 February.

Robinson, L. (2006) Acculturation in the United Kingdom. In D. L. Sam and J. W. Berry (eds) *The Cambridge Handbook of Acculturation Psychology.* Cambridge: Cambridge University Press.

Rodriguez, R. F. and Lopez, L. C. (2003) Mexican-American parental involvement with a Texas elementary school. *Psychology Reports,* 92(3, Part 1), 791–792.

Rogoff, B. (1990) *Apprenticeship in Thinking: Cognitive Development in Social Context.* Oxford: Oxford University Press.

Rogoff, B. and Chavajay, P. (1995) Whats Become of Research on the Cultural Basis of Cognitive-Development. *American Psychologist,* 50: 859–877.

Rogoff, B. and Morelli, G. (1989) Perspectives on children's development from cultural psychology. *American Psychologist,* 44: 343–348.

Rogoff, B. and Tudge, J. (1989) Culture and the Development of Childrens Action – a Cultural-Historical Theory of Developmental-Psychology. *Contemporary Psychology,* 34: 573–574.

Rohner, R. P. and Pettengill, S. M. (1985) Perceived Parental Acceptance–Rejection and Parental Control among Korean Adolescents. *Child Development,* 56: 524–528.

Root, M. P. (ed) (1992) *Racially Mixed People in America.* Newbury Park, CA: Sage.

Root, M.P. (ed) 1996) *The Multiracial Experience: Racial Dorders as the New Frontier.* Thousand Oaks, CA: Sage.

Rosenberg, M. (1979) *Conceiving the Self.* New York: Basic Books.

Rotheram, M. J. and Phinney, J. S. (1990) Patterns of Social Expectations among Black and Mexican-American Children. *Child Development,* 61: 542–556.

Rowe, J., Hundleby, M. and Garnett, L. (1989) *Child Care Now: A Survey of Placement Patterns.* London: BAAF.

Ruiz, R. A. (1981) Cultural and historical perspectives in counseling Hispanics. In D. W. Sue (ed) *Counseling the Culturally Different: Theory and Practice.* New York: Wiley.

Rushton, J. P. (1995) *Race, evolution and behavior: A life-history perspective.* New Brunswick, NJ: Transaction.

Rushton, A. and Minnis, H. (2000) Transracial placements. A commentary on a new adult outcome study. *Adoption and Fostering,* 24 (1): 53–58.

Sagi, A. (1990) Attachment Theory and Research from a Cross-Cultural Perspective. *Human Development,* 33: 10–22.

Sagi, A., Lamb, M. E., Lewkowicz, K. S., Shoham, R., Dvir, R. and Estes, D. (1985A) Security of Infant–Mother, Infant–Father, and Infant–Metapelet Attachments among Kibbutz-Reared Israeli Children. *Monographs of the Society for Research in Child Development,* 50: 257–275.

Sagi, A., Lamb, M. E., Shoham, R., Dvir, R. and Lewkowicz, K. S. (1985B) Parent–Infant Interaction in Families on Israeli Kibbutzim. *International Journal of Behavioral Development,* 8: 273–284.

Samovar, L. A. and Porter, R. E. (2002) *Communication between Cultures.* Belmont, CA: Wadsworth/Thomson Learning.

Samovar, L. A., Porter, R. E. and Jain, N. C. (1981) *Understanding Intercultural Communication,* 2nd edn. Belmont, CA: Wadsworth.

Sanders-Thompson, V. L. (1994) Socialization to race and its relationship to racial identification among African Americans. *Journal of Black Psychology,* 20(2): 175–188.

Scarr, S. and Weinberg, R. (1983) IQ test performance of black children adopted by white families. In S. Scarr (ed) *Race, Social Class and Individual Differences in IQ.* London: Lawrence Erlbaum.

Sears, D. (1988) Symbolic racism. In P. A. Katz and D. A. Taylor (eds) *Eliminating Racism: Profiles in Controversy.* New York: Plenum Publishers.

Sebring, D. L. (1985) 'Considerations in counseling interracial children', *Journal of Non-White Concerns in Personnel and Guidance,* 13: 3–9.

Segal, U. A. (1991) Cultural Variables in Asian Indian families. *The Journal of Contemporary Human Services*, 11: 233–41.

Segal, U. A. (1999) Children are abused in eastern countries. *International Social Work*, 42(1): 39–52.

Segall, M. H. (1999) *Human Behavior in Global Perspective: An Introduction to Cross-cultural Psychology*. Boston, Mass.: Allyn and Bacon.

Segall, M. H., Dasen, P. R., Berry John, W. and Poortinga Ype, H. (1990) *Human Behavior in Global Perspective: An Introduction to Cross-cultural Psychology*. Boston [Mass.]: London, Allyn and Bacon.

Segall, M. H., Lonner, W. J. and Berry, J. W. (1998) Cross-Cultural Psychology as a Scholarly Discipline: On the Flowering of Culture in Behavioral Research. *American Psychologist*, 53(10): 1101–10.

Serpell, R. (1974) Aspects of intelligence in a developing country. *Afr. Soc. Res.* 17: 578–596.

Servaes, J. (1988) Cultural identity in East and West. *The Howard Journal of Communications*, 1: 58–71.

Shackford, K. (1984) Interracial children: Growing up healthy in an unhealthy society. *Interracial Books for Children*, 15(6), 4–6.

Shade, B. J. (1991) Africa American Patterns of Cognition. In R. L. Jones (ed) *Black Psychology*. Hampton, VA: Cobb & Henry.

Shaw, A. (1988) *A Pakistani Community in Britain*. London: Blackwell.

Shaw, A. (2000) *Kinship and Continuity: Pakistani Families in Britain*. Amsterdam: Harwood Academic.

Shea, J. D. (1985) Studies of cognitive development in Papua New Guinea. *International Journal of Psychology*, 20: 33–61.

Shorter-Gooden, K. and Washington, N. C. (1996) Young, black and female: the challenge of weaving an identity. *Journal of Adolescence*, 19: 465–475.

Shweder, R. A. and Bourne, E. J. (1982) Does the concept of person vary cross-culturally? In A. J. Marsella and G. M. White (eds) *Cultural Conceptions of Mental Health and Therapy*. Boston: Reidel.

Simpson, G. E. and Yinger, J. M. (1985) *Racial and Cultural Minorities: An Analysis of Prejudice and Discrimination*. New York: Plenum Press.

Sinclair, R. and Hai, N. (2002) *Children of Mixed Heritage in Need in Islington*. London: National Children's Bureau.

Singer, E. (1998) Shared care for children. In M. Woodhead, D. Faulkner and K. Littleton (ed) *Cultural Worlds of Early Childhood*. London: Routledge.

Siraj-Blatchford, I. (1994) *The Early Years: Laying the Foundations for Racial Equality*. Stoke-on-Trent: Trentham Books.

Skellington, R., Morris, P. (1992) *'Race' in Britain Today.* London: Open University.

Skutnabb-Kangas, T. (1981) *Bilingualism or Not: The Education of Minorities.* Clevedon: Multilingual Matters.

Slaughter D. T. (1988) *Black Children and Poverty: A Developmental Perspective.* San Francisco: Jossey-Bass.

Small, J. (1986) Transracial placements: conflicts and contradictions. In S. Ahmed, J. Cheetham, and J. Small (eds) *Social Work with Blackchildren and their Families.* London: Batsford.

Smedley, A. (1993) *Race in North America: Origin and Evolution of a Worldview.* Boulder: Westview Press.

Smith, E. P. (1966, March) *Racial-ethnic Socialization: Family, School, and Community Influences.* Paper presented at the biennial meeting of the Society for Research in Adolescence, Boston, MA.

Smitherman, G. (1977) *Talkin and Testifyin: The Language of Black America.* Boston: Houghton Mifflin.

Smitherman-Donaldson, G. (1985) *Talkin and Testifyin: The Language of Black America.* Detroit: Wayne State University Press.

Sodowsky, G. R., Kwan, K. and Pannu, R. (1995) Ethnic identity of Asians in the United States: Conceptualization and illuustrations. In J. G. Ponterotto, J. M. Casas, L. A. Suzuki and C. M. Alexander (eds) *Handbook of Multicultural Counseling.* Thousand Oaks, CA: Sage.

Spearman, C. (1927) *The Abilities of Man: Their Nature and Measurement.* New York: Macmillan.

Spearman, C. E. (1927) *The Nature of 'Intelligence' and the Principles of Cognition.* New York: Macmillan.

Spencer, M. B. (1983) Children's cultural values and parental child rearing strategies. *Developmental Review,* 3(4): 351–370.

Spencer Margaret, B. (1984) Black children's race awareness, racial attitudes and self-concept: a reinterpretation. *Journal of Child Psychology and Psychiatry,* 25: 433–441.

Spencer, Margaret, B. (1988) Self concept development. In *Black Children and Poverty: A Developmental Perspective.* San Francisco: Jossey-Bass.

Spencer, Margaret, B., Brookins Geraldine, K. and Allen Walter, R. (1985) *Beginnings: the Social and Affective Development of Black Children.* Hillsdale, NJ: L. Erlbaum.

Spencer, M. B. (1982) Personal and Group Identity of Black-Children – an Alternative Synthesis. *Genetic Psychology Monographs,* 106: 59–84.

Spencer, M. B. and Dornbusch, S. (1990) Challenges in studying minority youth. In S, Feldman and G. Elliott(eds) *At the Threshold: The Developing Adolescent.* London: Harvard University Press.

Spencer, M. B. and Markstrom Adams, C. (1990) Identity processes among racial and ethnic minority children in America. *Child Development,* 61: 290–310.

Steinberg, L. D., Belsky, J. and Meyer, R. B. (1991) *Infancy, Childhood & Adolescence: Development in Context.* New York; McGraw-Hill.

Stephan, C. W. (1992) Mixed heritage individuals: Ethnic identity and trait characteristics. In M. P. Root (ed) *Racially Mixed People in America.* Newbury Park, CA: Sage.

Sternberg, R. J. (1985) *Beyond IQ: A Triarchic Theory of Human Intelligence.* Cambridge: Cambridge University Press.

Stevenson, H. C. (1994) Racial socialization in African American families: the art of balancing intolerance and survival. *The Family Journal: Counseling and Therapy for Couples and Families,* 2(3): 190–198.

Stevenson, H. C. (1995) Relationship of adolescent perceptions of racial socialization to racial identity. *Journal of Black Psychology,* 21(1): 49–70.

Stevenson, H. C. (1998) Theoretical considerations in measuring racial identity and socialization: Extending the self further. In R. L. Jones (ed) *African American Identity Development.* Hampton, VA: Cobb & Henry.

Stewart, W. A. (1970) Toward a history of American Negro dialect. In F. Williams (ed) *Language and Poverty; Perspectives on a Theme.* Chicago: Markham Pub. Co.

Stonequist, Everett, V. (1937) *The Marginal Man. A Study in Personality and Culture Conflict.* New York: Charles Scribner's Sons.

Stopes-Roe, M. and Cochrane, R. (1990) *Citizens of this Country: The Asian-British.* Clevedon: Multilingual Matters.

Straus, M. A. and Donnelly, D. A. (2001) *Beating the Devil Out of Them: Corporal Punishment in American Families and its Effects on Children.* 2nd edn. New York: Lexington Books.

Street, E. and Dryden, W. (1988) *Family Therapy in Britain.* Buckingham: Open University Press.

Sue, D. W., Arredondo, P. and McDavis, R. J. (1992) Multicultural Counseling Competencies and Standards – a call to the profession. *Journal of Multicultural Counselling and Development,* 20: 64–88.

Sue, D. W. and Sue, D. (1990) *Counseling the culturally different: theory and practice.* 2nd edn. New York: Wiley & Sons.

Sue, D. W. and Sue, D. (1999) *Counseling the Culturally Different: Theory and Practice.* New York: Wiley & Sons.

Sue, D. W. and Sue, D. (2003) *Counseling the culturally different: theory and practice.* 4th edn. New York: Wiley & Sons.

Super, C. M. and Harkness, S. (1986) The developmental niche: A conceptualization of the interface of child and culture. *International Journal of Behavioural Development*, 9: 545–570.

Super, C. M. and Harkness, S. (1994) The developmental niche. In W. J. Lonner and R. Malpass (eds) *Psychology and Culture*. Needham Heights, MA: Allyn & Bacon.

Super, C. M. and Harkness, S. (1997) The cultural structuring of child development. In J. W. Berry, P. R. Dasen and T. S. Saraswathi (eds) *Handbook of Cross-cultural Psychology* (Vol. 2). Boston: Allyn & Bacon.

Szapocznik, J., Scopetta, M. A., Kurtines, W. and Aranalde, M. A. (1978) *Theory and Measurement of Acculturation*. 12, 113–130.

Tajfel, H. (1978) *Differentiation between Social Groups*. London: Academic Press.

Tajfel, H. (1981) *Human Groups and Social Categories: Studies in Social Psychology*. Cambridge: Cambridge University Press.

Taub, D. J. and McEwen, M. K. (1992) The Relationship of Racial Identity Attitudes to Autonomy and Mature Interpersonal Relationships in Black-and-White Undergraduate Women. *Journal of College Student Development*, 33: 439–446.

Thoburn, J., Norford, L. and Rashid, S. P. (2000) *Permanent Family Placement for Children of Minority Ethnic Origin*. London: Jessica Kingsley Publishers.

Thoburn, J., Chand, A. and Procter, J. (2005) *Child Welfare Services for Minority Ethnic Families*. London: Jessica Kingsley Publishers.

Thomas Charles, W. (1971) *Boys no More: A Black Psychologist's View of Community*. Beverly Hills, Cal: Glencoe Press.

Thomas, L. (1998) Psychotherapy in the context of race and culture: an intercultural therapeutic approach. In Fernando, S. (ed) *Mental Health in a Multi-ethnic Society: A Multi-disciplinary Handbook*. London: Routledge.

Thompson, C. L. (1996) *Race, Culture and Counselling*. Buckingham: Open University Press.

Thompson, N. (1993) *Anti-discriminatory Practice*. Basingstoke: Macmillan.

Thompson, N. (1997) *Anti-discriminatory Practice*. 2nd edn. Basingstoke: Macmillan.

Thompson, N. (2001) *Anti-discriminatory Practice*. 3rd edn. Basingstoke: Macmillan.

Thompson, C. P., Anderson, L. P. and Bakeman, R. A. (2000) Effects of racial socialization and racial identity on acculturative stress in

African American college students. *Cultural Diversity and Ethnic Minority Psychology*, 6(2): 196–210.

Thornton, M. C., Chatters, L. M., Taylor, R. J. and Allen, W. R. (1990) Sociodemographic and Environmental Correlates of Racial Socialization by Black Parents. *Child Development*, 61: 401–409.

Thurstone, L. L. (1938) *Primary Mental Abilities*. Chicago: University of Chicago Press.

Ting-Toomey, S. (1981) Ethnic identity and close friendship in Chinese American college students. *International Journal of Intercultural Relations*, 5: 383–406.

Ting-Toomey, S. (1996) Managing intercultural conflicts effectively. In L. A. Samovar and R. E.Porter (eds) *Intercultural Communication: A Reader*. 8th edn. Belmont, CA: Wadsworth.

Tizard, B. and Phoenix, A. (1989) Black identity and transracial adoption. *New Community*, 15(3): 427–38.

Tizard, B. and Phoenix, A. (1993) *Black, White or Mixed Race: Race and Racism in the Lives of Young People of Mixed Parentage*. London: Routledge.

Tizard, B. and Phoenix, A. (2003) *Black, White or Mixed Race: Race and Racism in the Lives of Young People of Mixed Parentage*, 2nd edn. London: Routledge.

Tomlinson, S. (1984) *Home and School in Multicultural Britain*. London: Batsford Academic and Educational.

Triandis, H. C. (1981) Cultural Influences in Social-Behavior. *Revista Interamericana De Psicologia*, 15: 1–28.

Triandis, H. C. (1982) Cultures Consequences – International Differences in Work-Related Values. *Human Organization*, 41: 86–90.

Triandis, H. C. (1983) Some Dimensions of Intercultural Variation and Their Implications for Community Psychology. *Journal of Community Psychology*, 11: 285–302.

Triandis, H. C. (1989) The Self and Social-Behavior in Differing Cultural Contexts. *Psychological Review*, 96: 506–520.

Triandis, H. C. (1990) Toward Cross-Cultural Studies of Individualism and Collectivism in Latin-America. *Revista Interamericana De Psicologia*, 24: 199–210.

Triandis, H. C. (1994) *Culture and Social Behavior*. New York: London, McGraw-Hill.

Triandis, H. C. (1995) *Individualism and Collectivism*. Boulder: Westview Press.

Triandis, H. C. (1997) Where is culture in the acculturation model?

Applied Psychology – an International Review – Psychologie Appliquee-Revue Internationale, 46: 55–58.

Triandis, H. C. (2001) Individualism and collectivism: Past, present and future. In Matsumoto, D. (ed) *The Handbook of Culture and Psychology.* Oxford: Oxford University Press.

Tronick, E. Z., Winn, S. and Morelli, G. A. (1985) Multiple caretaking in the context of human evolution: Why don't the Efe know the Western prescription for child care? In M. Reite and T. Field (eds) *The Psychobiology of Attachment and Separation.* London: Sage.

Tronick, E. Z., Morelli, G. A. and Ivey, P. K. (1992) The Efe Forager Infant and Toddlers Pattern of Social Relationships – Multiple and Simultaneous. *Developmental Psychology,* 28: 568–577.

True, M. M., Pisani, L. and Oumar, F. (2001) Infant–mother attachment among the Dogon of Mali. *Child Development,* 72: 1451–1466.

Turner, J. C. and Social Science Research, C. (1981) *Social Identification and Intergroup Behaviour.* London: Social Science Research Council.

Tuckwell, G. (2002) *Racial Identity, White Counsellors and Therapists.* Buckingham: OUP.

Uba, L. (1994) *Asian Americans: Personality Patterns, Identity and Mental Health.* New York: Guilford Press.

Valsiner, J. (2000) *Culture and Human Development: An Introduction.* Thousand Oaks, CA: Sage Publications.

Van Ijzendoorn, M. H. (1990) Developments in Cross-Cultural Research on Attachment – Some Methodological Notes. *Human Development,* 33: 3–9.

Van Ijzendoorn, M. H. and Kroonenberg, P. M. (1988) Cross-Cultural Patterns of Attachment – a Meta-Analysis of the Strange Situation. *Child Development,* 59: 147–156.

Van Ijzendoorn, M. H. and Sagi, A. (1999) Cross cultural patterns of attachment: Universal and contextual dimensions. In J. Cassidy and P. R. Shaver (eds) *Handbook of Attachment; Theory, Research, and Clinical Applications.* New York: Guilford Press.

Van Ijzendoorn, M. H. and Kroonenberg, P. M. (1990) Cross-Cultural Consistency of Coding the Strange Situation. *Infant Behavior & Development,* 13: 469–485.

Verma, M. K., Corrigan, K. P., Firth, S. and Multilingual Matters, L. (1995) *Working with Bilingual Children: Good Practice in the Primary Classroom.* Clevedon: Multilingual Matters Ltd.

Vernon, P. E. (1969) *Intelligence and cultural environment.* London: Methuen.

Vontress, C. (1981) Racial and ethnic barriers in counseling, in P. Pedersen, J. G. Draguns, W. J. Lonner and J. E. Trimble (eds) *Counseling across Cultures.* Honolulu: University of Hawaii Press.

Vroegh, K. S. (1997) Transracial adoptees: Developmental status after 17 years. *American Journal of Orthopsychiatry,* 67: 568–575.

Vygotsky, L. S.(1978) *Mind in Society: the Development of Higher Psychological Processes.* Cambridge, Mass: Harvard University Press.

Wagner, N. N., Sue, S. and Endo, R. (1980) *Asian-Americans: Social and Psychological Perspectives, Vol. 2.* Ben Lomond, Calif.: Science and Behavior Books.

Wang, C. H. C. and Phinney, J. S. (1998) Differences in child rearing attitudes between immigrant Chinese mothers and Anglo-American mothers. *Early Development & Parenting,* 7: 181–189.

Ward, C. (1996) Acculturation. In D. Landis and R. Bhagat (eds) *Handbook of Intercultural Training.* 2nd ed. Thousand Oaks: Sage.

Ward, C. (2001) The A, B, Cs of Acculturation. In D. Matsumoto (ed) *The Handbook of Culture and Psychology.* Oxford: Oxford University Press.

Waterman, A. S. (1985) *Identity in Adolescence: Processes and Contents.* San Francisco: Jossey-Bass.

Weisner, T. S. and Gallimore, R. (1977) My brother's keeper: Child and sibling caretaking. *Current Anthropology,* 18 (2): 169–190.

Werbner, P. and Modood, T. (1997) *Debating Cultural Hybridity: Multicultural Identities and the Politics of Anti-racism.* London, Atlantic Highlands, NJ, USA: Zed Books.

Werner, E. E. (1979) *Cross-cultural Child Development.* Belmont, CA: Wadsworth.

Wheeler, L. and Reiss, H. (1988) On titles, citations and outlets. What do Mainstreamers Want? In M. Bond (ed) *The Cross-Cutural Challenge to Social Psychology.* London: Sage.

Wheeler, M. (1988) Influences on the Placement of Children in Care and a Social Workers Response. *Child Welfare,* 67(1): 25–37.

White, J. L. (1980) Toward a black psychology. In *Black Psychology,* Jones Reginald, L. (ed) New York: Harper and Row.

White, J. L. and Parham, T. A. (1990) *The Psychology of Blacks: An African-American Perspective.* Englewood Cliffs, NJ: Prentice Hall.

Whiting, B. B. and Whiting, J. W. M. (1975) *Children of Six Cultures: A Psycho-cultural Analysis.* Cambridge, MA: Harvard University Press.

Wiemann John, M., Coupland, N. and Giles, H. (1991) *'Miscommunication' and Problematic Talk.* Newbury Park, Calif.: London, Sage.

Williams, R. L. And Mitchell, H. (1981) The testing game. In R. Jones (ed) *Black Psychology*, 2nd edition. New York: Harper & Row.

Williams, RL. And Mitchell, H. (1991) The testing game. In R.Jones (ed) *Black Psychology*, 3nd edition. New York: Harper & Row.

Wilson, A. (1987) *Mixed Race Children: A Study of Identity*. London: Allen Unwin.

Wilson, A. N. (1978) *The Developmental Psychology of the Black Child*. New York: Africana Research Pubs.

Wober, M. (1975) *Psychology in Africa*. London: International African Institute.

Wolf, A. W., Lozoff, B., Latz, S. and Pauladetto, R. (1996) Parental theories in the management of sleep routines in Japan, Italy and the United States. In S. Harkness and C. M. Super (eds) *Parents' Cultural Belief Systems*. New York: Guilford Press.

Wong, A. (1986) Creole as a language of power and solidarity. In D. Sutcliffe and A. Wong (eds) *The Language of the Black Experience*. Oxford: Basil Blackwell.

Woodcock, J. (2003) Practical approaches to work with refugee children. In Dwivedi, K. (ed) *Meeting the Needs of Ethnic Minority Children*. London: Jessica Kingsley Publishers.

Woodhead, M. (1999) Reconstructing Developmental Psychology – Some First Steps. *Children & Society*, 13: 3–19.

Woodhead, M., Littleton, K., Faulkner, D. (1999) *Making Sense of Social Development*. London: Routledge.

Wright, C. (1992) *Race Relations in the Primary School*. London: David Fulton.

Yee, A. H., Fairchild, H. H., Weizmann, F. and Wyatt, G. E. (1993) Addressing Psychology Problems with Race. *American Psychologist*, 48: 1132–1140.

Yeh, C. J. and Huang, K. (1996) The collectivistic nature of ethnic identity development among Asian-American college students. *Adolescence*, 31: 645–661.

Yinger, J. M. (1976) Ethnicity in complex societies. In Lewis A. Coser and Ottoo N. Larsen (eds) *The Uses of Controversy in Sociology*. New York: Free Press.

Author index

217

Subject index